Genetic Programming - New Approaches and Successful Applications

Genetic Programming - New Approaches and Successful Applications

Editor

Asa Bensten

scitus
academics

Genetic Programming - New Approaches and Successful Applications
Edited by **Asa Bensten**

ISBN: 978-1-68117-264-4
Library of Congress Control Number: 2016937432

SCITUS Academics LLC,
www.scitusacademics.com
Box No. 4766, 616 Corporate Way,
Suite 2, Valley Cottage,
NY 10989

Notice

Printed in United States of America on Acid Free Paper

Preface

A genetic programming is sub-field of genetic algorithms. The main difference between genetic programming and genetic algorithms is how the solution is represented. Genetic programming creates computer programs in the lisp or scheme of computer languages. Genetic programming is an automatic technique used to create a computer program that approximately solves or solves a problem. Genetic programming addresses the challenge of getting a computer to solve an issue without explicitly programming it. This challenge requires an automatic system with a high-level problem statement and the output of which is a problem-solving work program. Genetic programming gradually increases the computer program population over a number of generations, starting with a primordial ooze of thousands of randomly created computer programs and using the Darwinian principle of natural selection, recombination, mutation, gene duplication, gene deletion and certain mechanisms of developmental biology. Genetic programming in particular begins with the initial population of randomly generated computer programs comprising primitive functions and terminals. The programs in the population are generally of different sizes and shapes.

The objective of this title is to demonstrate topical progress in the field of GP, both in the development of new theoretical approaches and in the development of applications that have successfully solved various real-world problems. The book is primarily intended for graduates, researchers and academics, although graduates who aspire to learn about the leading genetic programming techniques are hoped to benefit immensely.

Table of Contents

1

CHAPTER

GENETIC PROGRAMMING FOR THE DOWNSCALING OF EXTREME RAINFALL EVENTS ON THE EAST COAST OF PENINSULAR MALAYSIA

Sahar Hadi Pour, Sobri Bin Harun and Shamsuddin Shahid *

Department of Hydraulics & Hydrology, Faculty of Civil Engineering, Universiti Teknologi Malaysia, 81310 Johor Bahru, Malaysia

ABSTRACT

A genetic programming (GP)-based logistic regression method is proposed in the present study for the downscaling of extreme rainfall indices on the east coast of Peninsular Malaysia, which is considered one of the zones in Malaysia most vulnerable to climate change. A National Centre for Environmental Prediction reanalysis dataset at 42 grid points surrounding the study area was used to select the predictors. GP models were developed for the downscaling of three extreme rainfall indices: days with larger than or equal to the 90th percentile of rainfall during the north-east monsoon; consecutive wet days; and consecutive dry days in a year. Daily rainfall data for the time periods 1961–1990 and 1991–2000 were used for the calibration and validation of models, respectively. The results are compared with those obtained using the multilayer perceptron neural network (ANN) and linear regression-based statistical downscaling model (SDSM). It was found that models derived using GP can predict both annual and seasonal extreme rainfall indices more accurately compared to ANN and SDSM.

Keywords: genetic programming; downscaling; extreme rainfall indices; statistical downscaling model

1. INTRODUCTION

Climate change due to global warming will modify the climate in terms of both the mean and variability of rainfall [1,2]. Small changes in rainfall variability and the mean can produce relatively large changes in the probability of extreme rainfall events [3,4]. As the primary impacts of climate change on human life, environments, economies and societies result from extreme events, changes in extreme weather events due to global warming have become a major concern in recent years [2,5,6]. Therefore, reliable projection of future changes in extreme indices at the local scale is a major challenge in any climate region.

General circulation models (GCMs) are generally designed to simulate the present climate and project the future climate. However, GCMs cannot be used to project local- and regional-scale climates and their changes, because of their coarse spatial resolutions. Therefore, GCM simulations are downscaled into much finer spatial resolution for climate change impact studies at local and regional scales [7]. Two major downscaling approaches are often used: dynamical downscaling methods that are based on high-resolution regional climate models [8,9] and statistical downscaling methods based on some established statistical relationships between large-scale atmospheric variables (predictors) and local climate variables (predictands) [10,11]. Compared to dynamic downscaling, statistical downscaling requires simple computational skills to downscale GCM outputs in order to understand possible future changes in climate at the local scale [12].

A number of studies on downscaling extreme indices has been carried out in recent years [12,13,14,15,16,17]. However, this is still new in Malaysia and Southeast Asian countries, where studies of statistical downscaling have focused mainly on mean climate. Logistic regression is a popular technique for classifying information into two mutually exclusive and exhaustive categories [18]. It has been used for the downscaling of extreme rainfall indices in a number of research papers [19,20,21]. Logistic regression creates decision trees for the creation of decision rules. One of the main drawbacks of conventional logistic regression-based statistical downscaling procedures is that the performance of such models depends on theoretical assumptions and data restrictions. Furthermore, conventional statistical logistic regression methods show poor performance when the variable of interest is precipitation; the predictor/predictand relationships are very complex, and conventional downscaling methods may not work satisfactorily [22]. Genetic programming (GP) is a kind of non-parametric regression, which can relate the predictors and predictands and provide a predictive model identical to the analytical optimal solution when interrelationships between variables are poorly understood [23,24,25,26,27,28,29]. Genetic-based statistical logistic regression offers a clear advantage over the standard statistical logistic regression method [30,31]. It generates a set of logical expressions describing the structure of the data through iterative subsumption and probabilistically picks the most appropriate set to allow the system to predict in non-deterministic situations, while the achievement of this is not possible with current statistical logistic regression. Thus, the objective of the present study was to use a GP-based logistic regression method for the downscaling of rainfall extremes. The method is tested for the east coast of Peninsular Malaysia.

Three extreme rainfall indices that are important for the economy and livelihood of the population of the east coast of Peninsular Malaysia were downscaled: heavy rainfall days (days with larger than or equal to the 90th percentile of rainfall) during the north-east (NE) monsoon; consecutive dry days; and consecutive wet days in a year. The east coast of Peninsular Malaysia is one of the zones most vulnerable to climate change in the country [32]. It has been reported that extreme rainfall events have increased in Peninsular Malaysia in recent years [32,33,34]. Floods triggered by heavy rainfall are a major hydrological disaster, and almost every year, phenomena occur in the area. Deni *et al.* [33] reported that rainfall intensity increased in much of Peninsular Malaysia during the south-west (SW) monsoon. During the NE monsoon, total rainfall, the frequency of extreme rainfall events and rainfall intensity increased all over the peninsula [34]. It is anticipated that variability in inter-annual and inter-seasonal rainfall due to climate change will cause more hydrologic extremes on the east coast of Peninsular Malaysia and make people's livelihoods and local infrastructure more vulnerable. Therefore, downscaling extreme rainfall indices is very important for the creation of rational countermeasures in the context of climate change.

2. METHODOLOGY

2.1. Data and Sources

Rainfall data recorded at three stations, namely Besut, Dungun and Kemaman, on the east coast of Peninsular Malaysia were used to downscale the extreme rainfall indices using GP. The location of rainfall stations on the map of Peninsular Malaysia is shown in Figure 1a. The climate of the area can be loosely divided into four seasons: the NE monsoon from October to February; the SW monsoon from April to August; and two inter-monsoonal transitional periods in March and September. The east coast is considered as the wet belt of Peninsular Malaysia, with an annual rainfall of 2800 mm. Heavy rainfall on the east coast of Peninsular Malaysia is usually associated with the NE monsoon. Maximum precipitation usually occurs during the months of November and December. On the other hand, cloudless skies are observed during the SW monsoon. The topographic map of the study area, prepared using the Advanced Spaceborne Thermal Emission and Reflection Radiometer Global Digital Elevation Model, is shown in Figure 1b. The elevation in the area varies from −4 m on the narrow coastal plain to 2270 m in the interior mountainous region.

Daily rainfall data series for the time period 1961–2000 recorded at three locations in the study area were obtained from the Department of Irrigation and Drainage Malaysia. The predictors were obtained from the National Centre for Environmental Prediction (NCEP) reanalysis dataset [35]. Climate model data represent an aggregate over a grid box, and therefore, NCEP data are not an ideal representation of precipitation extremes computed from averages over stations. However, a number of studies have reported that the relationship between the extremes of gridded climatological datasets and observed point-level data from weather stations can be used to predict point-level extreme behavior from future runs of climate models [36,37,38,39,40,41].

Data quality control is a necessary step before the calculation of indices, because erroneous outliers can seriously impact index calculation and trends [42]. A number of quality control checks were carried out to identify errors, such as precipitation values below 0 mm, rainfall higher than 250 mm, more than 20 consecutive dry days during the NE monsoon and more than 20 consecutive wet days during the SW monsoon. Histograms of the data were also created to reveal problems in the dataset as a whole [43]. A Student's *t*-test was used to test the difference in the means between the two segments of the dataset to ensure the homogeneity of data. Differences between the sub-set series are not significant at the 95% level of confidence for any station.

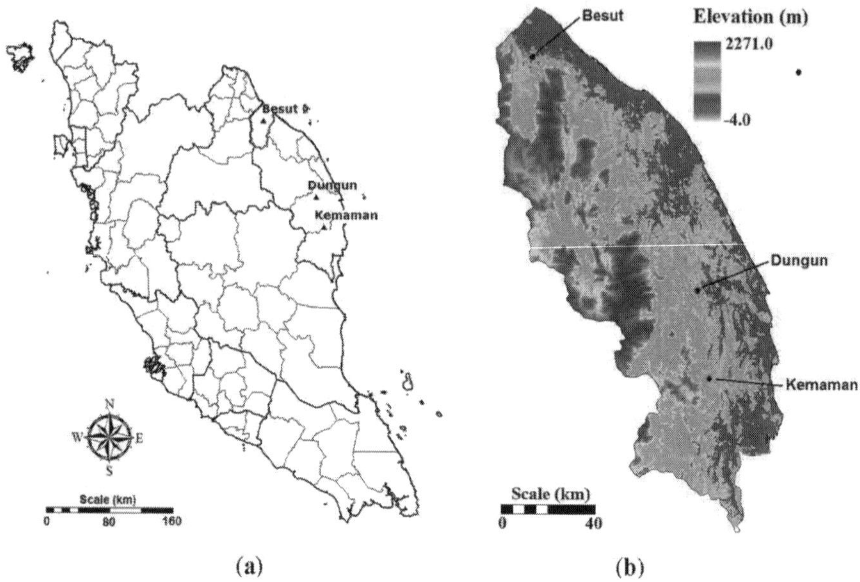

Figure 1. (**a**) Location of the rain gauge stations in Peninsular Malaysia; (**b**) terrain map of the study area.

Three extreme rainfall indices were computed for the present study. Table 1 provides descriptions of the indices. The indices were calculated on a seasonal or annual basis. In computing the percentile-based index, the percentile was calculated from the reference period 1961–1990, which is a normal climate period as defined by the World Meteorological Organization [44]. Heavy rainfall on the east coast of Peninsular Malaysia is usually associated with the NE monsoon. Therefore, only heavy rainfall days (the days with larger than or equal to the 90th percentile of rainfall) during the NE monsoon were downscaled in the present study.

Table 1. Definitions of precipitation indices used in the present study.

Index	Description	Unit
R90	Total number of days during NE monsoon in a year with rainfall ≥90th percentile of 1961–1990 daily rainfall	day
CDD	Maximum number of consecutive dry days (rainfall = 0) in a year	day
CWD	Maximum number of consecutive wet days (rainfall > 0) in a year	day

2.2. Selection of Predictors

One of the major challenges in climate downscaling, especially in downscaling extreme rainfall indices, is the selection of appropriate predictors. It is expected that predictors should be highly correlated with extreme rainfall indices. Furthermore, the predictors should be accurately projected by available GCMs for the future projection of climate. There are no general guidelines for the selection of predictors in different parts of the world, and therefore, a comprehensive search of predictors is necessary [45]. Twenty-six NCEP variables that are usually projected by various climate models, including the Hadley Centre Climate Model (HadCM), were used in the present study for the selection of predictors. The description of 26 NCEP variables is given in Table 2.

Table 2. Description of 26 NCEP variables used for predictor selection.

No.	Variables	Description	No.	Variables	Description
1	mslp	Mean sea level pressure	14	p5zh	500 hPa divergence
2	p_f	Surface airflow strength	15	p8_f	850 hPa airflow strength
3	p_u	Surface zonal velocity	16	p8_u	850 hPa zonal velocity
4	p_v	Surface meridional velocity	17	p8_v	850 hPa meridional velocity
5	p_z	Surface vorticity	18	p8_z	850 hPa vorticity
6	p_th	Surface wind direction	19	p800	850 hPa geopotential height
7	p_zh	Surface divergence	20	p8th	850 hPa wind direction
8	p5_f	500 hPa airflow strength	21	p8zh	850 hPa divergence
9	p5_u	500 hPa zonal velocity	22	rhum	Near surface relative humidity
10	p5_v	500 hPa meridional velocity	23	r500	Relative humidity at 500 hPa
11	p5_z	500 hPa vorticity	24	r850	Relative humidity at 850 hPa
12	p500	500 hPa geopotential height	25	shum	Near surface specific humidity
13	p5th	500 hPa wind direction	26	temp	Mean temperature

The climatic system is influenced by the combined action of multiple atmospheric variables in a wide tempo-spatial space. Any single circulation predictor and/or small tempo-spatial space are unlikely to be sufficient for climate projection, as they fail to capture key rainfall mechanisms based on thermodynamics and vapor content [46]. Following the suggestions of Wilby and Wigley [47], the regional synoptic circulation patterns that contributed to the anomalous rainfall pattern in Malaysia were considered in the selection of the spatial domain of each predictor, represented as 42 grid points surrounding the study area. All 26 daily NCEP variables at 42 NCEP grid points surrounding the study area (Figure 2) (total $26 \times 42 = 1092$) were individually correlated with local extreme rainfall events. The non-parametric Kendall tau correlation coefficient was used to measure the degree of association between NCEP variables and local extreme rainfall events. Finally, the NCEP variables that have a strong correlation with a particular rainfall event at a particular rainfall station were used for the selection of the final set of predictors through stepwise regression processes to downscale the corresponding rainfall event at that station.

2.3. Statistical Downscaling Model

The statistical downscaling model (SDSM) is a widely used downscaling tool developed by Wilby *et al.*[48]. The SDSM uses the multiple linear regression technique for the development of downscaling models. It develops each model by establishing the statistical relationship between the predictands and predictors as a first step and then simulates the future series of predictands by using the predicted data from GCMs. The SDSM uses two separate sub-models to determine the occurrence and the amount of conditional meteorological variables (or discrete variables), such as precipitation. Therefore, the SDSM can be classified as a conditional weather generator in which regression equations are used to estimate the parameters of daily precipitation occurrence and amount separately. Therefore, it is more sophisticated than a straightforward regression model [49].

2.4. Statistical Downscaling Using Multilayer Perceptron Artificial Neural Network

Multilayer perceptron (MLP) is the most popular, flexible and simplest type of artificial neural network (ANN), widely used to map non-linear relationships between predictors and predictands [50,51]. The main function of an ANN is to improve the performance function between the predicted and observed values. The MLP ANN is composed of an input layer, any number of hidden layers and an output layer of neurons [52,53]. Studies have revealed that statistical downscaling based on ANN models can present good non-linear regression models [54,55,56]. Therefore, ANN models have been used successfully for climate downscaling in many climatic regions [52,57].

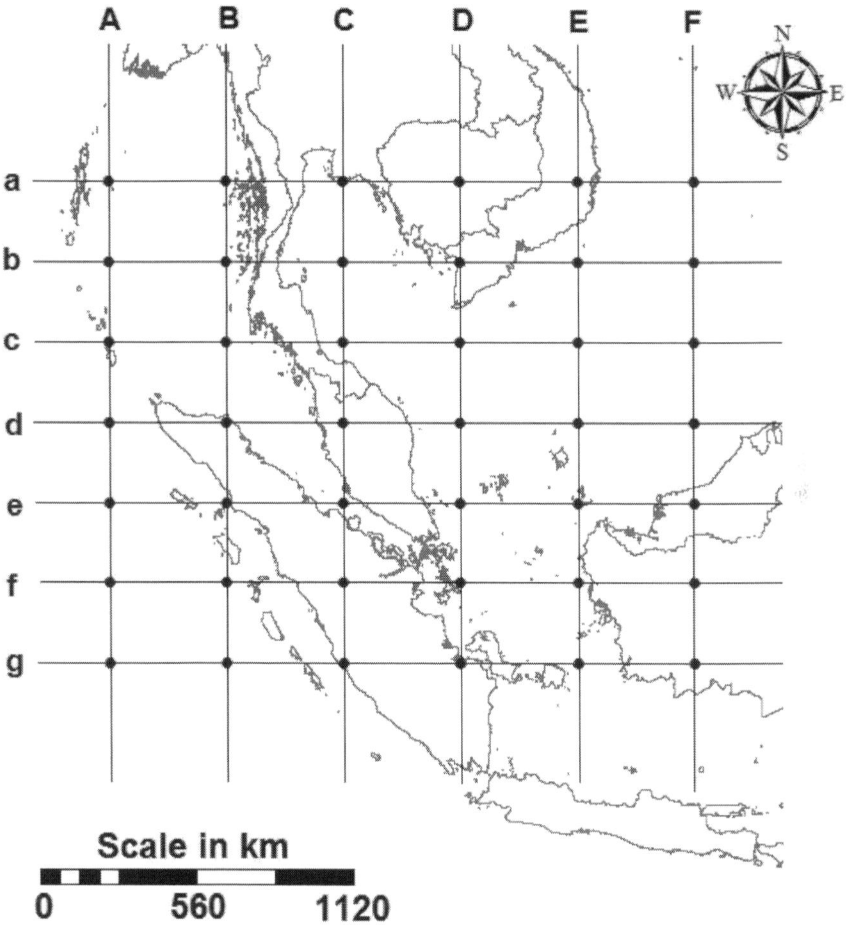

Figure 2. Location of NCEP grid points used to select the predictors.

The MLP neural network uses the following equations to model precipitation:

$$y_k = F\left(\sum_{j=1}^{h} w_j G(s_i) + b_k\right) \tag{1}$$

where F represents the linear activation function of the output neuron, b_k is the threshold and w_j represents the connection. G is the hyperbolic tangent sigmoid used as the activation function for the hidden nodes and can be expressed as follows:

$$G(s_i)=\frac{e^{S_i}-e^{-S_i}}{e^{S_i}+e^{-S_i}} \quad (2)$$

where s_i is the weighted sum of all incoming information and also referred to as the input signal:

$$s_i=\sum_{i=1}^{n} w_i x_i \quad (3)$$

where x_i is the input to the network (NCEP predictors) and w_i is the connection weight between nodes of the input and hidden layers.

2.5. Downscaling Using GP-Based Logistic Regression

Logistic regression follows the same principles of linear regression, except that the outcome is a dichotomous variable representing success or failure. It assumes that the probability of success or failure, $P(X)$, is related to X by the function. The general multiple logistic regression model can be represented in terms of p, *i.e.*, probability of success (or failure) as:

$$p=\frac{e^L}{1+e^L} \quad (4)$$

and, L=eβ0+β1+β2+...+ε, where β_0 is the intercept, β_1, β_2, ..., β_n are the slope coefficients and ε is the random error.

Like linear regression, the goal is to estimate the regression coefficients (β_0, β_1, β_2, ..., β_n) for a dataset. Unfortunately, the techniques used in linear regression to estimate the regression coefficients cannot be applied to logistic regression [18]. Traditionally, a stepwise regression procedure combined with the maximum likelihood method is used to determine significant predictors and their contribution to the probability of the target variable. The main disadvantage of stepwise regression with forward selection is that it can often result in biased selection of significant predictors [58]. In order to overcome this problem, a number of methods have been proposed, such as ridge regression, the least absolute shrinkage and selection operator [59], the elastic net [60], *etc.* However, these techniques often fail to infer sparse models or can exhibit undesirable behavior in the presence of highly correlated predictors [58]. Recently, GP has been proposed to overcome the inherent difficulties of logistic regression. Biesheuvel *et al.* [30] compared the performance of GP with logistic regression in diagnosing pulmonary embolism and reported that although the interpretation of a GP model is less intuitive, it is a promising technique for the development of prediction rules for diagnostic and prognostic purposes. Engoren *et al.* [31] also came to a similar conclusion and reported that GP can improve the prediction accuracy of logistic regression. The application of GP-based logistic regression has increased in recent years in different fields of science and technology [61,62,63,64].

In the present study, predictors (NCEP variables) were used to predict whether a rainfall event will occur or not. Therefore, the task of downscaling extreme indices is to find a model or function that maps the extreme rainfall indices from the predictors. The GP method is used to solve this problem by generating thousands of randomly-created computer programs. GP computer programs are often represented as symbolic expressions or an alternative representation of symbolic expressions given by expression trees. The tree representations consist of nodes and are of variable length. The nodes can either be non-terminal or terminal nodes; the former consist of functions that perform some action on one or more signals within the structure to produce an output signal, and the terminal nodes represent an input variable or a constant. The fitness of each program is computed according to its prediction ability, which is measured using a hit rate. A hit rate, also known as a success rate, is calculated as:

$$Hit\ Rate = \frac{\sum Success\ in\ Prediction}{\sum Success\ in\ Prediction + \sum Failure\ in\ Prediction} \quad (5)$$

After evaluating the fitness, better programs are selected for the next generation. Genetic operators, namely mutation and crossover, are used to generate offspring form the existing individuals. Crossover between two trees is carried out by randomly choosing a branch in each tree and switching them. Mutation is performed by choosing a node and changing its value or meaning, *i.e.*, the function symbol could become another function symbol or be deleted and the terminal value could be modified. The process is repeated until the termination conditions are met. The fittest program in the final generation is the prediction model of a particular extreme rainfall event [28,65].

The commercial software, Discipulus [66], is used for the development of GP-based logistic regression models. Discipulus is a general purpose GP system, which can be used for regression and binary classification problems. The software creates small programs with the technique of GP, which answer questions. For example, it can be used to decide whether a 90th percentile rainfall amount will occur during a specific day or not. Daily rainfall data for the time period 1961–1990 were used as the GP learning set, and the data for the time period 1991–2000 were used for validation.

3. RESULTS

3.1. Selection of Predictors

For the selection of predictors, the NCEP variables from 42 grid points surrounding the study area were individually correlated with local rainfall events. The NCEP variables from different grid points, having high correlation with heavy rainfall event at Dungun station, are shown in Figure 3a. In the figure, the capital letter in an NCEP variable name represents the column and the lower case letter represents the row of the NCEP grid point, as shown in Figure 2. The number in brackets represents the NCEP variable, as described in Table 1. Therefore, Cd(23) represents relative humidity at 500 hPa at the grid point located in column "C" and row "d". Eleven NCEP variables from different grid points were found to have high correlation with a heavy rainfall event. These NCEP variables were used to select the final set of predictors for the downscaling using stepwise multiple regression. Stepwise multiple regression is a way of choosing predictors of a particular dependent variable on the basis of statistical criteria, such as an F-test or adjusted R-squared test. Stepwise multiple regression adds and removes predictors, in a stepwise manner, until there is no justifiable reason to add or remove more. Therefore, it allows the selection of the subset of independent variables that is the best predictor. The plot of regression coefficients between different subsets of independent variables and 90th percentile rainfall events at Dungun station is shown in Figure 3b. The figure shows that the model performance increases with the inclusion of more NCEP variables. However, it does not increase substantially after the inclusion of more variables with three independent variables, namely Cd(23), Db(2) and Db(3). Therefore, these three NCEP variables were finally chosen as predictors for the downscaling of heavy rainfall days at Dungun station.

(a)

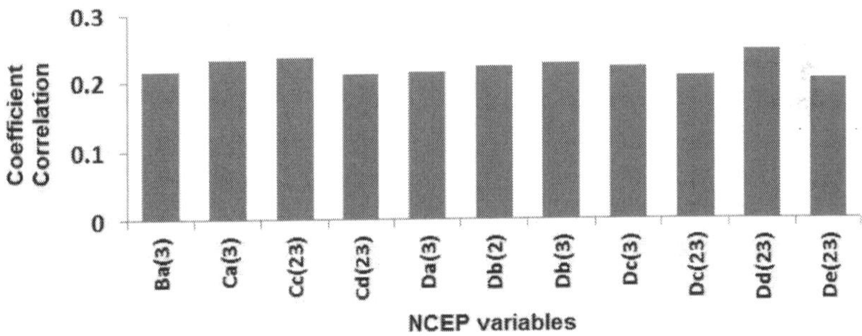

(b)

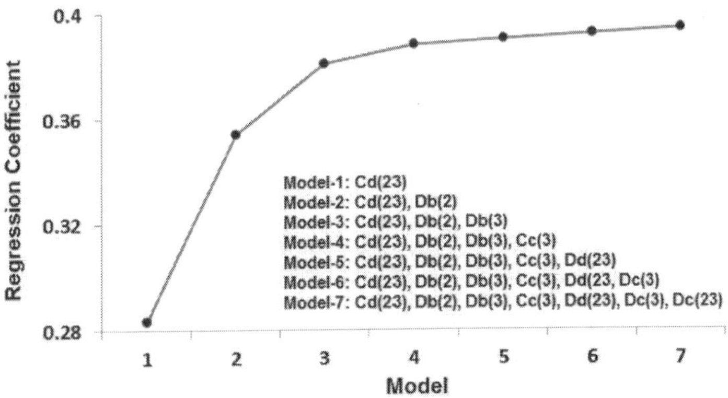

Figure 3. (**a**) The NCEP variables from different grid points with good correlation with heavy rainfall events during the NE monsoon; (**b**) the plot of regression coefficients between different subsets of NCEP variables and heavy rainfall events at Dungun station.

The process produced the same set of NCEP variables for all three stations. The NCEP variables selected as predictors for different rainfall indices are given in Table 3. NCEP variables at grid points located in the NE direction have more influence on the rainfall of the study area. This is justifiable, as the rainfall in the study area is influenced by the NE monsoon.

Table 3 shows that the NCEP variables selected for downscaling rainfall indices are relative humidity at 500 and 850 hPa, surface airflow strength and surface zonal velocity. Precipitation at a location depends on the available air moisture content and flow of moist air. Relative humidity at 500 and 850 hPa represents the water vapor available in the air; surface airflow strength represents the regime of near surface air flow and surface zonal velocity on the equator cause zonal wind stress. Therefore, selection of these variables is physically plausible for rainfall downscaling. Other researchers also used those variables as predictors for rainfall downscaling in Malaysia [67,68]. It is very important to remember that the predictors used for downscaling should be reliably simulated by GCMs. The predictors selected in the present study are well simulated by many GCMs, including Hadley Centre Coupled Model, version 2 (HadCM2), Canadian Global Coupled Model, version 2 (CGCM2), *etc.* Therefore, these predictors have been widely used for the downscaling and projection of future rainfall [67,68,69].

Table 3. NCEP variables used to build downscaled models.

Event	Predictor	Code	Description
90th percentile rainfall event	P1	Cd(23)	Relative humidity at 500 hPa at grid point Cd
	P2	Db(2)	Surface airflow strength at grid point Db
	P3	Dc(3)	Surface zonal velocity at grid point Dc
Rainfall event	P1	Cd(23)	Relative humidity at 500 hPa at grid point Cd
	P2	Dd(24)	Relative humidity at 850 hPa at grid point Dd
	P3	Db(3)	Surface zonal velocity at grid point Db

3.2. Downscaling Using GP

The goal of a GP downscaling process is to produce an algebraic expression or model that best describes the daily rainfall from predictors. For this purpose, the GP algorithm works with solution candidates, which are tree structure representations of symbolic expressions. The function set used for non-terminal nodes includes +, −, ×, /, %, square root, log, as well as logical and other commonly-used trigonometric operators. As the goal is to find the extreme rainfall from NCEP variables, the terminal nodes must consist of selected NCEP variables, as well as constants. The obtained results are discussed below.

3.2.1. Downscaling Heavy Rainfall Days

A GP model for the downscaling of the days with larger than or equal to 90th percentile rainfall was developed first. The amounts of 90th percentile daily rainfall over the normal climate period (1961–1990) defined by the World Meteorological Organization [44] are 23.2, 24.6 and 25.8 mm at Besut, Dungun and Kemaman stations, respectively. GP-based logistic regression was used to decide whether 90th percentile rainfall will occur or not during a day from the NCEP variables.

The GP software (Discipulus) used in the present study performs multiple runs by default. In the present study, 100 runs were used to produce a wide range of results. Termination of each run was considered as 200 generations without any improvement in fitness function. The distribution of results from multiple GP runs includes a distributional tail of excellent solutions. The best solution is selected based on the hit rate. The highest overall hit rates were obtained in downscaling heavy rainfall days in run 52 after 652 generations at Besut station, in run 47 after 712 generations at Dungun and in run 34 after 512 generations at Kemaman. The highest overall hit rates obtained at different stations is given in Table 4. It can be seen from the table that GP is able to model the 90th percentile rainfall index in 78.3%–81.1% of cases during calibration and 75.9%–78.0% of cases during validation. This means that GP-based logistic regression is successful in downscaling heavy rainfall days in more than 78.3% of cases. The best tree structure representations of symbolic expressions produced by GP in downscaling heavy rainfall days at Besut station is shown in Figure 4. The simplified equations obtained from the GP structures that can be used to downscale the number of heavy rainfall days in the vicinity of three rainfall stations is given in Table 5.

Table 4. Overall hit rates during training and validation of genetic programming (GP) models in downscaling rainfall indices.

Rainfall Indices	Station Name	Hit Rate (%)	
		Training	Validation
Days with larger than or equal to 90th percentile rainfall	Besut	81.1	78.0
	Dungun	80.1	76.8
	Kemaman	78.3	75.9
Rainy days	Besut	86.1	82.0
	Dungun	84.5	80.2
	Kemaman	83.9	81.0

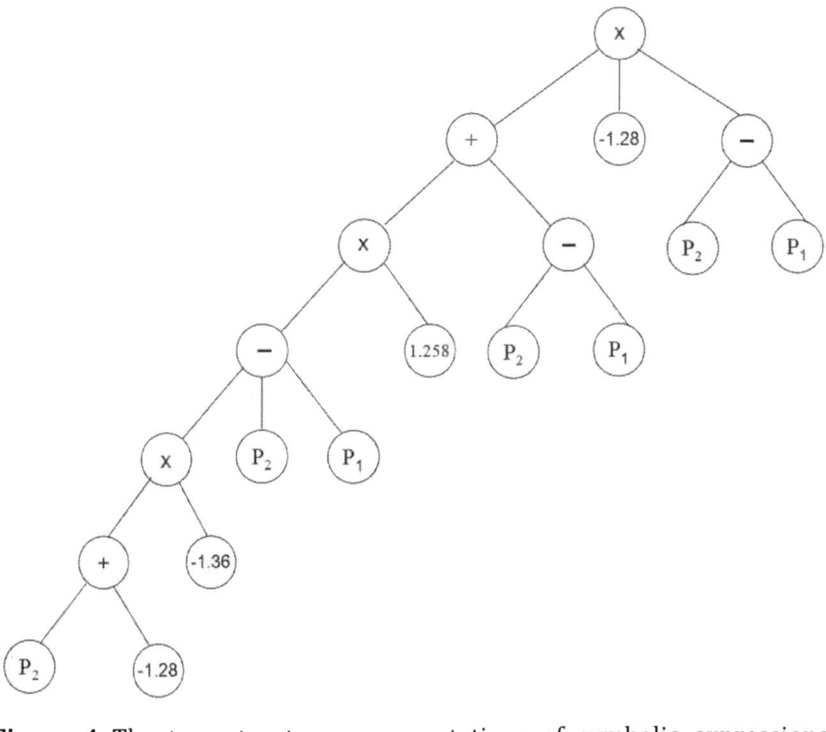

Figure 4. The tree structure representations of symbolic expressions produced by GP for heavy rainfall event downscaling at Besut (descriptions of P_1, P_2 and P_3 are given in Table 3).

Table 5. The simplified equations derived by GP for the downscaling of extreme rainfall indices (descriptions of P_1, P_2 and P_3 are given in Table 3).

Rainfall Indices	Station Name	Equation
Days with larger than or equal to 90th percentile rainfall	Besut	$-1.28[P_2 - P_1 + 1.258[P_2 - P_1 - 1.36[P_2 + P_3]]] \times [P_2 - P_1]$
	Dungun	$[P_2 + P_1 - 2.56[P_2 + P_1 - 3.26[P_1 + P_2 + P_3]]] \times 1.23P_2$
	Kemaman	$-1.11[P_2 - P_1 + 1.56[P_2 - P_1 - 1.45[P_2 + P_3]]] \times [P_2 - P_1 + P_3]$
Rainy days	Besut	$(P_3 - P_1 + P_2) - 1.51(P_3 \times P_2 - P_1) + 1.14(P_1 - P_3 + sqrt(P_1))$
	Dungun	$1.23 \times (P_1 + P_2) - 1.26(P_3 \times P_2 - P_1) + 0.86(P_1 - P_2)$
	Kemaman	$2.34 \times P_2 - 2.13(P_3 \times 1.54 - P_1) + 1.45(P_1 - P_3 \times P_1)$

3.2.2. Downscaling Consecutive Wet and Dry Days

For downscaling of consecutive wet and dry days, a GP model was developed to predict whether rainfall will occur or not during a day. This produced a binary time series for the whole period, which was used to compute the consecutive wet and dry days in a year.

The GP model required different numbers of generations to give the highest overall hit rates at different stations. The best hit rates in downscaling rainy days at different stations is given in Table 4. It can be seen from the table that GP-based logistic regression was successful in downscaling rainfall days in 83.9%–86.1% of cases during calibration and 80.2%–82.0% of cases during validation. The best tree structure produced by the GP in downscaling rainy days at Besut is shown in Figure 5. The simplified equations obtained from the structures that can be used for downscaling rainy days at different stations are given in Table 5.

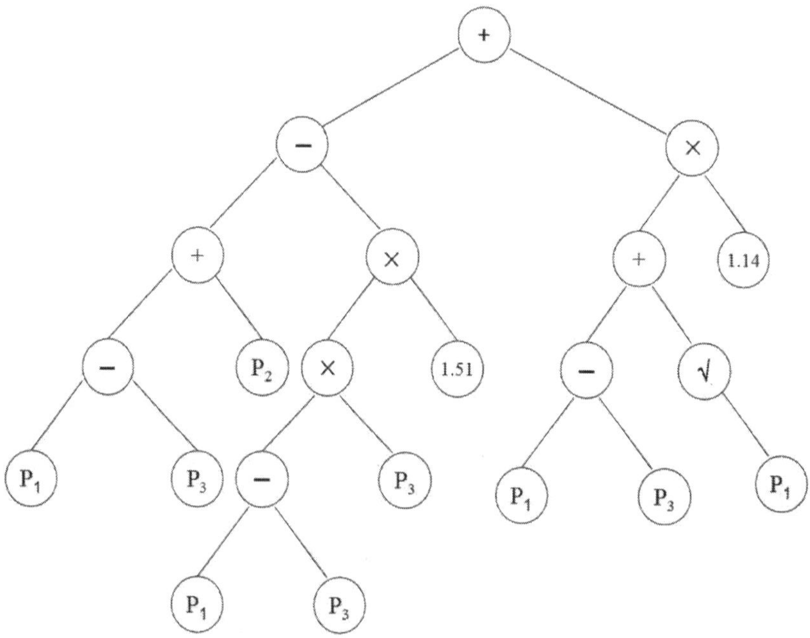

Figure 5. The tree structure representations of symbolic expressions produced by GP for the downscaling of rainy days at Besut (descriptions of P_1, P_2 and P_3 are given in Table 3).

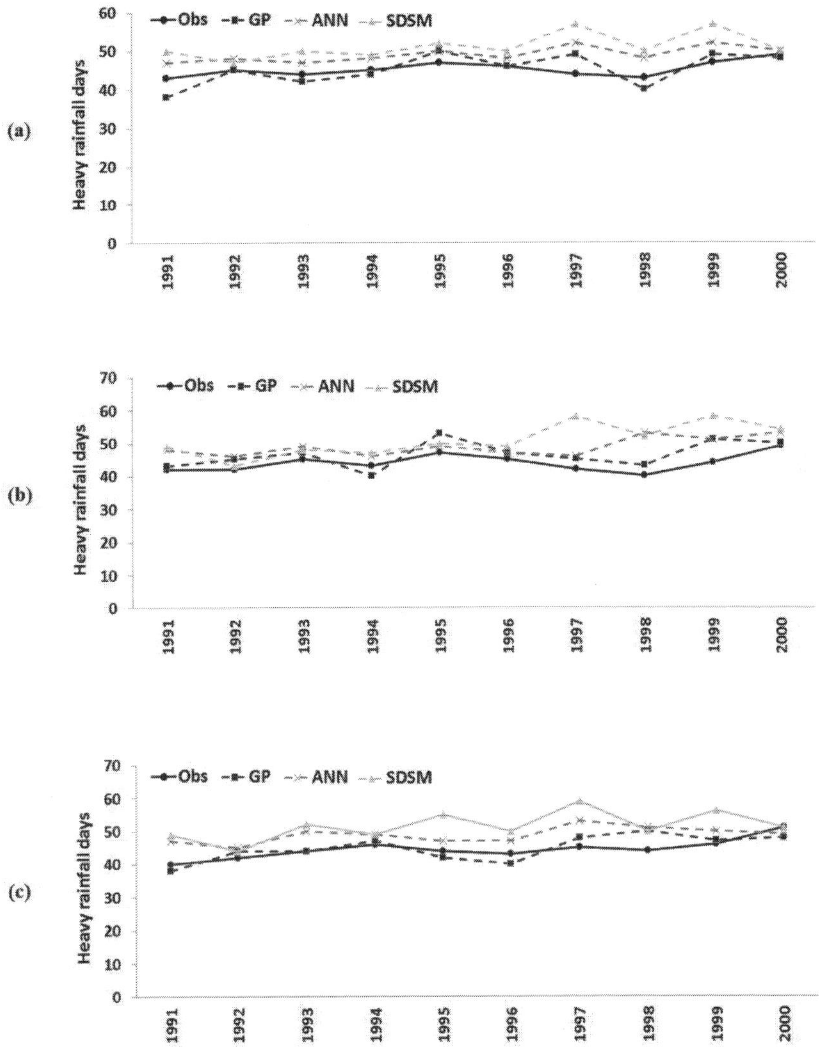

Figure 6. Observed number of heavy rainfall days and those downscaled by GP, the ANN and the statistical downscaling model (SDSM) during model validation at: (**a**) Besut; (**b**) Dungun; and (**c**) Kemaman.

3.3. Downscaling Using ANN

A feed-forward learning-based three-layer MLP ANN developed in MATLAB was used in the present study to downscale extreme rainfall indices. The same predictors used in GP (Table 3) were also used in the

ANN. Like GP, an ANN is used to decide whether rainfall will occur or not during a day from the NCEP variables. Data for the time periods 1961–1990 and 1991–2000 were used for calibration and validation of the ANN model, respectively. The ANN was run 100 times, and the obtained results from each run were stored. A termination criterion for a single run was chosen as 200 generations without improvement. The best ANN model was selected based on the hit rate. The results were then compared with those obtained using GP and the SDSM.

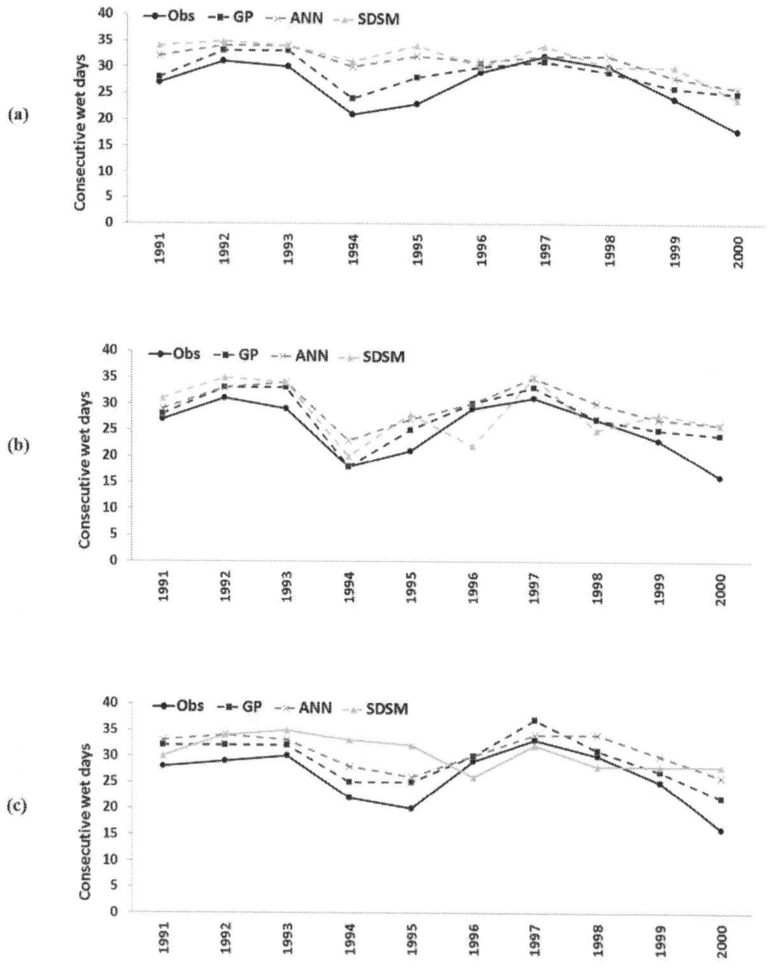

Figure 7. Observed number of consecutive wet days and those downscaled by GP, the ANN and the SDSM during model validation at: (**a**) Besut; (**b**) Dungun; and (**c**) Kemaman.

3.4. Downscaling Using the SDSM

The SDSM package was also used to downscale daily rainfall with the same predictors used for GP (given in Table 3). Daily rainfall data for the time periods 1961–1990 and 1991–2000 were used for calibration and validation of the SDSM, respectively. The extreme rainfall indices were then estimated from the daily rainfall downscaled by the SDSM. In the present study, extreme rainfall indices during the validation period were computed and compared with observed and GP-based downscaled results.

3.5. Comparison of Results

Comparisons of observed and downscaled heavy rainfall days during monsoon, as well as consecutive wet days and consecutive dry days in a year over the model validation period (1991–2000) are shown inFigure 6, Figure 7 and Figure 8, respectively. It can be seen in Figure 6 that all of the methods estimated the number of heavy rainfall days successfully over the evaluation period. However, the downscaled output from GP is closer to the observed values compared to those estimated by the ANN and the SDSM. In most of the years, both the ANN model and SDSM overestimated the number of heavy rainfall days. Compared to the ANN, the SDSM overestimated heavy rainfall days more often. On the other hand, GP underestimated the number of days in certain years, but the estimated GP values were found to be very close to observed values in almost all of the years and at all of the stations. The root mean squared error (RMSE) and correlation coefficient (expressed as r^2) between observed and downscaled values during validation are given in Table 6. The table shows that the errors in estimation of the number of heavy rainfall days by GP are always significantly less compared to ANN and SDSM estimations. The correlation coefficient between observed values and GP downscaled values during the validation period was also found to be higher compared to ANN and SDSM downscaling.

Similar results were obtained for consecutive wet days and consecutive dry days in a year. It can be seen from Figure 7 that the number of consecutive wet days in a year was overestimated by the ANN model and SDSM in most of the years at all three stations during the validation period. GP also overestimated the number of consecutive wet days in certain years. However, GP downscaled values are found to be closer to observed values compared to those downscaled by the ANN and SDSM at all of the stations. Table 6 shows that the errors in the number of consecutive wet days in a year estimated by GP is always significantly less compared to ANN and SDSM estimations. The correlation coefficient between observed and GP downscaled values during the validation period was also found to be higher.

(a)
(b)
(c)

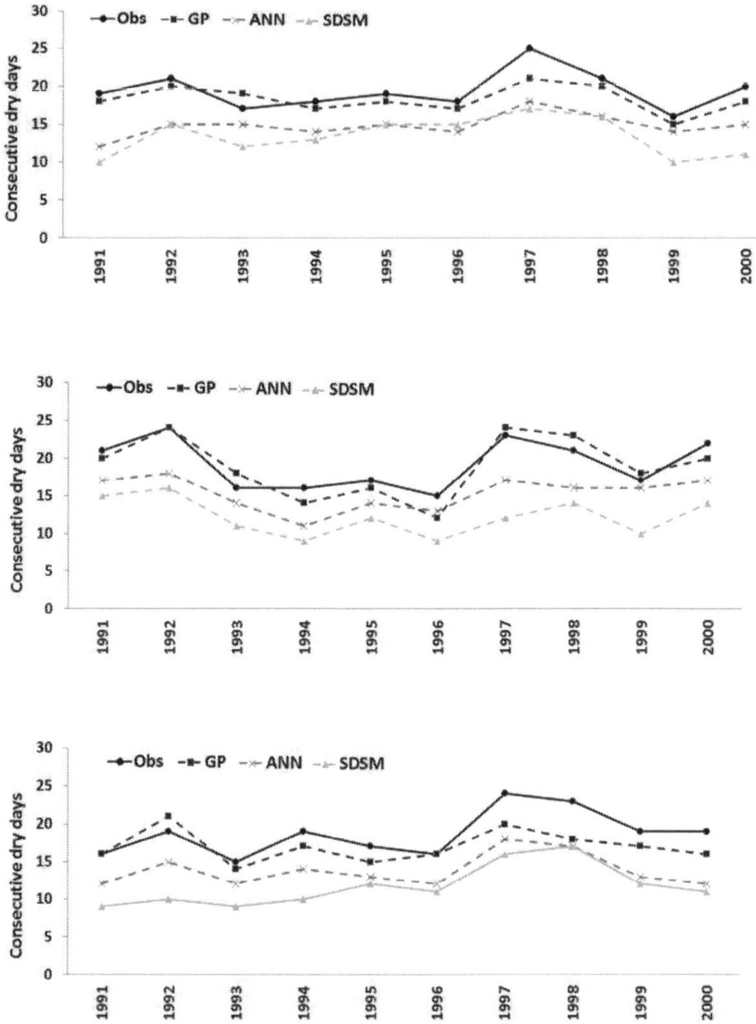

Figure 8. Observed number of consecutive dry days and those downscaled by GP, the ANN and the SDSM during model validation at (**a**) Besut; (**b**) Dungun; and (**c**) Kemaman.

Errors in GP downscaling of the number of consecutive dry days in a year were found to be similar to those in the estimations of the other two extreme indices. It can be seen from Figure 8 that the downscaled number of consecutive dry days in a year by GP, the ANN and SDSM is less than the observed number of days in most of the years at all three stations. However, GP downscaled values are still found to be closer compared to those downscaled by the ANN and SDSM.

Comparison of observed and downscaled heavy rainfall days during different months of the NE monsoon, as well as continuous wet days and continuous dry days during NE and SW monsoons at different stations during model validation is shown in Figure 9. It can be seen from Figure 9 that seasonal or monthly variations in extreme rainfall indices are well reconstructed by GP compared to those by the ANN and SDSM. In the case of heavy rainfall days, the SDSM was found to downscale almost to the same number in all of the NE monsoon months. The ANN is able to show some variation in the number of heavy rainfall days, but not like GP. It can also be noted from the values in Figure 9 that all of the methods overestimated the number of heavy rainfall days in most of the months. Still, the values estimated by GP are closer to the observed values compared to those estimated by the ANN and SDSM. The RMSEs between the observed and estimated number of heavy rainfall days using different methods during model validation are given inTable 7. The table shows that the error in the estimation of the number of heavy rainfall days by GP is always less compared to the ANN and SDSM.

Table 6. The RMSEs and correlation coefficients (r^2) between observed and downscaled extreme indices estimated by GP, the ANN and the SDSM during model validation.

Indices	Station	GP		ANN		SDSM	
		RMSE	r^2	RMSE	r^2	RMSE	r^2
90th percentile rainfall days	Besut	1.08	0.75	1.31	0.58	2.16	0.43
	Dungun	1.14	0.73	1.83	0.58	2.69	0.41
	Kemaman	1.13	0.67	1.62	0.61	2.57	0.51
Consecutive wet days	Besut	1.02	0.88	1.73	0.80	1.95	0.65
	Dungun	1.05	0.89	1.54	0.83	1.74	0.61
	Kemaman	1.10	0.96	1.66	0.92	2.20	0.46
Consecutive dry days	Besut	1.06	0.83	1.55	0.73	1.99	0.67
	Dungun	1.04	0.91	1.65	0.87	2.28	0.85
	Kemaman	1.23	0.82	1.60	0.82	2.26	0.77

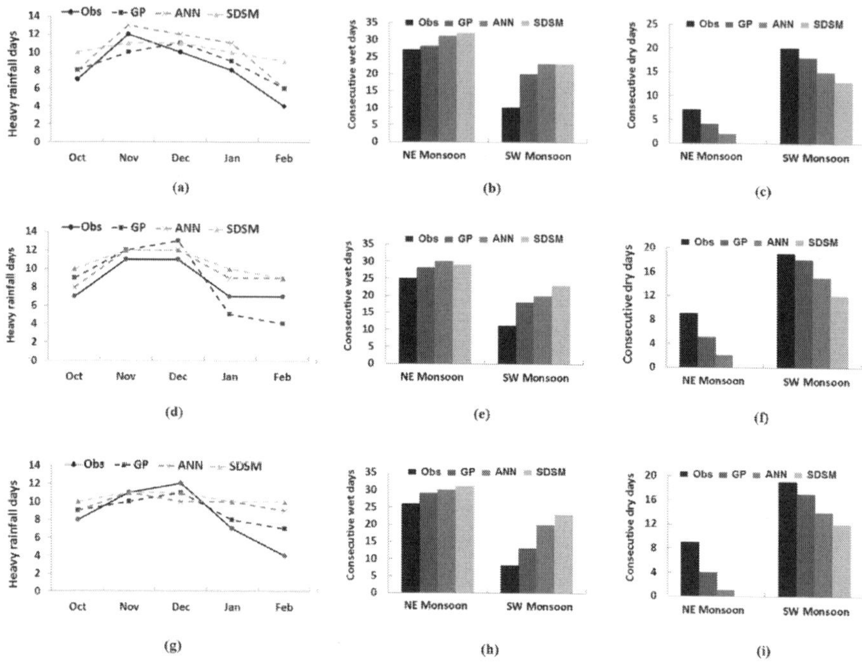

Figure 9. Monthly/seasonal distribution of: (**a**) heavy rainfall days, (**b**) consecutive wet days and (**c**) consecutive dry days at Besut; (**d**) heavy rainfall days; (**e**) consecutive wet days and (**f**) consecutive dry days at Dungun; and (**g**) heavy rainfall days, (**h**) consecutive wet days and (**i**) consecutive dry days at Kemaman.

Table 7. The RMSE in downscaled seasonal extreme indices using GP, the ANN and the SDSM during model validation.

Indices	Station	GP	ANN	SDSM
90th percentile rainfall days	Besut	1.66	2.18	3.16
	Dungun	1.68	2.35	2.45
	Kemaman	1.80	3.12	3.54
Consecutive wet days	Besut	5.02	6.80	6.96
	Dungun	3.81	5.15	6.32
	Kemaman	2.92	6.96	7.91
Consecutive dry days	Besut	1.80	3.54	4.95
	Dungun	2.06	4.03	5.70
	Kemaman	2.69	4.72	5.70

The number of consecutive wet days in two major seasons (SW monsoon and NE monsoon) was overestimated by the ANN and SDSM during the validation period at all three stations (Figure 9). GP also overestimated the number of consecutive wet days, but GP downscaled values were found to be closer to observed values compared to those downscaled by the ANN and SDSM in both of the seasons and at all of the stations. Table 7 shows that the errors in estimation of seasonal consecutive wet spells estimated by GP are always less compared to those estimated by the ANN and SDSM. Errors in the downscaling number of seasonal dry spells are also found to be less for GP. It can be seen from Figure 9 that downscaled lengths of seasonal dry spells estimated by GP, the ANN and the SDSM are lower than the observed number of consecutive dry days in both seasons at all of the stations. However, GP downscaled values were still found to be closer compared to those downscaled by the ANN and SDSM.

4. CONCLUSIONS

Downscaling daily rainfall is an extremely difficult task, as the relations between predictors and predictands are often difficult to map. This is especially true for Malaysia, where relations between local rainfall and ocean-atmospheric circulation parameters are not clearly understood. The application of GP shows that extreme rainfall indices in a tropical area, like the east coast of Peninsular Malaysia, can be downscaled with reasonable accuracy. It is expected that the GP-based methodology proposed in the present study can be used as a reliable tool for the projection of extreme rainfall indices at the local and regional scale, where climate projection under different climate change scenarios is important.

It should be noted that extreme weather phenomena often occur at small scales; thus, coarse resolution models may not always be able to simulate extreme rainfall events accurately. In projecting future climates using downscaling models, it should be remembered that GCMs designed with a single run for long-term climate projection are apparently not dependent on the initial model conditions, as they are soon destroyed after a short period of simulation. These models, as a result, tend to diagnose tendencies of future climate states rather than precise predictions of whether particular events are likely to occur [70]. Downscaled models contain considerable uncertainties, and quantification of uncertainty for the outputs of downscaling models is very important. Studies can be carried out in the future to quantify the uncertainty in GP-based models in the downscaling of extreme rainfall indices on the east coast of Peninsular Malaysia.

ACKNOWLEDGMENTS

We are grateful to the Ministry of Higher Education (Malaysia) and Universiti Teknologi Malaysia for financial support of this research through the Fundamental Research Grant Scheme (FRGS) research project (Vote No. R.J130000.7822.4F541). A course on scientific writing and publication was given by Universiti Teknologi Malaysia (UTM) in 2013. The feedback from the facilitators at this course is gratefully acknowledged.

AUTHOR CONTRIBUTIONS

Sahar Hadipour and Sobri Bin Harun jointly conducted data quality assessments and modelling. Sahar Hadipour also wrote the first draft of the paper. Shamsuddin Shahid coordinated the research and contributed to writing the article.

REFERENCES

1. Shahid, S.; Harun, S.B.; Katimon, A. Changes in diurnal temperature range in Bangladesh during the time period 1961–2008. *Atmos. Res.* **2012**, *118*, 260–270.

2. IPCC. Summary for policymakers. In *Climate Change 2013: The Physical Science Basis. Contribution of the Working Group I to the Fifth Assessment Report of the Intergovernmental Panel on Climate Change*; Cambridge University Press: Cambridge, UK/New York, NY, USA, 2013.

3. Su, B.D.; Jiang, T.; Jin, W.B. Recent trends in observed temperature and precipitation extremes in the Yangtze River basin, China. *Theor. Appl. Climatol.* **2006**, *83*, 139–151.

4. Shahid, S. Trends in extreme rainfall events of Bangladesh. *Theor. Appl. Climatol.* **2011**, *104*, 489–499.

5. Shahid, S. Rainfall variability and the trends of wet and dry periods in Bangladesh. *Int. J. Climatol.* **2010**, *30*, 2299–2313.

6. Gao, T.; Xie, L. Multivariate regression analysis and statistical modeling for summer extreme precipitation over the Yangtze River Basin, China. *Adv. Meteorol.* **2014**.

7. Solman, S.A. Regional climate modeling over South America: A review. *Adv. Meteorol.* **2013**.

8. Laprise, R. Regional climate modelling. *J. Comput. Phys.* **2008**, *227*, 3641–3666.

9. Liu, Y.; Xie, L.; Morrison, J.M.; Kamykowski, D. Dynamic downscaling of the impact of climate change on the ocean circulation in the Galápagos Archipelago. *Adv. Meteorol.* **2013**.

10. Wilby, R.L.; Charles, S.P.; Zorita, E.; Timbal, B.; Whetton, P.; Mearns, L.O. Guidelines for Use of Climate Scenarios Developed from Statistical Downscaling Methods. Supporting Material of the Intergovernmental Panel on Climate Change. Available online: (accessed on 24 November 2014).

11. Do Hoai, N.; Udo, K.; Mano, A. Downscaling global weather forecast outputs using ANN for flood prediction. *J. Appl. Math.* **2011**.

12. Khalili, M.; van Nguyen, V.T.; Gachon, P. A statistical approach to multi-site multivariate downscaling of daily extreme temperature series. *Int. J. Climatol.* **2013**, *33*, 15–32.

13. Fan, L.; Chen, D.; Fu, C.; Yan, Z. Statistical downscaling of summer temperature extremes in northern China. *Adv. Atmos. Sci.* **2013**, *30*, 1085–1095.

14. Flaounas, E.; Drobinski, P.; Vrac, M.; Bastin, S.; Lebeaupin-Brossier, C.; Stéfanon, M.; Borga, M.; Calvet, J.C. Precipitation and temperature space-time variability and extremes in the Mediterranean region: Evaluation of dynamical and statistical downscaling methods. *Clim. Dynam.* **2013**, *40*, 2687–2705.

15. Bürger, G.; Sobie, S.R.; Cannon, A.J.; Werner, A.T.; Murdock, T.Q. Downscaling extremes: An intercomparison of multiple methods for future climate. *J. Clim.* **2013**, *26*, 3429–3449.

16. White, C.J.; McInnes, K.L.; Cechet, R.P.; Corney, S.P.; Grose, M.R.; Holz, G.K.; Katzfey, J.J.; Bindoff, N.L. On regional dynamical downscaling for the assessment and projection of temperature

and precipitation extremes across Tasmania, Australia. *Clim. Dynam.* **2013**, *41*, 3145–3165.

17. Jeong, D.I.; St-Hilaire, A.; Ouarda, T.B.M.J.; Gachon, P. Projection of future daily precipitation series and extreme events by using a multi-site statistical downscaling model over the great montréal area, Québec, Canada. *Hydrol. Res.* **2013**, *44*, 147–168.

18. Christensen, R. *Log-Linear Models and Logistic Regression*, 2nd ed.; Springer Verlag: New York, NY, USA, 1997.

19. Fealy, R.; Sweeney, J. Statistical downscaling of precipitation for a selection of sites in Ireland employing a generalised linear modelling approach. *Int. J. Climatol.* **2007**, *27*, 2083–2094.

20. Yang, W.; Bardossy, A.; Caspary, H.J. Downscaling daily precipitation time series using a combined circulation- and regression-based approach. *Theor. Appl. Climatol.* **2010**, *102*, 439–454.

21. Levavasseur, G.; Vrac, M.; Roche, D.M.; Paillard, D.; Martin, A.; Vandenberghe, J. Present and LGM permafrost from climate simulations: Contribution of statistical downscaling. *Clim. Past.* **2011**, *7*, 1225–1246.

22. Hashmi, M.Z.; Shamseldin, A.Y.; Melville, B.W. Statistical downscaling of watershed precipitation using gene expression programming (GEP). *Environ. Model. Softw.* **2011**, *26*, 1639–1646.

23. Banzhaf, W.; Nordin, P.; Keller, R.E.; Francone, F.D. *Genetic Programming: An Introduction*; Morgan Kaufmann, Inc.: San Francisco, CA, USA, 1998.

24. Coulibaly, P. Downscaling daily extreme temperatures with genetic programming. *Geophys. Res. Lett.***2004**.

25. Shahid, S.; Hasan, M.; Mondal, R.U. Modeling monthly mean maximum temperature using genetic programming. *Int. J. Soft Comput.* **2007**, *2*, 612–616.

26. Liu, X.; Coulibaly, P.; Evora, N. Comparison of data-driven methods for downscaling ensemble weather forecasts. *Hydrol. Earth Syst. Sci.* **2008**, *12*, 615–624.

27. Hashmi, M.Z.; Shamseldin, A.Y.; Melville, B.W. Statistical downscaling of precipitation: State-of-the-art and application of

Bayesian multi-model approach for uncertainty assessment. *Hydrol. Earth Syst. Sci. Discuss.* **2009**, *6*, 6535–6579.

28. Kisi, O.; Shiri, J. Precipitation forecasting using wavelet-genetic programming and wavelet-neuro-fuzzy conjunction models. *Water Resour. Manag.* **2011**, *25*, 3135–3152.

29. Zerenner, T.; Venema, V.; Simmer, C. Atmospheric Downscaling Using Genetic Programming. Available online: (accessed on 24 November 2014).

30. Biesheuvel, C.J.; Siccama, I.; Grobbee, D.E.; Moons, K.G. Genetic programming outperformed multivariable logistic regression in diagnosing pulmonary embolism. *J. Clin. Epidemiol.* **2004**, *57*, 551–560.

31. Engoren, M.; Habib, R.H.; Dooner, J.J.; Schwann, T.A. Use of genetic programming, logistic regression, and artificial neural nets to predict readmission after coronary artery bypass surgery. *J. Clin. Monit. Comput.* **2013**, *27*, 455–464.

32. Yusuf, A.A.; Francisco, H.A. *Climate Change Vulnerability Mapping for Southwest Asia*; Economy and Environment Program for Southeast Asia (EEPSEA): Singapore, 2009.

33. Deni, S.M.; Suhaila, J.; Zin, W.Z.W.; Jemain, A.A. Spatial trends of dry spells over Peninsular Malaysia during monsoon seasons. *Theor. Appl. Climatol.* **2010**, *99*, 357–371.

34. Suhaila, J.; Deni, S.M.; Zin, W.Z.W.; Jemain, A.A. Spatial patterns and trends of daily rainfall regime in Peninsular Malaysia during the southwest and northeast monsoons: 1975–2004. *Meteorol. Atmos. Phys.* **2010**, *110*, 1–8.

35. Kalnay, E.; Kanamitsu, M.; Kistler, R.; Collins, W.; Deaven, D.; Gandin, L.; Iredell, M.; Saha, S.; White, G.; Woollen, J.; *et al.* The NCEP/NCAR 40-year reanalysis project. *Bull. Amer. Meteor. Soc.* **1996**, *77*, 437–470.

36. Friederichs, P.; Hense, A. Statistical downscaling of extreme precipitation events using censored quantile regression. *Mon. Weather Rev.* **2007**, *135*, 2365–2378.

37. Wang, J.F.; Zhang, X.B. Downscaling and projection of winter extreme daily precipitation over North America. *J. Clim.* **2008**, *21*, 923–937.

38. Mannshardt-Shamseldin, E.C.; Smith, R.L.; Sain, S.R.; Mearns, L.O.; Cooley, D. Downscaling extremes: A comparison of extreme value distributions in point-source and gridded precipitation data. *Ann. Appl. Stat.* **2010**, *4*, 484–502.

39. Kallache, M.; Vrac, M.; Naveau, P.; Michelangeli, P.A. Nonstationary probabilistic downscaling of extreme precipitation. *J. Geophys. Res.* **2011**.

40. Leanna, M.M.; King, S.I.; Sarwar, KR.; McLeod, A.I.A.; Slobodan, P.; Simonovic, P. The effects of climate change on extreme precipitation events in the Upper Thames River Basin: A comparison of downscaling approaches. *Can. Water Resour. J.* **2012**, *37*, 253–274.

41. Bürger, G.; Murdock, T.Q.; Werner, A.T.; Sobie, S.R.; Cannon, A.J. Downscaling extremes—An intercomparison of multiple statistical methods for present climate. *J. Clim.* **2012**, *25*, 4366–4388.

42. You, Q.; Kang, S.; Aguilar, E.; Yan, Y. Changes in daily climate extremes in the eastern and central Tibetan Plateau during 1961–2005. *J. Geophys. Res.* **2008**.

43. Aguilar, E.; Peterson, T.C.; Ramírez Obando, P.; Frutos, R.; Retana, J.A.; Solera, M.; Soley, J.; González García, I.; Araujo, R.M.; Rosa Santos, A.; *et al.* Changes in precipitation and temperature extremes in CentralAmerica and northern South America, 1961–2003. *J. Geophys. Res.* **2005**.

44. WMO. *The Role of Climatological Normals in A Changing Climate*; WCDMP-No. 61, WMO-TD No. 1377, World Climate Data and Monitoring Programme; World Meteorological Organization: Geneva, Switzerland, 2007.

45. Tripathi, S.; Srinivas, V.V.; Nanjundiah, S.R. Support vector machine approach to downscale precipitation in climate change scenarios. *J. Hydrol.* **2006**, *330*, 621–640.

46. Wilby, R. Statistical downscaling of daily precipitation using daily airflow and seasonal teleconnection indices. *Clim. Res.* **1998**, *10*, 163–178.

47. Wilby, R.L.; Wigley, T.M.L. Precipitation predictors for downscaling: Observed and general circulation model relations relationhips. *Int. J. Climatol.* **2000**, *20*, 641–661.

48. Wilby, R.L.; Dawson, C.W.; Barrow, E.M. SDSM—A decision support tool for the assessment of regional climate change impacts. *Environ. Model. Softw.* **2002**, *17*, 145–157.

49. Tavakol-Davani, H.; Nasseri, M.; Zahraie, B. Improved statistical downscaling of daily precipitation using SDSM platform and data-mining methods. *Int. J. Climatol.* **2012**, *33*, 2561–2578.

50. Dawson, C.W.; Wilby, R.L. Hydrological modeling using artificial neural networks. *Prog. Phys. Geogr.***2004**, *25*, 80–108.

51. Chadwick, R.; Coppola, E.; Giorgi, F. Anartificial neural network technique for downscaling GCM outputs to RCM spatial scale. *Nonlinear Proc. Geoph.* **2011**, *18*, 1013–1028.

52. Harpham, C.; Dawson, C.W. The effect of different basis functions on a radial basis function network for time series prediction: A comparative study. *Neurocomputing* **2006**, *69*, 2161–2170.

53. Hsieh, W.W. *Machine Learning Methods in the Environmental Sciences: Neural Networks and Kernels*; Cambridge University Press: Cambridge, UK, 2009.

54. Haylock, M.R.; Cawley, G.C.; Harpham, C.; Wilby, R.L.; Goodess, C.M. Downscaling heavy precipitation over the United Kingdom: A comparison of dynamical and statistical methods and their future scenarios. *Int. J. Climatol.* **2006**, *26*, 1397–1415.

55. Karamouz, M.; Fallahi, M.; Nazif, S.; Rahimi Farahani, M. Long lead rainfall prediction using statistical downscaling and articial neural network modeling. *Trans. A: Civ. Eng.* **2009**, *16*, 165–172.

56. Gardner, M.W.; Dorling, S.R. Artificial neural networks (the multilayer perceptron)—A review of applications in the atmospheric sciences. *Atmos. Environ.* **1998**, *32*, 2627–2636.

57. Cannon, A.J. Probabilistic multisite precipitation downscaling by an expanded Bernoulli-Gamma density network. *J. Hydrometeorol.* **2008**, *9*, 1284–1300.

58. Makalic, E.; Schmidt, D.F. Review of modern logistic regression methods with application to small and medium sample size problems. *Lecture Notes Comput. Sci.* **2011**.

59. Tibshirani, R. Regression shrinkage and selection via the lasso. *J. R. Stat. Soc. B* **1996**, *58*, 267–288.

60. Zou, H.; Hastie, T. Regularization and variable selection via the elastic net. *J. R. Stat. Soc. B* **2005**, *67*, 301–320.

61. Hunter, A. Using multiobjective genetic programming to infer logistic polynomial regression models. Experimental Supplement. In Proceedings of the 15th European Conference on Artificial Intelligence, Lyon, France, 21–26 July 2002.

62. Siccama, I.; Keijzer, M. *Genetic Programming as a Method to Develop Powerful Predictive Models for Clinical Diagnosis*; Association for Computing Machinery (ACM) Press: Washington, DC, USA, 2005; pp. 164–166.

63. Helfand, B.T.; Loeb, S.; Meeks, J.J.; Fought, A.J.; Kan, D.; Catalona, W.J. Pathological outcomes associated with the 17q prostate cancer risk variants. *J. Urol.* **2009**, *181*, 2502–2507.

64. Ratner, B. *Statistical and Machine-Learning Data Mining: Techniques for Better Predictive Modeling and Analysis of Big Data*; Taylor & Francis: New York, NY, USA, 2011.

65. Koza, J.R. *Genetic Programming: A Paradigm for Genetically Breeding Populations of Computer Program to Solve Problem*; Technical Report STAN-CS-90-1314; Stanford University Computer Science Department: Stanford, CA, USA, 1990.

66. Francone, F.D. *Discipulus™ Software Owner's Manual, Version 3.0 Draft*; Machine Learning Technologies Inc.: Littleton, CO, USA, 1998.

67. Hassan, Z.; Shamsudin, S.; Harun, S.B. Application of SDSM and LARS-WG for simulating and downscaling of rainfall and temperature. *Theor. Appl. Climatol.* **2012**, *116*, 243–257.

68. Tukimat, N.N.A.; Harun, S.B. The projection of future rainfall change over Kedah, Malaysia with the statistical downscaling model. *Malays. J. Civ. Eng.* **2013**, *23*, 67–79.

69. Hessami, M.; Gachon, P.; Ouarda, T.B.M.J.; St-Hilaire, A. Automated regression-based statistical downscaling tool. *Environ. Model. Softw.* **2008**, *23*, 813–834.

70. Cullen, H. *The Weather of the Future: Heat Waves, Extreme Storms, and Other Scenes from a Climate-Changed Planet*; HarperCollins Publishers: New York, NY, USA, 2010.

2

CHAPTER

GENETIC PROGRAMMING: EFFICIENT MODELING TOOL IN HYDROLOGY AND GROUNDWATER MANAGEMENT

J. Sreekanth[1, 2, 3] and Bithin Datta[1, 2]

[1] *CSIRO Land and Water, Ecosciences Precinct, Australia*

[2] *Discipline of Civil and Environmental Engineering, School of Engineering and Physical Sciences, James Cook University, Townsville, Australia*

[3] *CRC for Contaminant Assessment and Remediation of the Environment, Mawson Lakes, Australia*

1. INTRODUCTION

With the advent of computers a wide range of mathematical and numerical models have been developed with the intent of predicting or approximating parts of hydrologic cycle. Prior to the advent of conceptual or process based models, physical hydraulic models, which are reduced scale representations of large hydraulic systems, were used commonly in water resources engineering. Fast development in the computational systems and numerical solutions of complex differential equations enabled development of conceptual models to represent physical systems in almost all arenas of life including hydrological and water resources systems. Thus, in the last two decades large number of mathematical models was developed to represent different processes in the hydrological cycle. Hydrological models can be broadly classified in to three.

1. Physical models
2. Conceptual models
3. Statistical / Black box models

Physical models are reduced scale representations of the actual hydrological system and the responses obtained from these models are up-scaled to estimate the responses of the real system. Conceptual models are based on different individual processes or components of a hydrological process. For example, in modelling the watershed response to a storm event a conceptual model make use of different equations to compute different components like subsurface flow, evapo-transpiration, channel flow, groundwater flow, surface run off etc. The third type of modelling involves using mathematical and statistical techniques to fit a model to a data set which then relates the dependent variable to the independent variables. This type of modelling includes regression models, response matrix, transfer functions, neural networks, support vector machine etc. The most widely used "black box" type modelling approach in hydrology and water resources literature is neural networks. Genetic programming is a potential tool to develop simple and efficient functional relationship between hydrological variables. In spite of the wide range of possible applications in hydrology and water resources, GP has not been widely reported in the hydrology and water resources literature. The focus of this chapter is to discuss the potential applicability of genetic programming to develop simple and computationally efficient hydrological models, in light of a few studies reported in the recent years. The key points discussed are as follows;

1. GP's ability to develop simple models with interpretability to overcome the curse of "black box" nature of data intensive models.
2. Lesser number of parameters used in GP models as compared to parallel neural network architectures.
3. GP's ability to parsimoniously identify the significance of the modelling inputs.

1.1. Genetic Programming as a Modelling Tool

Genetic programming belongs to and is one of the latest members in the family of evolutionary computation. Evolutionary computation refers to the group of computational techniques which are inspired by and emulate the natural process of evolution which resulted in the formation of the entire variety of organisms present on earth. Just as the way evolution and natural selection has resulted in the formation of organisms that are competent and best suitable inhabitants to live in any natural environment, the principle has been applied in computational science to evolve solutions to complex engineering problems which are subject to random and chaotic environments similar to the circumstances in which natural evolution has occurred. Evolutionary computation forms the basic principle behind the evolutionary algorithms like genetic algorithm (GA), genetic programming (GP), Evolutionary programming, evolution strategy, differential evolution. Evolutionary algorithms, widely used in mathematical optimization, are in general based on the application of evolutionary principles like selection, cross-over and mutation to a "population" of candidate solutions over a number of generations to find the optimal solutions to an engineering problem. Genetic algorithm is, for example, a widely used optimization techniques using these principles as the basic "operators" of the algorithm. Genetic programming [1] is similar to genetic algorithm in this aspect that it uses these genetic operators selection, cross-over and mutation in its algorithms. However, the uniqueness of genetic programming is that it performs these operators over symbolic expression or formulae or programs rather than over numbers which represent the candidate solutions. Thus, in genetic programming the candidate solutions are symbolic expressions or formulae. In a modelling framework these symbolic expressions or formulae or programs are candidate models to simulate a physical phenomenon. The parse tree notations of two parent and offspring genetic programs are shown in figure 1. Thus the optimal formula that is evolved by genetic programming can be used as a best fit model for predicting the physical phenomenon under consideration.

In figure 1, two parent programs to model a physical phenomenon are shown. After testing these programs for their modelling performance, they are operated by cross-over operator. That is, parts of the programs are crossed over at the dashed locations to generate the offspring programs. Also, mutation is illustrated by arbitrarily changing the parameter 2 to 6.

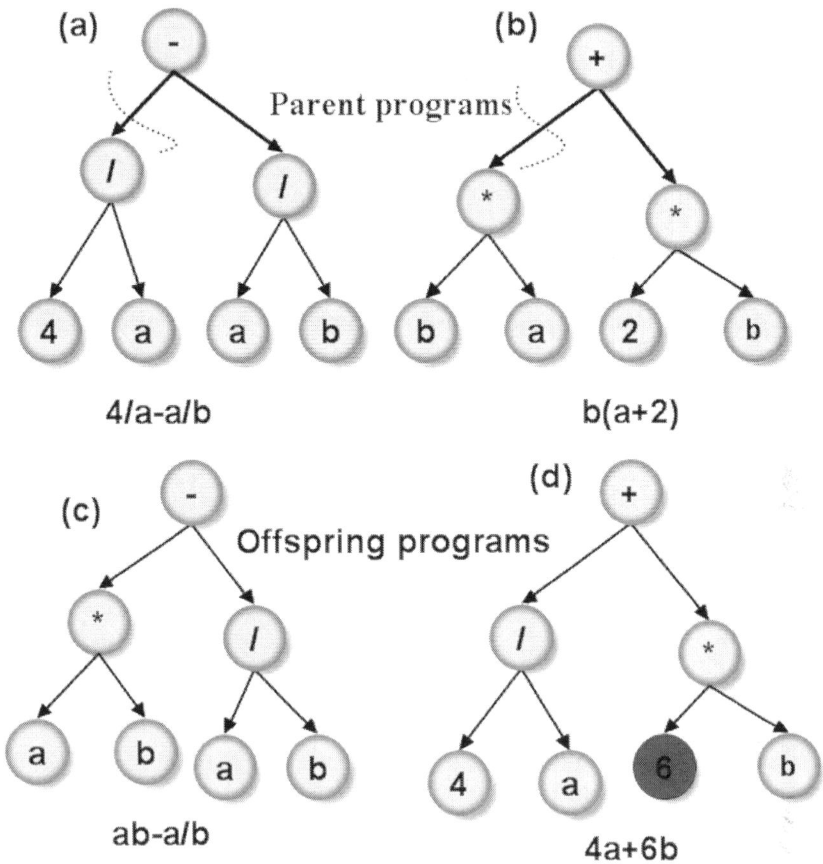

Figure 1. Symbolic representation of parent and offspring genetic programs

In the last decade a few studies in the broad area of hydrology have utilized genetic programming based models for making hydrological predictions. The utility of GP in developing rainfall-runoff models, which are highly non-linear models was addressed in [2] They combined the use of GP based models with other conceptual models in deriving useful hydro-climatic models. It was concluded that GP was able to develop more robust models in that the functional relationships between different model inputs could be easily identified thus resulting in more transparency of the "black box" type of modelling. Another study [3] applied genetic programming and artificial neural networks in hydrology to model the effect of rain on the runoff flow in an urban basin. This study also illustrated the possibility of including the physical basis of the problem in the GP based model. Another research in this direction [4] compared three different artificial intelligence techniques viz, neural networks, adaptive neuro-fuzzy inference system (ANFIS), and genetic programming for discharge routing of a river in Turkey. The study revealed that GP displayed a better edge over the other two modelling approaches in all the statistics compared like the mean absolute error (MAE), mean squared relative error (MSRE) and correlation coefficient. Kisi et al (2010) [5] developed a wavelet gene expression programming (WGEP) for forecasting daily precipitation and compared it with wavelet neuro-fuzzy models (WNF). The results showed that WGEP models are effective in forecasting daily precipitation with better performance over WNF models. Selle [6] utilized genetic programming to systematically develop alternative model structures with different complexity levels for hydrological modelling with the objective of testing whether GP can be used to identify the dominant processes within the hydrological system. Models were developed for predicting the deep percolation responses under surface irrigated pastures to different soil types, water table depths and water ponding times during surface irrigation. The dominant process in the model prediction as determined from the models generated using genetic programming was found to be comparable to those determined using conceptual models. Thus it was concluded that Genetic programming can be used to evaluate the structure of hydrological models. A common aspect of GP based modelling that all these studies reported is the fact that the GP modelling resulted in fairly simpler models which could be easily interpreted for the physical significance of the input variables in making a prediction. Jyothiprakash and Magar (2012) [12] performed a comparative study of reservoir inflow models developed using ANN, ANFIS and linear GP for lumped and distributed data. The study reported superior performance of GP models over ANN and ANFIS models.

2. SIMPLE AND INTERPRETABLE HYDROLOGICAL MODELS USING GENETIC PROGRAMMING

The major drawback of all the data driven modelling approaches is the black box nature of these models, i.e., the user cannot easily identify what is happening in model which computes the outputs corresponding to the inputs supplied to the model. One of the key advantages of genetic programming as a modelling tool is its ability to develop simple hydrological models. The simplicity of the models is close associated with their interpretability. The simpler the models are the better they can be interpreted. This in turn helps in assessing the contributions of different members of the predictor set or inputs in making a particular prediction. Selle and Muttil (2011) utilized this capability of GP to test the structure of hydrological models to predict deep percolation response in surface irrigated pastures. Data obtained using lysimeter experiments were used to develop simple models using genetic programming. The developed models were simple and interpretable which helped in identifying the dominant processes involved in the deep percolation process. Often the developed models could be expressed as simple algebraic equations. The dominant processes identified compared well with the same as used in conceptual models. The study also investigated the recurrence of the models developed using GP in multiple runs and found out that they were consistently coming up with the same model for a given level of complexity of the model. However, the study also reported that as the level of complexity increases recurrence of the generated model were affected and the physical interpretability of the models decreases and hence careful understanding of the complexity of the system is to be considered before a level of complexity is chosen for the GP models.

This however, illustrates that carefully developed GP models remain mathematically simple and are readily interpretable to the extent that the dominant processes which influence the prediction could be readily identified from the model structure. When carefully implemented models can throw light into and identify the key physical processes contributing to the phenomenon predicted and hence the development of the model. This is an important feature lacking from many of the data mining based prediction models resulting from which these modelling approaches are often earmarked as "black-box" models. "Black-box" nature of the prediction models often result in the limited use of such models for practical predictive applications.

2.1. Model Complexity of GP and Neural Networks – Comparative Study

The authors had conducted a study [7] to evaluate the complexity of predictive models developed using Genetic programming in comparison with models developed using neural networks. The models based on GP and neural network were developed as potential surrogate models to a complex numerical groundwater flow and transport model. The saltwater intrusion levels at monitoring locations resulting due to the excitation of the aquifer by pumping from a number of groundwater pumping wells were modelled by using GP and neural networks. The pumping rates at these groundwater well locations for three different stress periods were the inputs or independent variables for the model. The resulting salinity levels at the monitoring locations were the dependent variables or outputs.

The GP and ANN based surrogate models were trained based on the training and validation data generated using a three dimensional coupled flow and transport simulation model FEMWATER. The GP models were developed using a software Discipulus, which uses a linear genetic programming algorithm. The ANN surrogate models were developed using a feed forward back propagation algorithm implemented in the software neuroshell. The input data considered were the pumping rates at eleven well locations over three different time periods, constituting 33 input variables. Since pumping at each location can take any real value between the prescribed minimum and maximum these input variables constitute a 33 dimensional continuous space, each dimension representative of a pumping rate at a particular location in a particular stress period. Hence efficient training of the GP and ANN models required carefully chosen input data which is representative of the entire input space. Latin hypercube sampling was performed to choose uniformly distributed input samples from the 33 dimensional input space. An input sample is a vector of 33 values of pumping rate at 11 well locations during three stress periods. The salinity level at each observation location is the dependent variable or output. The values of the outputs required for training the GP and ANN models were generated by running the FEMWATER model. The numerical simulation model was run numerous times to generate the output data set corresponding to each input vector. The input-output data set generated following this procedure was divided into two sets with three quarters of the data in one set and the rest in the other. The larger set was used for training GP and ANN models and the smaller one was used for validating the models. The members of the training and validation sets for both GP and ANN were chosen randomly.

The ANN used in the study was trained in the supervised training mode using a back propagation algorithm. The objective function considered for both the GP and ANN training was minimization of the total root mean square error (RMSE) of the prediction. The prediction error was calculated as the difference between the model (GP or ANN) predicted values and the actual from the numerical model generated data set.

The input-hidden-output layer architecture for the ANN model was optimized by trial and error. Both GP and ANN models had 33 input variables and 3 outputs. The number of hidden neurons in the ANN model was determined by adding 1 hidden neuron during each trial. A sigmoid transfer function and a learning rate of 0.1 were used. In developing the model the back propagation algorithm modifies the connection weights connecting the input-hidden and output neurons by an amount proportional to the prediction error in each iteration and repeats this procedure numerous times till the prediction errors are minimized to a pre-specified level. Thus for any given model architecture (model structure) the neural network model optimizes the connection weights to accomplish satisfactory model predictions. Where as the genetic programming modelling approach is different in that it evolves the optimal model architecture and their respective parameters in achieving satisfactory predictions.

The GP models developed used a population size of 500, mutation and cross over frequencies of respectively 95 and 50 percent. The number of generations were not specified a priory, instead the evolutionary process was stopped when the fitness function was less than a critical value. In order to achieve the simplest models, the mathematical operators where initially kept a minimum and then further operators were added into the functional set. In this manner, initially addition and subtraction were alone added in this set and later the operators multiplication, arithmetic and data transfer were added into the set.

The predictive performance of the GP and ANN models on an independent set of data were found to be satisfactory in terms of the correlation coefficient and minimized RMSE. Figure 2 and 3respectively shows the ANN and GP predictions of salinity levels at three monitoring locations corresponding to the their corresponding values from the numerical simulation model A dissection of the GP and ANN models were performed to evaluate the model complexity. The modelling framework of the GP models essentially has a functional set and a terminal set. The functional set comprises of the mathematical operations like addition, subtraction, division, multiplication, trigonometric functions etc. The terminal set of GP comprises of the model parameters which are also optimized simultaneously as the model structure is optimized. In our study the developed GP models used a maximum terminal set size of 30. i.e., satisfactory model predictions could be achieved with only 30 parameters for the GP model.

The functional operators essentially develop the structure of the GP models by operating on the input variables. In the GP modelling framework this model structure is not pre-specified unlike the ANN models. Instead, the model structure is evolved in the course of model development by testing numerous different model structures. This approach definitely provides scope for the development of improved model structures as against the ANN method. In the ANN approach where comparatively only a few models are tested in the trial and error approach which does not implement an organized search for better model architectures. The only components that are optimized during the development of the ANN model are the connection weights. Thus the model structure is rigid and is retained as determined by the trial and error procedure. This gives lesser flexibility in adapting the model structure with respect to the process being modelled. In our study it was found that while GP models required only 30 parameters in developing the model the number of connection weights in the ANN models was 1224. This is a metric of the simplicity of the GP models as against the ANN models. Fromfigures 2 and 3 it is observed that despite the simplicity of the model and much lesser number of parameters used GP predictions are very similar to the ANN model predictions. For each hidden neuron added into the ANN architecture the number of connection weights increases by a number equal to the total number of inputs and outputs. Hence there is a geometric increase in the number of connection weights with increase in the number of hidden neurons in ANN architecture.

The comparison of the number of parameters in itself testifies the ability of the genetic programming framework to develop simpler models. The impact of the number of parameters on the model is on the uncertainty of the predictions made using the model. The more the number of parameters, the more uncertainty in them and hence this uncertainty propagates into the predictions made.

3. PARSIMONIOUS SELECTION OF INPUT VARIABLES

Another key feature of the genetic programming based modelling approach is the ability of genetic programming to identify the relative importance of the independent variables chosen as the modelling inputs. Many often in hydrological applications it is uncertain which variables are important to be included as inputs in modelling a physical phenomenon. Similarly time series models are used quite often in predicting or forecasting hydrological variables. For example the river stages measured on a few consecutive days can be used to forecast the river stage for the following days. In doing so the number of past days' flow to be included as inputs into the time series model depends on the size and shape of the catchment and many similar parameters. Most often rigorous statistical tests like auto-correlation studies are conducted to determine whether an independent variable is significant to be included in the model development or not. Once included most often it is not possible to eliminate from most of the modelling frameworks because of the earlier mentioned rigidity of the model structure. For example, in neural networks an insignificant model input should be ideally assigned zero connection weights to the output. However, these connection weights most often don't assume the zero value but converge to very small values near zero. This results in the insignificant variable being influencing the predictions made by a small amount. These results in uncertainties in the predictions made.

The evolutionary process of determining the optimum model structure helps GP to identify and eliminate insignificant variables from the model development. The authors conducted a study dissecting the neural network and GP models developed in the same study described above to evaluate the parsimony in the selection of inputs for model development. GP evolves the best model structure and parameters by testing millions of alternate model structures. The relative importance of the each independent variable in the model development was computed by the recurrence of each independent variable in the best 30 models developed by GP. Thus, if an input appears in all the 30 models its impact factor is 1 and if one independent variable appears in none of the best 30 models its impact factor is 0.

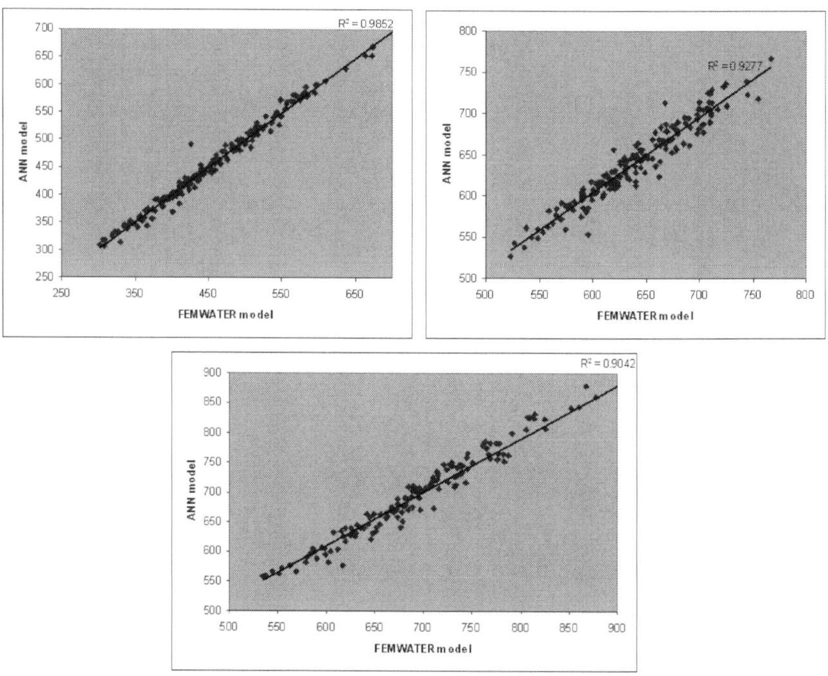

Figure 2. Salinity predictions at three locations by the ANN models

To determine the significance of the inputs in the neural network model a connection weights method was used [7]. In this method the significance of each input is computed as a function of the connection weights which connects it to the output through the hidden layer. The formulae used in [7] were used to compute this;

1. First step in this approach was to compute the product of the input-hidden layer and hidden output layer weights. The, divide this by the sum of products of absolute values of the input-hidden and hidden output layer weights of all input neurons. This is given by Qih in (2)

$$P_{i,h} = |W_{i,h}| \times |W_{h,o}| \tag{1}$$

$$Q_{ih} = \frac{P_{ih}}{\sum_{i=1}^{ni} P_{ih}} \tag{2}$$

2. Divide the sum of the Qih for each hidden neuron by the sum for each hidden neuron of the sum for each input neuron of Qih , for each *i*. The relative importance of all output weights attributable to the given input variable is then obtained. The relative importance is then mapped to a 0-1 scale with the most important variables assuming a value of 1. A RI value of 0 indicates an insignificant variable.

$$RI = \frac{\sum_{h=1}^{nh} Q_{ih}}{\sum_{h=1}^{nh}\sum_{i=1}^{ni} Q_{ih}} \tag{3}$$

In this manner, the significance of each independent variable (input) to the model was quantified in a 0-1 range as impact factor and relative importance respectively for GP and ANN models. These values for GP and ANN models are plotted in figures 4,5 and 6.

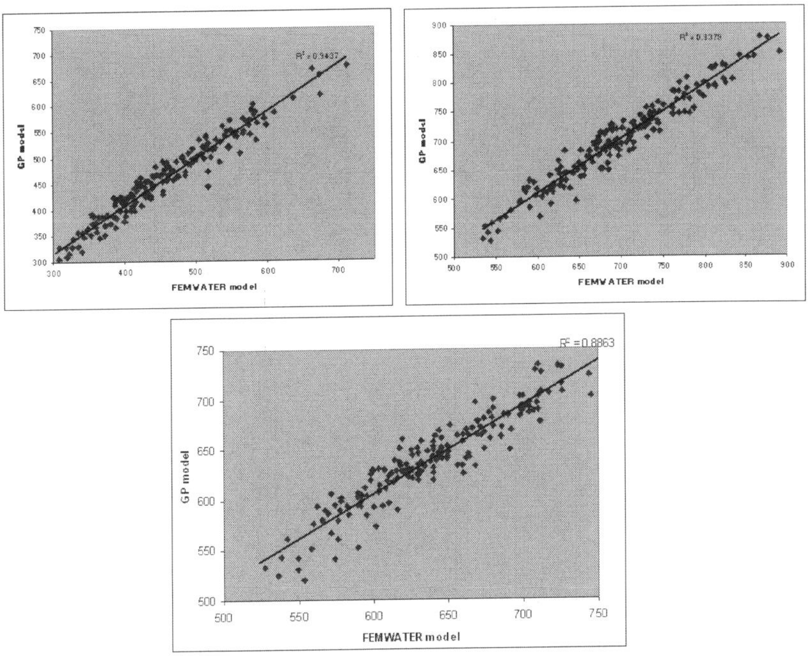

Figure 3. Salinity predictions at three locations by the ANN models

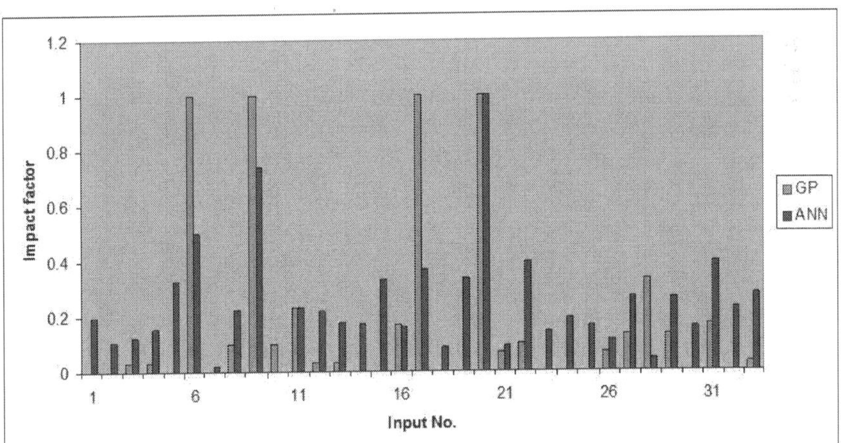

Figure 4. Impact factors of input variables in predicting Salinity at location 1.

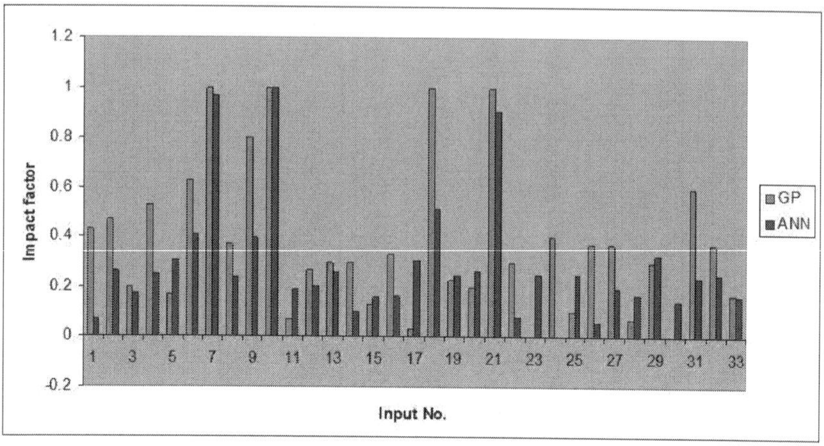

Figure 5. Impact factors of input variables in predicting Salinity at location 2.

From these figures it can be observed that all the variables considered has a non-zero impact in the developed ANN models. Whereas, GP is able to assign zero impact factor to those inputs which are not significant and thus able to eliminate them from the model. This helps in developing simpler models and reducing the predictive uncertainty. In figure 4 it can be seen that GP identified 13 inputs with zero impact factor. This implies that the pumping values corresponding to these inputs have negligible effect on the salinity levels at the observation location. Thus 13 out of the 33 inputs considered are eliminated from the GP models resulting in much simpler models compared to the ANN models where all the 33 inputs take part in predicting the salinity even though some of them are having very less impact on the predictions made. The ability of GP to eliminate insignificant variables is because of the evolutionary nature of model structure optimization. By performing cross-over, mutation and selection of candidate models over a number of generations GP is able to derive the optimum model structure with the most important input variables which are relevant to the model prediction. This inturn help in developing simpler models with fewer uncertainties in the model prediction.

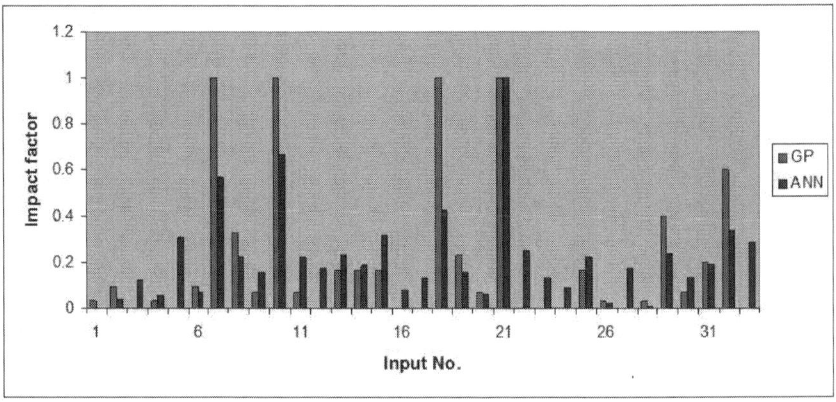

Figure 6. Impact factors of input variables in predicting Salinity at location 3.

4. MULTIPLE PREDICTIVE MODEL STRUCTURES USING GP

The advent of GP as a modelling tool has paved the way for researches exploring the possibility of multiple optimal models for predicting hydrological processes. Genetic programming, in its evolutionary approach to derive optimal model structures and parameters, tests millions of model structures which can mimic the physical process under consideration. Researches have found that multiple models can be identified using GP which are considerably different in model structures but able to make consistently good predictions. Parasuraman and Elshorbagy [8] developed genetic programming based models for predicting the evapo-transporation. In doing so, multiple optimal GP models were trained and tested and they were applied to quantify the uncertainty in those models. Another study by the authors [9] developed ensemble surrogate models for predicting the aquifer responses to pumping in terms of salinity levels at observation locations. An ensemble of surrogate models based on GP was developed and the ensemble was used to get model predictions with improved reliability levels. The variance of the model predictions were used as the measure of uncertainty in the modelling process.

5. GP AS SURROGATE MODEL FOR SIMULATION-OPTIMIZATION

A very important application of data intensive modelling approaches is to develop surrogate models to computationally complex numerical simulation models. As detailed elsewhere in this article, the authors have utilized GP in developing potential surrogates to a complex density dependent groundwater flow and transport simulation model. The potential utility of the surrogates is to replace the numerical simulation model in simulation-optimization frameworks. Simulation-optimization models are used to derive optimal management decisions using optimization algorithms in which a numerical simulation models is run to predict the outcome of implementing the alternative management options. For example, the authors developed simulation-optimization models to develop optimal management decisions for coastal aquifers. The optimal pumping from the coastal aquifer can be decided only by considering the impact of any alternative pumping strategy on saltwater intrusion. For this the numerical simulation model needs to be integrated with the optimization algorithm and the impact of each candidate pumping strategy is predicted by using the simulation model iteratively. This involve a lot of computational burden as thousands of numerical model runs are required before an optimal pumping strategy is identified.

GP was used a surrogate model within the optimization algorithm as a substitute of the numerical simulation model in our study (Sreekanth and Datta, 2010). Previous studies have used artificial neural networks as surrogate models to replace groundwater numerical simulation models. Emily et a1 (2005) used genetic programming based surrogate models for groundwater pollution source identification. In our study (Sreekanth and Datta, 2010), it was found that genetic programming could be used as a superior surrogate model in such application with definite advantages. The study intended to develop optimal pumping strategies for coastal aquifers in which the total pumping could be maximized and at the same time limiting the saltwater intrusion at pre-specified limits. In doing so, the effect of pumping on the salinity levels was predicted using trained and tested GP models. The GP models were externally coupled to a genetic algorithm based optimization model to derive the optimal management strategies. The results of the GP based simulation-optimization was then compared to the results obtained using an ANN-based simulation-optimization model. The ability of GP in parsimoniously identifying the model inputs helped in reducing the dimension of the decision space in which modelling and optimization was carried out. The smaller dimension of the modelling space helped in reducing the training and testing required to develop the surrogate models. The study identified that GP has potential applicability in developing surrogate models with potential application in simulation-optimization methodology to solve environmental management problems.

6. CONCLUSION

The aim of this chapter is to introduce genetic programming as a potential modelling tool for hydrology and water resources applications. Genetic programming belongs to the broad class of evolutionary computational tools developed in recent years. Compared to the vast number of data mining and artificial intelligence applications in hydrology and water resources, the application of GP has been limited in spite of its potential applicability in a wide range of modelling applications. This chapter illustrates a few applications of GP as a modelling tool in the broad area of water resources modelling and management. The studies have found GP to be a useful tool for such applications with some advantages over other artificial intelligence techniques. The major findings reported in this chapter are enumerated as follows;

1. Genetic programming is able to develop simple models for developing the time series forecast models. When compared to the complex architecture of neural networks the GP models are simpler and easy to analyse. This is particularly relevant in developing transparent models for predicting natural phenomena. Complex neural network architectures make ANN model more or less "black-box" in nature, where as simpler GP models makes it easy to analyse the physical significance of each input in the model development.

2. In GP modeling, the optimum model architecture is evolved by GP after testing, most often, millions of alternate model structures and parameters as against the trial and error approach being followed by other artificial intelligence modeling approaches like neural networks. This helps in converging to global optimal solutions in minimizing the error criteria used for model development. Thus GP is able to develop global optimum models for predicting/forecasting hydrological processes and time series.

3. Genetic programming has the capability of parsimoniously selecting the variables for model development from the potential inputs. This helps to prevent redundancy in model development in terms of unnecessary inputs and parameters. In course of the model development GP determines the significance of each input in the model development in an efficient way so that the totally

insignificant inputs are eliminated from the model. As shown in the results approaches like neural network models are also able to identify the relative significance of the inputs, they are less efficient in achieving this because of the rigidity of the model structure and connection weights.

These key advantages of GP modeling are illustrated using realistic example in the broad area of hydrology and groundwater management for time series model development and conclusions are drawn which establishes the potential of genetic programming as a modeling and prediction tool for hydrology and water resources application.

REFERENCES

1. J. R. Koza, 1994Genetic programming as a means for programming computers by natural selection. Statistics and Computing, 4287112
2. V. Babovic, M. Keijzer, 2002Rainfall runoff modelling based on genetic programming. Nordic Hydrology, 335331346
3. J. R. Rabunal, J. Puertas, J. Suarez, D. Rivero, 2006Determination of the unit hydrograph of a typical urban basin using genetic programming and artificial neural networks Hydrological Processes, 214476485
4. Rahman Khatibi, Mohammad Ali Ghorbani, Mahsa Hasanpour Kashani and Ozgur Kisi2011Coparison of three artificial intelligence techniques for discharge routing, Jorunal of Hydrology, 403(3-4), 201-212.
5. Ozgur Kisi and Jalal Shiri2010Precipitation forecasting using wavelet genetic programming and wavelet neuro fuzzy conjunction models, Water Resources Management, 25(13), 3135-3152.
6. Benne Selle, Nithin Muttil2010Testing the structure of a hydrological model using genetic programming, Journal of Hydrology, 397(1-2), 1-9.
7. J. Sreekanth, Datta. Bithin, 2011Comparative evaluation of Genetic Programming and Neural Networks as potential surrogate models for coastal aquifer management, Journal of Water Resources Management, 2532013218doi:s11269-011-9852-8)

8. K. Parasuraman, A. Elshorbagy, 2008Toward improving the reliability of hydrologic prediction: Model structure uncertainty and its quantification using ensemble-based genetic programming framework. Water Resources Research, 44(12).
9. J. Sreekanth, Datta. Bithin, 2011Coupled simulation-optimization model for coastal aquifer management using genetic programming based ensemble surrogate models and multiple realization optimization, Water Resources Research, 47, W04516, doi:WR009683
10. J. Sreekanth, Datta. Bithin, 2010Multi-objective management of saltwater intrusion in coastal aquifers using genetic programming and modular neural network based surrogate models, Journal of Hydrology, 393 (3-4), 245-256
11. Zechman. Emily, Mirghani. G. Baha, Mahinthakumar, S. Ranji, Ranjithan, 2005A genetic programming based surrogate model development and its application to a groundwater source identification problem, ASCE conf. Proc. 173, 341.
12. V. Jyothiprakash, Magar. R. B. And, 2012Multi-step ahead daily and hourly intermittent reservoir inflow prediction using artificial intelligence techiniques using lumped and distributed data, Journal of Hydrology, 450293307

3
CHAPTER

PREDICTING HIGH OR LOW TRANSFER EFFICIENCY OF PHOTOVOLTAIC SYSTEMS USING A NOVEL HYBRID METHODOLOGY COMBINING ROUGH SET THEORY, DATA ENVELOPMENT ANALYSIS AND GENETIC PROGRAMMING

Yi-Shian Lee [1,*] **and Lee-Ing Tong** [2]

[1]*Research Center for Psychological and Educational Testing, National Taiwan Normal University, HePing East Rd., Section 1, Taipei 106, Taiwan*

[2]*Department of Industrial Engineering Management, National Chiao Tung University, 1001 Ta-Hsuch Rd., Hsunchu 300, Taiwan*

ABSTRACT

Solar energy has become an important energy source in recent years as it generates less pollution than other energies. A photovoltaic (PV) system, which typically has many components, converts solar energy into electrical energy. With the development of advanced engineering technologies, the transfer efficiency of a PV system has been increased from low to high. The combination of components in a PV system influences its transfer efficiency. Therefore, when predicting the transfer efficiency of a PV system, one must consider the relationship among system components. This work accurately predicts whether transfer efficiency of a PV system is high or low using a novel hybrid model that combines rough set theory (RST), data envelopment analysis (DEA), and genetic programming (GP). Finally, real data-set are utilized to demonstrate the accuracy of the proposed method.

Keywords: photovoltaic systems; rough set theory; data envelopment analysis; genetic programming; hybrid model

1. INTRODUCTION

Although traditional energy resources, such as oil and coal, account for the largest proportion of energy worldwide, they also produce more pollution than solar energy. As environmental awareness and the need to reduce pollution have increased, solar energy has become an important energy source in industrialized countries. Photovoltaic systems convert solar energy into electrical energy. However PV systems are not yet popular and their transfer efficiency must be improved. Hence, engineers have used various combinations of system components to increase the transfer efficiency of PV systems. Generally, the transfer efficiency of a PV system is only 6–20% [1]. According to the options of experts in PV energy of Taiwan, a transfer efficiency exceeding 9% is considered high and that ≤9% is considered low [2]. Generally, engineers or energy managers must judge if a PV system belongs to one category or the other, thus, a reliable prediction model is needed to determine whether the transfer efficiency of a PV system is high or low. Managers or decision-makers in the PV field will then be able to identify the critical components using the prediction model and improve to transfer efficiencies. Thus, this work develops a novel and efficient prediction model to determine whether transfer efficiency of a PV system is high or low.

In applications of discriminating models, most studies utilized different approaches to construct an effective prediction model [3,4,5,6,7]. These models were constructed using conventional statistical methods, such as discriminant analysis and logistic regression, or artificial intelligence (AI) methods, such as artificial neural networks (ANNs) and support vector machines (SVMs). Ong *et al.* [8] demonstrated that a discriminating model constructed using an ANN-based method is more accurate than a model constructed using traditional statistical methods, especially when data-sets are non-linear. However, ANN-based discriminating models have poor prediction accuracy when applied to small samples and input variables are irrelevant [9]. Additionally, hidden layers in an ANN are difficult to explain and the relationship between input variables and output variables in an ANN or SVM cannot be expressed by a mathematical equation. Genetic programming (GP) has recently been applied in many fields to construct classification or prediction models. Since GP does not require any assumptions about the relationships between dependent and independent variables to construct a prediction model [10], GP can be applied to both small and large samples [8]. In some applications, GP has better prediction accuracy than ANN-based methods. For examples, Ong *et al.* [8] utilized GP to construct a more satisfactory credit scoring model than ANN model; Muttil and Lee [11] utilized GP to predict coastal algal blooms and claimed GP can obtain more effective prediction model than ANN in their analytical case. In prediction or classification applications, GP can be used to construct a mathematical equation [10,11,12]. Moreover, a comparison of the performance of classification models indicated that GP outperforms conventional statistical methods and ANNs [13].

Measuring and monitoring energy efficiency have become important issues in many fields [14]. Some studies have utilized data envelopment analysis (DEA) to assess energy efficiency. For instance, Boyd and Pang [15] examined the relationship between productivity and energy intensity utilizing DEA to assess productivity. Hu and Kao [16] developed an energy efficiency index utilizing DEA. This index is used to determine the energy-saving target ratio (ESTR) for seventeen APEC countries. Based on the importance of energy efficiency and the ability of DEA to determine the ratio between input and output variables, this work adopts DEA to evaluate the input/output efficiency of PV systems using multiple inputs, such as texture type, selection of a PV module, and PV module capacity, and one output (transfer efficiency of PV systems).

Moreover, identifying significant input variables is important when constructing an effective prediction model. Many conventional methods, such as correlation analysis, have been utilized to identify the significant input variables for predicting the output variable. However, such methods are restricted by some assumptions, such as a linear relationship among variables and normality, and large data-sets. Thus, a technique that provides a knowledge system contained in a data-set and clear attribute selection under different classes is desirable. Rough set theory (RST) can be utilized as a soft computing tool to deal with data-sets with poor information and remove irrelevant attributes from a dataset [17]. Notably, RST has been applied in many real-world classification problems [18,19,20].

To construct an efficient prediction model that determines whether the transfer efficiency of a PV system is high or low, this work uses input/output efficiency of a PV system as the predictive variable and enhances prediction accuracy using a novel hybrid model combining RST with GP; this model is called the RST-GP model. Because of its robust reliability in knowledge systems, RST is utilized during the first stage to identify significant input variables. During the second stage, significant independent variables obtained from RST are utilized as input variables for GP to construct a prediction model that can determine whether the transfer efficiency of a PV system is high or low. This remainder of this paper is organized as follows.Section 2 reviews the PV system literature. Section 3 briefly reviews the DEA model used to evaluate the input/output efficiency of a PV system. Section 4 describes RST and GP. Section 5 elucidates the proposed hybrid model. Section 6 analyzes and compares the outcomes of the proposed and existing hybrid models.Section 7 gives conclusions.

2. AN OVERVIEW OF PV SYSTEM

This section introduces the structure of PV system and factors influencing PV system transfer efficiency.

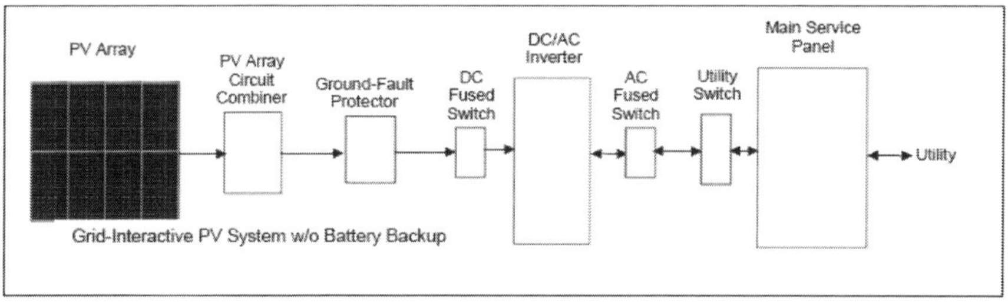

Figure 1. A diagram of a PV system [21].

2.1. PV System

A PV system primarily consists of a solar cell, an electrical conditioner, an inverter, and a system controller. A PV system uses an inverter to transform light energy into electrical energy. Figure 1 shows the PV system process.

2.2. Factors Influencing PV Systems

Gregg *et al.* [22] noted that numerous complex factors influence the efficiency of PV systems. These factors can be classified as internal or external factors. Internal factors include PV system texture, the azimuthal angle, transformation of the PV inverter, and selection of direct current (DC) voltage and an inverter. Among the internal factors, PV system texture, the most important factor, influences PV system transfer efficiency. Single crystal and polycrystals are common in PV systems. The azimuthal angle of a PV system is that at which most light is received given the absence of obstacles; thus, azimuthal angle varies with PV system location. The PV inverter transforms light energy into electrical energy. Selection of DC voltage and the inverter both influence PV system transfer efficiency. However, in the real world, the transformation of light energy into electrical energy is affected by dynamic changes in sunshine. Accordingly, the optimal transfer efficiency of a PV inverter cannot be attained in practice.

The two major external factors are described as follows: first, the amount of solar radiation strongly influences PV system transfer efficiency. Thus, the degree of solar radiation must also be considered when determining PV system transfer efficiency. Second, the temperature of a PV system affects the amount of electrical energy converted from light energy. Thus, determining the optimal temperature in a real environment is a major goal for energy experts.

2.3. Evaluating PV System Transfer Efficiency

Transfer efficiency of a PV system is the percentage of energy converted from light energy. The transfer efficiency formula is:

$$\text{Transfer efficiency}\ (\%) = \frac{P_{mou}}{P_{in}} \times 100\% \tag{1}$$

where Pmou is maximum output electrical energy, and Pin is input light energy. As transfer efficiency increases, the amount of energy a PV system generates increases.

3. USING DEA TO DETERMINE EFFICIENCIES

Notably, DEA is a linear programming (LP)-based technique for evaluating decision-making units (DMUs) and deals with many decision-making problems by converting multiple output and input variables into a single comprehensive performance measure [23]. DEA is an extensively utilized non-parametric data analysis technique. For instance, Hu and Kao [16] utilized DEA to construct an energy efficiency index. This index is used to determine the energy-saving target ratio (ESTR) for seventeen Asia-Pacific Economic Cooperation (APEC) countries. Tsai *et al.* [23] applied DEA with other measures to assess the magnitude of performance differences between leading telecom carriers. Guo and Tanaka [24] utilized a fuzzy DEA model to solve an efficiency evaluation problem with given fuzzy input and output data. Wu *et al.* [25] used the DEA-neural network approach to evaluate branch efficiency for a large Canadian bank. Additional detailed descriptions of DEA can be found elsewhere [26,27,28].

DEA, developed by Charnes, Cooper, and Rhodes (CCR) [28], was based on Farrell's (1957) pioneering study of efficiency measures (relative efficiency or productivity of a specific DMU) [29]. Suppose data for each DMU, j=1,2,...,n, comprise q positive outputs, yrj, r=1,2,...,q, and p positive inputs, xij, i=1,2,...,p. Let h_o (o=1,2,...,n) be the DMU whose relative efficiency is to be maximized. The DEA model is displayed as LP as follows:

$$\text{Maximize } h_o = \frac{\sum_{r=1}^{q} u_{ro} y_{ro}}{\sum_{i=1}^{p} v_{io} x_{io}} \tag{2}$$

$$\text{Subject to } \frac{\sum_{r=1}^{q} u_r y_{rj}}{\sum_{i=1}^{p} v_i x_{ij}} \leq 1$$

$$u_r, v_i \geq 0; \quad i = 1,2,\ldots,p; \quad r = 1,2,\ldots,q$$

where uro, vio are the variable weights of given to the *r*th output and *i*th input of the *o*th DMU, respectively. Furthermore, uro and vio are decision variables of LP modeling used to determine the relative efficiency of DMU_o. Obviously, the maximum value (efficiency score), ho, cannot exceed 1. If ho=1, the DMU_o is called the constant returns to scale (CRS) frontier [30]. There are two CCR models in practice. One minimizes input variables, and the other maximizes output variables. In this work, in order to obtain maximum energy efficiency, the maximized output variables of the CCR model are utilized to obtain the optimal value for the objective function, ho.

4. ROUGH SET THEORY AND GENETIC PROGRAMMING

This section reviews the basic concepts of RST and GP.

4.1. Basic Concepts of Rough Set Theory

Pawlak [31] developed RST as a data-mining approach in 1982. RST has proved effective for data-sets with poor information or ambiguity and it can be applied in many fields [32,33,34]. Walczak and Massart [35] provided a detailed description of RST.

An information system can be represented as S=(*U*, *R*, *V*, *f*), where *U* is the universe (a finite set of objects, $U=\{x_1,x_2,\ldots,x_n\}$), *R* is a finite set of attributes (features and variables), V=∪r∈RVr, where V_r is the domain of attribute *r*, and f:U×R→V is an information function such that f(x,r)∈Vr for all x∈U and r∈R. In RST, highly accurate good-quality approximations are very important when extracting decision rules. Let P⊆R and X⊆U, the lower approximation of *X* in *S* by *P* is denoted as $\underline{P}X$, and the upper approximation of *X* in *S* by *P* is denoted as $\overline{P}X$ and are derived as follows:

$$\underline{P}X = \{x \in U \mid Ind(R) \subset X\} \tag{3}$$

$$\overline{P}X = \{x \in U \mid U / Ind(R) \cap X \neq \phi\} \tag{4}$$

where:

$$U / Ind(R) = \left\{(x_i, x_j) \in U \cdot U, f(x_i, r) = f(x_j, r), \forall r \in R\right\} \tag{5}$$

From Equations (3),(4), the boundary can be represented as follows:

$$PN_p\left(X\right) = \overline{P}X - \underline{P}X \tag{6}$$

Hence, reducts can be obtained utilizing approximation spaces. Given an information system S=(U,R), and then the reduct *RED*(*P*), the minimal set of attributes is P⊆R, such that rP(U)=rR(U) where:

$$r_P(U) = \frac{\sum_{i=1}^{n} card(\underline{P}(X_i))}{card(U)} = \frac{\sum_{i=1}^{n} |\underline{P}(X_i)|}{|U|} \tag{7}$$

where rp(U) is the ratio of all *P*-correctly classified objects to all objects (*U*) in the system. Furthermore, core is common to all reducts. For instance, *COR*(*P*) is the core of *P* when COR(P)=∩RED(P). Reduction is a feature subset selection process. The selected feature subset retains its explanation ability and has minimal redundancy [36]. Core analysis results can be represented as a reference of important attributes in a knowledge system. Several RST-based reduction and feature-selection algorithms have been developed. For instance, Wen *et al.* [37] applied RST and a grey model to analyze the factors influencing gas breakdown. Li *et al.* [38] developed a grey-based rough set approach to solve a supplier-selection problem. Thangavel and Pethalakshmi [39] reviewed studies using RST-based feature selection.

4.2. Genetic Programming

Koza [40] developed GP as a novel algorithm for computer programs that exploits evolution in solving model structure identification problems and performs symbolic regression [41]. The basic concepts of GP resemble those of genetic algorithms (GAs), and include mutation, crossover, and reproduction [10]. Unlike GAs, GP uses a generic parse-tree representation to replace the logic number of the genetic state (0 and 1). Additionally, GP can construct an optimal forecasting equation through symbolic regression. The main advantage of symbolic regression is that it is not limited to any functional form or normality assumption for data-sets. For instance, GP is more flexible in symbolic setting than conventional regression method or data-mining approach (e.g., ANN). Notably, GP is also widely utilized in practical applications such as in forecasting [10,11,12,42] and classification [8,43].

Functions or statements in GP have operators ({+, −, ×, ÷, *log*, and *exp*}) and a trigonometric function ({*sin,cos*, and *tan*}). Hence, a GP parse tree (Figure 2) can be applied to a simple example: *cos*[8*x*] − *sec*[5*y*]. When selecting input variables, GP automatically finds variables that contribute most to the model [11,42] and does not have any restriction for data size, as compared to an ANN or large data-set [8,43].

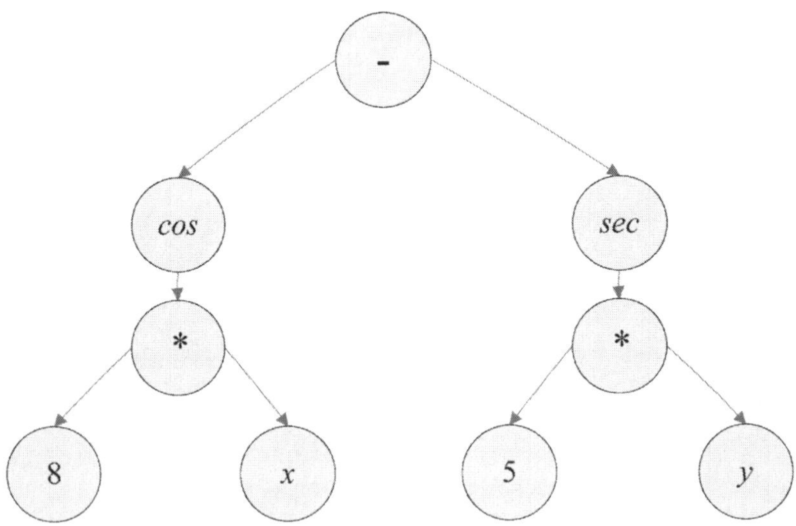

Figure 2. Example of GP parse tree representation.

5. THE PROPOSED HYBRID PREDICTION MODEL

This work develops a four-step procedure for predicting whether the transfer efficiency of a PV system is high or low. The proposed prediction model is as follows:

Step 1: Collect transfer efficiencies of PV systems with various component combinations. These components are independent variables and transfer efficiency is a binary output variable (*i.e.*, high or low) in the proposed prediction model.

Step 2: RST selects the significant independent variables of a PV system based on its robust reliability in knowledge system [36,37,38,39]. The importance of feature selection based on RST (*i.e.*, core analysis) can be explained as follows [44]:

$$\sigma_{(C,D)}(a)=\frac{\gamma_C(D)-\gamma_{C-\{a\}}(D)}{\gamma_C(D)}=1-\frac{\gamma_{C-\{a\}}(D)}{\gamma_C(D)} \tag{8}$$

where $\gamma C(D)$ denotes the degree of dependence between conditional features *C* (the variables of PV systems) and decision feature *D* (*i.e.*, the high or low PV transfer efficiency), $\gamma C-\{a\}(D)$ denotes the degree of dependence between removing a conditional feature (such as *a* condition feature) from *C* and decision feature *D*. $\sigma(C,D)(a)$ denotes the variation of degree of dependence between removing *a* from *C* with all condition features *C*. When $\sigma(C,D)(a)$ is large, feature *a* importantly affects the decision attribute *D*.

Step 3: The DEA evaluates energy efficiency (*i.e.*, the input/output ratio) of a PV system. The input variables in DEA are obtained in Step 2 and the output variable in DEA is transfer efficiency of a PV system. The DMU values obtained from DEA represent energy efficiencies of PV systems.

Step 4: GP constructs a classification model for predicting whether transfer efficiency of a PV system is high or low. For the GP model, this work utilizes the significant independent variables obtained in Step 2 and the input/output ratio obtained in Step 3 as input variables of GP and binary transfer efficiency (*i.e.*, high or low) of a PV system is the output variable of GP. Table 1 presents parameter settings of the GP model. The parameters of GP are obtained by trial-and-error approach.

Table 1. The settings of GP model.

Items	Content
Population size	400
Maximum number of generation	1000
Function set	+, −, ×, ÷, *sin*, *cos*, *exp*, *log* constant
Crossover rate	0.8
Mutation rate	0.02

In Step 2, RST is utilized to select the significant independent variables of PV systems because adopting significant independent variables can yield good accuracy for constructing a prediction model [36]. Moreover, RST can not only deal with small data-sets but also requires no statistical assumptions (such as a linear relationship between input variables with output variable). In Step 3, DEA is utilized to evaluate the energy efficiency of PV systems because the index (energy efficiency of PV systems) efficiently provides sufficient information for evaluating the economic-value of PV systems. In Step 4, GP is utilized to construct a prediction model because of its high performance in forecasting and classification. Furthermore, GP yields good forecasts using only small data-sets [42]. Hence, RST, DEA, and GP are integrated herein to predict the high or low transfer efficiency of PV systems, and the model thus developed is called the RST-DEA-GP model.

6. EMPIRICAL ANALYSIS

A real data-set of transfer efficiency of PV systems collected from a Taiwanese research organization is utilized to demonstrate the effectiveness of the proposed model. The data used in Step 1 concern 38 PV systems. Each PV system contains 18 variables (e.g., texture type, capacity for PV-transfer, and number of inverters) and binary transfer efficiency (e.g., low or high). The low and high transfer efficiencies of the PV systems are coded as 0 and 1, respectively. The data-set comprises 38 PV systems–15 with low and 23 with high transfer efficiencies.

Table 2. Selected significant variables from RST and DMU variable from DEA.

Variables	Description	Importance (obtained from RST)
X_1	Texture type	0.6424
X_2	The output power of inverter	0.5715
X_3	The selection of PV module	0.4817
X_4	The number of inverter	0.3914
X_5	The weights of PV module	0.3367
X_6	The selection of inverter	0.2893
X_7	PV module capacity	0.2567
X_8	The selection of DC voltage	0.2638
X_9	The location of PV setting	0.2476
X_{10}	DMU (obtained from DEA)	—

In Step 2 of the proposed hybrid model, RST is utilized to identify significant independent variables of PV systems. The RST algorithm can be constructed using MATLAB software. The RST results indicate that nine independent variables (X_1–X_9) are significant (Table 2) because that the importance value of nine independent variables are greater than 0.2. It has not a clear criterion to determine the threshold value (importance value). Moreover, the nine independent variables (X_1–X_9) have high correlation to output variable (the low or high transfer efficiencies of PV systems). The correlation coefficient are greater than 0.6. Also, based on the opinion of experts in PV energy in Taiwan, these nine variables importantly influence for the transfer efficiency of PV systems.

In Step 3, DEA is utilized to evaluate the DMU value of each PV system. Table 2 shows the DMU value (X_{10}). In applying DEA, input variables of DEA are the nine significant variables obtained in Step 2 and the output variable of DEA is PV system transfer efficiency. The DEA algorithm can be executed by LINGO software. Table 3 lists the DMU values of the PV systems. In Step 4, the significant independent variables obtained in Step 2 and DMU obtained in Step 3 are utilized as input variables for GP to predict the high or low level of PV system transfer efficiency. To demonstrate the effectiveness of the proposed hybrid model, some basic classification models such as *K* Nearest Neighbor (KNN), Naive Bayes (NB), SVM, ANN, and GP are utilized as benchmark models. The basic classification models belong to data-mining techniques and can obtain better prediction performance than traditional linear statistical method (e.g., linear regression) [8,10].

Table 3. The results of DMU value of each PV system by utilizing DEA.

No	DMU	No	DMU
PV001	1.0000	PV023	0.7735
PV002	0.9482	PV024	0.8059
PV003	0.9879	PV025	1.0000
PV004	0.8392	PV026	1.0000
PV005	1.0000	PV027	1.0000
PV006	1.0000	PV028	1.0000
PV007	1.0000	PV029	1.0000
PV008	1.0000	PV030	0.6981
PV009	1.0000	PV031	0.6417
PV010	0.6902	PV032	0.6608
PV011	0.9215	PV033	0.4919
PV012	0.5153	PV034	1.0000
PV013	0.4955	PV035	0.8274
PV014	0.9667	PV036	0.4947
PV015	0.7484	PV037	0.8405
PV016	1.0000	PV038	0.9944
PV017	0.6144		
PV018	0.8630		
PV019	1.0000		
PV020	0.8630		
PV021	1.0000		
PV022	0.8832		

Although some studies [36] have also adopted hybrid classification models that combine RST, DEA, and SVM to predict business failures, the RST of their proposed methodology did not identify how to obtain the important variables based on a clear equation. This study [36] only adopted the RSES software tool [45] to select important variables. Furthermore, the SVM model performs well only with large data-sets, and collecting large data-sets for PV systems is difficult. Hence, the use of a suitable classification model for small data-sets is important for constructing a high-precision prediction model.

In order to compare the accuracy of hybrid prediction model when adding DEA or nor, this work does some design of experiments for prediction models. The proposed model, named RST-DEA-GP model, which adopts the significant variables obtained by RST and the DMU variable obtained in DEA as input variables for GP (model I). The RST-GP model adopts only the significant variables, X_1–X_9, as the input variables for GP (model II). In both models I and II, this work adopts leave-one-out cross validation to test the accuracy of the prediction model.

Table 4 and Table 5 show the analytical results for hybrid models I and II, respectively. Model I has an average correct classification rate of 92.10%, and that of model II is 84.21%. Hence, adding DEA provides more information than adopting significant input variables only and enhances prediction model accuracy.

Table 4. RST-DEA-GP model (model I) results with both significant variables and DMU.

Actual class	Classified class	
	1 (High-level)	2 (Low-level)
1 (High-Level)	22 (95.65%)	1 (4.35%)
2 (Low-Level)	2 (13.33%)	13 (86.67%)

Average correct classification rate: 92.10%.

Table 5. RST-GP model (model II) results with only significant variables.

Actual class	Classified class	
	1 (High-level)	2 (Low-level)
1 (High-Level)	21 (91.30%)	2 (8.70%)
2 (Low-Level)	4 (26.67%)	11 (73.33%)

Average correct classification rate: 84.21%.

The RST-SVM-based models are also utilized to predict whether PV systems have high or low transfer efficiency. The RST-DEA-SVM model uses both significant variables obtained from RST and DMU as input variables of SVM (model III). The RST-SVM model, which utilizes only significant attributes, is model IV. In constructing the SVM model, this work utilizes STATISTICA software to generate a classification model. Some studies [46,47] utilized the Gaussian kernel function to enhance prediction performance. For the SVM model, parameters settings are the Gaussian kernel function, $C =$ 3, and r=0.129, which can generate an appropriate prediction model. Table 6 and Table 7 summarize prediction results for the confusion matrix utilizing models III and IV, respectively. Based on RST-SVM-based model results, adding DEA improves the correct classification rate from 78.94% to 81.57%.

Table 6. RST-DEA-SVM model (model III) results with significant variables and DMU.

Actual class	Classified class	
	1 (High-level)	2 (Low-level)
1 (High-Level)	20 (86.96%)	3 (13.04%)
2 (Low-Level)	4 (26.67%)	11 (73.33%)

Average correct classification rate: 81.57%.

Table 7. RST-SVM model (model IV) results with only significant variables.

Actual class	Classified class	
	1 (High-level)	2 (Low-level)
1 (High-Level)	20 (86.96%)	3 (13.04%)
2 (Low-Level)	5 (33.33%)	10 (66.67%)

Average correct classification rate: 78.94%.

Furthermore, two RST-ANN-based prediction models are applied. One uses the significant variables obtained from RST and the DMU variable obtained from DEA as input variables for an ANN (model V, named RST-DEA-ANN model). The RST-ANN model utilizes only significant variables as input variables for the ANN (model VI). This work uses Qnet2000 software to construct the ANN classification model. Cybenko [48] demonstrated that utilizing one hidden layer is sufficient when modeling any complex system. Hence, the appropriate network models are 10-5-1 and 9-7-1 for nodes of the input layer, hidden layer, and output layer for models V and VI, respectively. Table 8 and Table 9 summarize prediction results for the confusion matrix utilizing models V and VI, respectively. Similarly, from the results of RST-SVM-based model, RST-ANN is also obvious that adding DEA can improve the correct classification rate from 76.31% to 81.57%.

Table 8. RST-DEA-ANN model (model V) results with both significant variables and DMU.

Actual class	Classified class	
	1 (High-level)	2 (Low-level)
1 (High-Level)	21 (91.30%)	2 (8.70%)
2 (Low-Level)	5 (33.37%)	10 (66.67%)

Average correct classification rate: 81.57%.

Table 9. RST-ANN model (model VI) results with only significant variables.

Actual class	Classified class	
	1 (High-level)	2 (Low-level)
1 (High-Level)	19 (82.61%)	4 (17.39%)
2 (Low-Level)	5 (33.33%)	10 (66.67%)

Average correct classification rate: 76.31%.

With the same analysis of the above classification models (model I to VI), two RST-KNN-based and RST-NB-based prediction models are applied to predict whether PV systems have high or low transfer efficiency. This work also adopts STATISTICA to construct the KNN and NB classification models, respectively. For KNN classification, one uses the significant variables obtained from RST and the DMU variable obtained from DEA as input variables for a KNN (model VII, named RST-DEA-KNN model). The RST-KNN model utilizes only significant variables as input variables for the KNN (model VIII). Table 10 and Table 11summarize prediction results for the confusion matrix utilizing models VII and VIII, respectively. Based on RST-KNN-based model results, adding DEA improves the correct classification rate from 73.68 % to 76.31%.

Table 10. RST-DEA-KNN model (model VII) results with both significant variables and DMU.

Actual class	Classified class	
	1 (High-level)	2 (Low-level)
1 (High-Level)	19 (82.61%)	4 (17.39%)
2 (Low-Level)	5 (33.33%)	10 (66.67%)

Average correct classification rate: 76.31%.

Table 11. RST-KNN model (model VIII) results with only significant variables.

Actual class	Classified class	
	1 (High-level)	2 (Low-level)
1 (High-Level)	18 (78.26%)	5 (21.74%)
2 (Low-Level)	5 (33.33%)	10 (66.67%)

Average correct classification rate: 73.68%.

For NB classification, one uses the significant variables obtained from RST and the DMU variable obtained from DEA as input variables for a NB (model IX, named RST-DEA-NB model). The RST-NB model utilizes only significant variables as input variables for the NB (model X). Table 12 and Table 13 summarize prediction results for the confusion matrix utilizing models IX and X, respectively. Based on RST-NB-based model results, adding DEA improves the correct classification rate from 73.68 % to 76.31%.

Table 12. RST-DEA-NB model (model IX) results with both significant variables and DMU.

Actual class	Classified class	
	1 (High-level)	**2 (Low-level)**
1 (High-Level)	19 (82.61%)	4 (17.39%)
2 (Low-Level)	5 (33.33%)	10 (66.67%)

Average correct classification rate: 76.31%.

Table 13. RST-NB model (model X) results with only significant variables.

Actual class	Classified class	
	1 (High-level)	**2 (Low-level)**
1 (High-Level)	19 (82.61%)	4 (17.39%)
2 (Low-Level)	6 (40%)	9 (60%)

Average correct classification rate: 73.68%.

To compare the performance of models I to XII with that of basic classification models (GP, SVM, ANN, KNN, and NB models), the latter, basic classification models are utilized to construct the prediction model. Additionally, the original 18 variables of the PV system are taken into account as the input variables of each basic classification model and the output variable is the binary transfer efficiency (high or low) of a PV system. The results (average correct classification rate) of the basic classification models, based on leave-one-out cross validation are: GP (84.21%, model XI), SVM (78.94%, model XII), ANN (78.94%, model XIII), KNN (71.05%, model XIV), and NB (68.42%, model XV). To determine the computational demands of all classification models (model I to XV), the computing time of each is calculated (Table 14).

Table 14. Computational time of different models (seconds).

Model	Computational time
Model I (RST-DEA-GP)	65.13
Model II (RST-GP)	62.34
Model III (RST-DEA-SVM)	60.17
Model IV (RST-SVM)	56.49
Model V (RST-DEA-ANN)	63.28
Model VI (RST-ANN)	60.67
Model VII (RST-DEA-KNN)	55.23
Model VIII (RST-KNN)	53.28
Model IX (RST-DEA-NB)	54.87
Model X (RST-NB)	52.81
Model XI (GP)	51.78
Model XII (SVM)	50.46
Model XIII (ANN)	51.39
Model XIV (KNN)	48.23
Model XV (NB)	46.26

These analytical results demonstrate that the proposed hybrid model is more accurate than other hybrid models in predicting whether the transfer efficiency of PV systems is high or low. Although the computational time of the proposed model exceeds that of the other models, its prediction of whether the transfer efficiency of PV systems is low or high is very precise. Notably, adding the DMU variable, obtained from DEA, as an independent variable to the GP, SVM, ANN, KNN and NB models yields more information than considering only significant variables, and enhances the classification accuracy rate of the proposed model. Finally, the proposed model can obtain greater performance than only adopting one classification model (GP).

7. CONCLUSIONS

Accurately predicting high or low transfer efficiency of a PV system is difficult since many uncertain factors may influence correct classifications of real-world data. This work makes four important contributions to the existing literature. First, adding DEA provides additional information for constructing a model that can predict high or low transfer efficiency of PV systems. Second, the results of RST can allow managers or decision-makers in the PV field to identify the critical components. Third, the proposed hybrid model has better classification results than existing hybrid models, regardless of whether only significant variables are adopted or significant variables and the DMU variable are adopted. Fourth, the proposed model also has the lowest misclassification rate among all models tested. Therefore, the proposed RST-DEA-GP model can accurately predict whether a PV system has high or low transfer efficiency.

Future work can apply grey theory to determine whether a PV system has high or low transfer efficiency based on uncertain information. Second, in order to demonstrate the effectiveness of the proposed hybrid prediction model, it will be utilized to predict more different country PV systems.

REFERENCES

1. Bureau of Energy, Ministry of Economic. Available online: (accessed on 13 February 2012).
2. Industrial Technology Research Institute. Available online: (accessed on 13 February 2012).
3. Zhou, X.; Liu, K.Y.; Wong, S.T.C. Cancer classification and prediction using logistic regression with Bayesian gene selection. *J. Biomed. Inf.* **2004**, *37*, 249–259.
4. Worth, A.P.; Cronin, M.T.D. The use of discriminant analysis, logistic regression and classification tree analysis in the development of classification models for human health effects. *J. Mol. Struct. Theochem.* **2003**, *622*, 97–111.
5. Kurt, I.; Ture, M.; Kurum, A.T. Comparing performances of logistic regression, classification and regression tree, and neural networks for predicting coronary artery disease. *Expert Syst. Appl.* **2008**,*34*, 366–374.

6. Huang, Z.; Chen, H.; Hsu, C.J.; Chen, W.H.; Wu, S. Credit rating analysis with support vector machines and neural networks: a market comparative study. *Decis. Support Syst.* **2004**, *37*, 543-558.
7. Luts, J.; Ojeda, F.; Plas, R.V.D.; Moor, B.D.; Huffel, S.V.; Suykens, J.A.K. A tutorial on support vector machine-based methods for classification problems in chemometrics. *Anal. Chim. Acta* **2010**, *665*, 129–145.
8. Ong, C.S.; Huang, J.J.; Tzeng, G.H. Building credit scoring models using genetic programming. *Expert Syst. Appl.* **2005**, *29*, 41–47.
9. Nath, R.; Rajagopalan, B.; Ryker, R. Determining the saliency of input neural classifiers. *Comput. Oper. Res.* **1997**, *24*, 767–773.
10. Lee, D.G.; Lee, B.W.; Chang, S.H. Genetic programming model for long-term forecasting of electric power demand. *Electr. Power Syst. Res.* **1997**, *40*, 17–22.
11. Muttil, N.; Lee, J.H.W. Genetic programming for analysis and real-time prediction of coastal algal blooms. *Ecol. Model.* **2005**, *189*, 363–376.
12. Liong, S.Y.; Gautam, T.R.; Khu, S.T.; Babovic, V.; Muttil, N. Genetic Programming: a new paradigm in rainfall-runoff modelling. *J. Am. Water Res. Assoc.* **2002**, *38*, 557–584.
13. Zhang, Y.; Bhattacharyya, S. Genetic Programming in classifying large-scale data: an ensemble method. *Inf. Sci.* **2004**, *163*, 85-101.
14. Ang, B.W. Monitoring changes in economy-wide energy efficiency: From energy-GDP ratio to composite efficiency index. *Energy Policy* **2006**, *34*, 574–582.
15. Boyd, J.X.; Pang, T.G. Estimating the linkage between energy efficiency and productivity. *Energy Policy* **2000**, *28*, 289–296.
16. Hu, J.L.; Kao, C.H. Efficiency energy-saving targets for APEC economies. *Energy Policy* **2007**, *35*, 373–382.
17. Pawlak, Z. Rough sets and intelligent data analysis. *Inf. Sci.* **2002**, *147*, 1–12.
18. Ahn, B.S.; Cho, S.S.; Kim, C.Y. The integrated methodology of rough set theory and artificial neural network for business failure prediction. *Expert Syst. Appl.* **2000**, *18*, 65–74.

19. Leung, Y.; Fischer, M.M.; Wu, W.Z.; Mi, J.S. A rough set approach for the discovery of classification rules in interval-valued information systems. *Int. J. Approx. Reason.* **2008**, *47*, 233–246.

20. Dembczynski, K.; Greco, S.; Slowinski, R. Rough set approach to multiple criteria classification with imprecise evaluations and assignments. *Eur. J. Oper. Res.* **2009**, *198*, 626–636.

21. A Guide to Photovoltaic (PV) System Design and Installation. Available online: (accessed on 13 February 2012).

22. Gregg, A.; Parker, T.; Swenson, R. A "real world" examination of PV system design and performance. In Proceeding of the IEEE Photovoltaic Specialists Conference, Austin, TX, USA, June 2005; pp. 1587–1592.

23. Tsai, H.C.; Chen, C.M.; Tzeng, G.H. The comparative productivity efficiency for global telecoms. *Int. J. Prod. Econ.* **2006**, *103*, 509–526.

24. Guo, P.; Tanaka, H. Fuzzy DEA: a perceptual evaluation method. *Fuzzy Sets Syst.* **2001**, *119*, 149–160.

25. Wu, D.; Yang, Z.; Liang, L. Using DEA-neural network approach to evaluate branch efficiency of a large Canadian bank. *Expert Syst. Appl.* **2006**, *31*, 108–115.

26. Banker, R.D.; Charnes, A.; Cooper, W.W. Some models for estimating technical and scale inefficiencies in data envelopment analysis. *Manag. Sci.* **1984**, *30*, 1078–1092.

27. *Data Envelopment Analysis: Theory, Methodology and Applications*; Charnes, A., Cooper, W.W., Lewin, A.Y., Seiford, L.M., Eds.; Springer: Boston, MA, USA, 1995.

28. Charnes, A.; Cooper, W.W.; Rhodes, E. Measuring the efficiency of decision making units. *Eur. J. Oper. Res.* **1978**, *2*, 429–444.

29. Farrell, M.J. The measurement of productive efficiency. *J. R. Stat. Soc. Ser. A. Gen.* **1957**, *120*, 253–289.

30. Chen, Y.; Ali, A.I. Output-input ratio analysis and DEA frontier. *Eur. J. Oper. Res.* **2002**, *142*, 476–479.

31. Pawlak, Z. Rough sets. *Int. J. Comput. Inf. Sci.* **1982**, *11*, 341–356.

32. Shyng, J.Y.; Wang, F.K.; Tzeng, G.H.; Wu, K.S. Rough set theory in analyzing the attributes of combination values for the Insurance Market. *Expert Syst. Appl.* **2007**, *32*, 56–64.

33. Swiniarski, R.W.; Skowron, A. Rough set methods in feature selection and recognition. *Pattern Recogn. Lett.* **2003**, *24*, 833-849.

34. Zhai, L.Y.; Khoo, L.P.; Fok, S.C. Feature extraction using rough set theory and genetic algorithms an application for the simplification of product quality evaluation. *Comput. Ind. Eng.* **2002**, *43*, 661–676.

35. Walczak, B.; Massart, D.L. Tutorial rough sets theory. *Chemom. Intell. Lab. Syst.* **1999**, *47*, 1–16.

36. Yeh, C.C.; Chi, D.J.; Hsu, M.F. A hybrid approach of DEA, rough set and support vector machines for business failure prediction. *Expert Syst. Appl.* **2010**, *37*, 1535–1541.

37. Wen, K.L.; Wang, C.W.; Yeh, C.K. Apply rough set and GM (h,N) model to analyze the influence factor in gas breakdown. In Proceeding of IEEE International Conference on Systems, Man, and Cybernetics Society, London, UK, April 2007; pp. 2771–2775.

38. Li, G.D.; Yamaguchi, D.; Nagai, M. A grey-based rough decision-making approach to supplier selection. *Int. J. Adv. Manuf. Technol.* **2008**, 1032–1040.

39. Thangavel, K.; Pethalakshmi, A. Dimensionality reduction based on rough set theory: A review. *Appl. Soft Comput.* **2009**, *9*, 1–12.

40. Koza, J. *Genetic Programming: On the Programming of Computers by Natural Selection*; MIT Press: Cambridge, MA, USA, 1992.

41. Davidson, J.W.; Savic, D.A.; Walters, G.A. Symbolic and numerical regression: Experiments and applications. *Inf. Sci.* **2003**, *150*, 95–117.

42. Lee, Y.S.; Tong, L.I. Forecasting energy consumption using a grey model improved by incorporating genetic programming. *Energy Convers. Manag.* **2011**, *52*, 147–152.

43. Huang, J.J.; Tzeng, G.H.; Ong, C.S. Two-stage genetic programming (2SGP) for the credit scoring model. *Appl. Math. Comput.* **2006**, *174*, 1039–1053.

44. Wen, K.L.; Nagai, M.; Chang, T.C.; Wen, H.C. *An Introduction to Rough Set Theory and Application*; Wu-Nan Book Co. Ltd.: Taipei, Taiwan, 2008.

45. Komorowski, K.; Ohrn, A.; Skowron, A. The ROSETTA rough set software system. In *Handbook of Data Mining and Knowledge Discovery*; Klosgen, W., Zytkow, J., Eds.; Oxford University Press: New York, NY, USA, 2002.

46. Pai, P.F.; Lin, C.S. A hybrid ARIMA and support vector machines model in stock price forecasting.*Omega* **2005**, *33*, 497–505.

47. Chen, K.Y.; Wang, C.H. A hybrid SARIMA and support vector machines in forecasting the production values of the machinery industry in Taiwan. *Expert Syst. Appl.* **2007**, *32*, 254–264.

48. Cybenko, G. Approximation by superpositions of a sigmoidal function. *Math. Control Signal. Syst.* **1989**, *2*, 303–314.

4

CHAPTER

GENETIC PROGRAMMING: A NOVEL COMPUTING APPROACH IN MODELING WATER FLOWS

Shreenivas N. Londhe and Pradnya R. Dixit

[1] *Vishwakarma Institute of Information Technology, Kondhwa (bk), Pune, India*

1. INTRODUCTION

The use of artificial intelligence in day to day life has increased since late 20th century as seen in many home appliances such as microwave oven, washing machine, camcorder etc which can figure out on their own what settings to use to perform their tasks optimally. Such intelligent machines make use of the soft computing techniques which treat human brain as their role model and mimic the ability of the human mind to effectively employ modes of reasoning that are approximate rather than exact. The conventional hard computing techniques require a precisely stated analytical model and often a lot of computational time. Premises and guiding principles of Hard Computing are precision, certainty, and rigor [1]. Many contemporary problems do not lend themselves to precise solutions such as recognition problems (handwriting, speech, objects and images), mobile robot coordination, forecasting, combinatorial problems etc. This is where soft computing techniques score over the conventional hard computing approach. Soft computing differs from conventional (hard) computing in that, unlike hard computing, it is tolerant of imprecision, uncertainty, partial truth, and approximation. The guiding principle of soft computing is to exploit the tolerance for imprecision, uncertainty, partial truth, and approximation to achieve tractability, robustness and low solution cost [1]. The principal constituents, i.e., tools, techniques of Soft Computing (SC) are Fuzzy Logic (FL), Neural Networks (NN), Evolutionary Computation (EC), Machine Learning (ML) and Probabilistic Reasoning (PR). Soft computing many times employs NN, EC, FL etc, in a complementary rather than a competitive way resulting into hybrid techniques like Adaptive Neuro-Fuzzy Interface System (ANFIS).

The application of soft computing techniques in the field of Civil Engineering started since early nineties and since encompassed almost all fields of Civil Engineering namely Structural Engineering, Construction Engineering and Management, Geotechnical Engineering, Environmental Engineering and lastly Hydraulic Engineering which is the focus of this chapter. The technique of ANN is now well established in the field of Civil Engineering to model various random and complex phenomena. Other techniques such as FL and EL caught attention of many research workers as a complimentary or alternative technique to ANN, particularly after knowing the drawbacks of ANN [2]. The soft computing tool of Genetic Programming which is essentially classified as an Evolutionary Computation (EC) technique has found its foot in the field of Hydraulic Engineering in general and modeling of water flows in particular since last 12 years or so. Modeling of water flows is perhaps the most daunting task ever faced by researchers in the field of Hydraulic Engineering owing to the randomness involved in many natural processes associated with the water flows. In pursuit of achieving more and more accuracy in estimation/forecasting of water related variables the researchers have made of use Genetic Programming for various tasks such as forecasting of runoff with or without rainfall, forecasting of ocean waves, currents, spatial mapping of waves to name a few. The present chapter takes a stalk of the applications of GP to model water flows which will enable the future researchers who want to pursue their research in this field. The chapter is organized as follows. Next section deals with basics of GP. A review of applications of GP in the field of Ocean Engineering is presented in the next section followed by review of applications in the field of hydrology. Few applications in the field of Hydraulics are discussed in the subsequent section. It may be noted that papers published in reputed international journals are only considered for review. Two case studies are presented next which are based on publications of the first author. The concluding remarks and future scope as envisaged by the authors are discussed at the end.

2. THE EVOLUTIONARY COMPUTATION

The paradigm of evolutionary processes distinguishes between an organism's genotype, which is constructed of genetic material that is inherited from its parent or parents, and the organism's phenotype, which is the coming to full physical presence of the organism in a certain given environment and is represented by a body and its associated collection of characteristics or phenotypic traits. Within this paradigm, there are three main criteria for an evolutionary process to occur as per [3] and they are

- Criterion of Heredity: Offspring are similar to their parents: the genotype copying process maintains a high fidelity.
- Criterion of Variability: Offspring are not exactly the same as their parents: the genotype copying process is not perfect.
- Criterion of Fecundity: Variants leave different numbers of offspring: specific variations have an effect on behavior and behavior has an effect on reproductive success.

The evolutionary techniques can be differentiated into four main streams of Evolutionary Algorithm(EA) development [4] namely Evolution Strategies (ES), Evolutionary Programming (EP), Genetic Algorithms (GA) and Genetic Programming (GP) [5]. However, all evolutionary algorithms share the common property of applying evolutionary processes in the form of selection, mutation and reproduction on a population of individual structures that undergo evolution. The criterion of heredity is assured through the application of a crossover operator, whereas the criterion of variability is maintained through the application of a mutation operator. A selection mechanism then 'favours' the more fit entities so that they reproduce more often, providing the fecundity requirement necessary for an evolutionary process to proceed.

3. GENETIC PROGRAMMING:

Like genetic algorithm (GA) the concept of Genetic Programming (GP) follows the principle of 'survival of the fittest' borrowed from the process of evolution occurring in nature. But unlike GA its solution is a computer program or an equation as against a set of numbers in the GA and hence it is convenient to use the same as a regression tool rather than an optimization one like the GA. GP operates on parse trees rather than on bit strings as in a GA, to approximate the equation (in symbolic form) or computer program that best describes how the output relates to the input variables. A good explanation of various concepts related to GP can be found in [5] Koza (1992). GP starts with a population of randomly generated computer programs on which computerized evolution process operates. Then a 'tournament' or competition is conducted by randomly selecting four programs from the population. GP measures how each program performs the user designated task. The two programs that perform the task best 'win' the tournament. GP algorithm then copies the two winner programs and transforms these copies into two new programs via crossover and mutation operators i.e. winners now have the 'children.' These two new child programs are then inserted into the population of programs, replacing the two loser programs from the tournament. Crossover is inspired by the exchange of genetic material occurring in sexual reproduction in biology. The creation of offspring's continues (in an iterative manner) till a specified number of offspring's in a generation are produced and further till another specified number of generations are created. The resulting offspring at the end of all this process (an equation or a computer program) is the solution of the problem. The GP thus transforms one population of individuals into another one in an iterative manner by following the natural genetic operations like reproduction, mutation and cross-over. Figure 1 shows general flowchart of GP as given by [5].

The tree based GP corresponds to the expressions (syntax trees) from a 'functional programming language' [5]. In this type, Functions are located at the inner nodes; while leaves of the tree hold input values and constants. A population of random trees representing the programs is initially constructed and genetic operations are performed on these trees to generate individuals with the help of two distinct sets; the terminal set T and the function set F.

Population: These are the programs initially constructed from the data sets in the form of trees to perform genetic operations using Terminal set and Function set. The function set for a run is comprised of operators to be used in evolving programs eg. addition, subtraction, absolute value, logarithm, square root etc. The terminal set for a run is made up of the values on which the function set operates. There can be four types of terminals namely inputs, constant, temporary variables, conditional flags. The population size is the number of programs in the population to be evolved. Larger population can solve more complicated problem. The maximum size of population depends upon RAM of the computer and length of programs in the population.

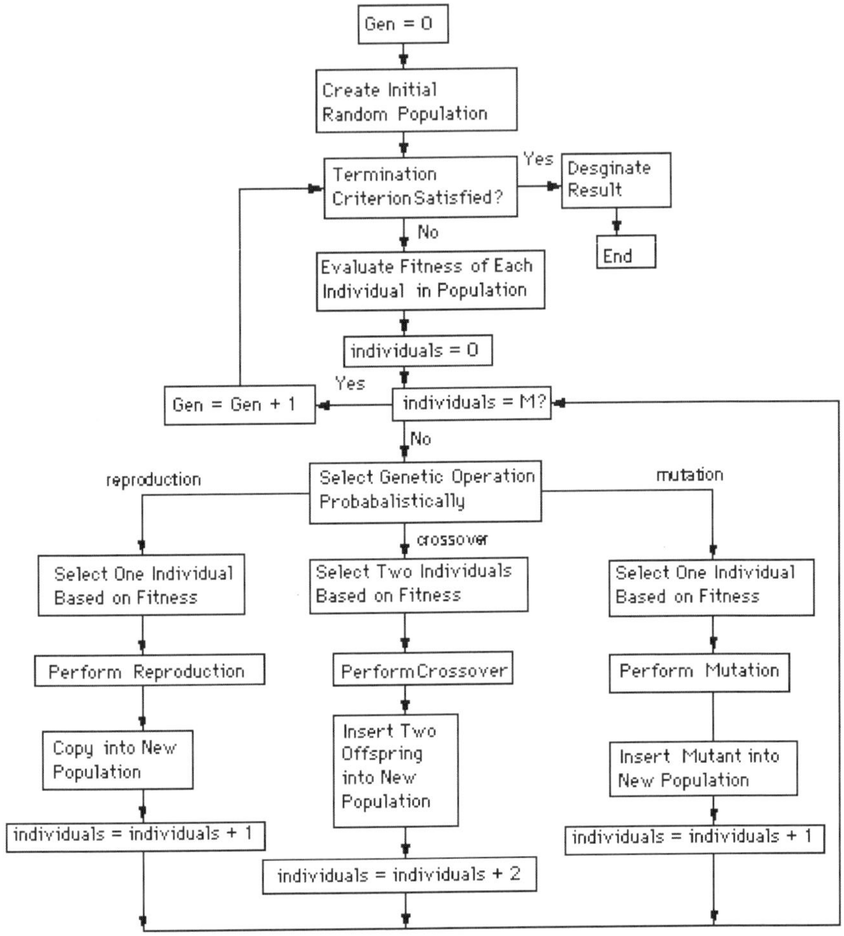

Figure 1. Flowchart of Genetic programming (Ref: [5])

4. GENETIC OPERATIONS

Cross over: Two individuals (programs) are chosen as per the fitness called parents. Two random nodes are selected from inside such program (parents) and thereafter the resultant sub-trees are swapped, generating two new programs. The resulting individuals are inserted into the new population. Individuals are increased by 2. The parents may be identical or different. The allowable range of cross over frequency parameter is 0 to 100%

Mutation: One individual is selected as per the fitness. A sub-tree is replaced by another one randomly. The mutant is inserted into the new population. Individuals are increased by 1. The allowable range of mutation frequency parameter is 0 to 100%

Reproduction: The best program is copied as it is as per the fitness criterion and included in the new population. Individuals are increased by 1. Reproduction rate = 100 – mutation rate – (crossover rate * [1 – mutation rate])

The second variant of GP is Linear genetic Programming (LGP) which uses a specific linear representation of computer programs. The name 'linear' refers to the structure of the (imperative) program representation only and does not stand for functional genetic programs that are restricted to a linear list of nodes only. On the contrary, it usually represents highly nonlinear solutions. Each individual (Program) in LGP is represented by a variable-length sequence of simple C language instructions, which operate on the registers or constants from predefined sets. The function setof the system can be composed of arithmetic operations (+, -, X, /), conditional branches, and function calls (f{x, x^n, sqrt, e^x,sin, cos, tan, log, ln }). Each function implicitly includes an assignment to a variable which facilitates use of multiple program outputs in LGP. LGP utilizes two-point string cross-over. A segment of random position and random length of an instruction is selected from each parents and exchanged. If one of the resulting children exceeds the maximum length, this cross-over is abandoned and restarted by exchanging equalized segments. An operand or operator of an instruction is changed by mutation into another symbol over the same set. The readers are referred to [7] and [8] for further details.

Gene-Expression Programming (GEP) is an extension of GP, developed by [5]. The genome is encoded as linear chromosomes of fixed length, as in Genetic Algorithm (GA); however, in GEP the genes are then expressed as a phenotype in the form of expression trees. GEP combines the advantages of both its predecessors, GA and GP, and removes their limitations. GEP is a full fledged genotype/phenotype system in which both are dealt with separately, whereas GP is a simple replicator system. As a consequence of this difference, the complete genotype/phenotype GEP system surpasses the older GP system by a factor of 100 to 60,000. In GEP, just like in other evolutionary methods, the process starts with the random generation of an initial population consisting of individual chromosomes of fixed length. The chromosomes may contain one or more than one genes. Each individual chromosome in the initial population is then expressed and its fitness is evaluated using one of the fitness function equations available in the literature. These chromosomes are then selected based on their fitness values using a roulette wheel selection process. Fitter chromosomes have greater chances of selection for passage to the next generation. After selection, these are reproduced with some modifications performed by the genetic operators. In Gene Expression Programming, genetic operators such as mutation, inversion, transposition and recombination are used for these modifications. Mutation is the most efficient genetic operator, and it is sometime used as the only means of modification. The new individuals are then subjected to the same process of modification, and the process continues until the maximum number of generations is reached or the required accuracy is achieved.

5. WHY USE GP IN MODELING WATER FLOWS?

It is a known fact that many variables in the domain of Hydraulic Engineering are of random nature having a complex underlying phenomenon. For example the generation of ocean waves which are primarily functions of wind forcing is a very complex procedure. Forecasting of the ocean waves is an essential prerequisite for many ocean-coastal related activities. Traditionally this is done using numerical models like WAM and SWAN. These models are extremely complex in development and application besides being highly computation-intensive. Further they are more useful for forecasting over a large spatial and temporal domain. The accuracy levels of wave forecasts obtained through such numerical models again leaves scope for exploration of alternative schemes. These numerical models suffer from disadvantages like requirement of exogenous data, complex modeling procedure, rounding off errors and large requirement of computer memory and time and there is no guarantee that the results will be accurate. Particularly when point forecasts were required the researchers therefore used the data driven techniques namely ARMA, ARIMA and since last two decades or so the soft computing technique of Neural Networks. A comprehensive review of applications of ANN in Ocean Engineering is done by [9]. Although wave forecasting models were developed using Artificial Neural Networks by many research workers their was scope for use of another data driven techniques in that the ANN based models generally were unable to forecast extreme events with reasonable accuracy and the accuracy of forecasts decreases with increase in lead time as reported in many research papers. This became an ideal situation for the entry of another soft computing tool of GP which functions in a completely different way than ANN in that it does not involve any transfer function and evolves generations and generations of 'offspring' based on the 'fitness criteria' and genetic operations as explained in the earlier section the researchers thought, may be useful to capture the underlying trends better than ANN technique and can be used as a regressive tool. Same can be said about another important variable in hydraulic engineering "runoff or stream flow".

The rainfall -runoff modeling is very complex procedure and many numerical schemes are available as well as a large number of attempts by ANNs are also been made [2, 10, 11]. Thus Genetic Programming entered in rainfall-runoff modeling. It was also found that GP results were superior to that of M5 Model Trees another data driven modeling technique [12, 13]. Apart from these two variables the use of GP for modeling for many hydraulic engineering processes was found necessary for similar reasons. A review of these applications particularly in Ocean Engineering, Hydrology and Hydraulics (all grouped under Hydraulic Engineering) will be presented in the next three sections.

6. APPLICATIONS IN OCEAN ENGINEERING

As mentioned earlier papers published in reputed international journals are considered in this chapter. Primarily the applications of GP in Ocean Engineering were found for modeling of oceanic parameters like waves, water levels, zero cross wave periods, currents, wind, sediment transport and circular pile scour. Table 1 shows applications of GP in the field of Ocean Engineering listed chronologically followed by their review. This will facilitate the reader to have a glance of the work which would be presented next.

One of the earlier applications was done to retrieve missing informationin wave records along the west coast of India [14]. Such a need arises many times due to malfunctioning of instrument or drift of wave measuring buoy making it inoperative as a result of which data is not measured and it is lost forever. Filling up the missing significant wave height (Hs) values at a given location based on the same being collected at the nearby station(s) was done using GP. The wave heights were measured at an interval of 3 hours. Data at six locations around Indian coastline was used in this exercise. Out of the total sample size of four years the observations for the initial 25 months were used to evaluate the final or optimum GP program or equation while those for the last 23 months were employed to validate the performance and achieve gap in-filling with different quanta of missing information. It was found that both tree based and linear GP models worked in similar fashion as far as accuracy of estimation was considered. The data

Table 1. Applications of GP in Ocean Engineering

REF. NO.	YEAR	AUTHOR	TITLE OF PAPER	JOURNAL/PUBLICATION
14	2007	Kalra R., Deo M.C.	Genetic Programming to retrieve missing information in wave records along the west coast of India	Applied Ocean Research
25	2007	Singh, A. K., Deo M.C., Sanil Kumar V.	Combined Neural network – genetic programming for sediment transport	Journal of Maritime Engineering, The Institution of Civil Engineers, Issue MAO
16	2007	Charhate S. B., Deo M. C., Sanil Kumar V.	Soft and Hard Computing Approaches for Real Time Prediction of Currents in a Tide Dominated Coastal Area	Journal of Engineering for the Maritime Environment. Proceedings of the Institution of Mechanical Engineers, London, M4
15	2008	Ustoorikar K.S., Deo, M. C.	Filling up Gaps in wave data with Genetic Programming	Marine Structures

18	2008	Jain., P., Deo M. C.	Artificial intelligence tools to forecast ocean waves in real time	The Open Ocean Engineering Journal
22	2008	Charhate, S. B., Deo, M. C., Londhe S. N.	Inverse modeling to derive wind parameters from wave measurements	Applied Ocean Research
17	2008	Gaur, S., and Deo, M. C.	Real time wave forecasting using genetic programming	Ocean Engineering
06	2008	Londhe S. N.	Soft computing approach for real-time estimation of	Ocean Engineering

22	2008	Charhate, S. B., Deo, M. C., Londhe S. N.	Inverse modeling to derive wind parameters from wave measurements	Applied Ocean Research
17	2008	Gaur, S., and Deo, M. C.	Real time wave forecasting using genetic programming	Ocean Engineering
06	2008	Londhe S. N.	Soft computing approach for real-time estimation of missing wave heights	Ocean Engineering
23	2009	Charhate, S. B., Deo, M. C., Londhe S. N.	Genetic programming for real time prediction of offshore wind	International Journal of Ships and Offshore Structures

26	2009	Guven, A., Azmathulla, H. Md., Zakaria, N.A.	Linear genetic programming for prediction of circular pile scour	Ocean Engineering
24	2009	Daga, M., Deo, M. C.	Alternative data-driven methods to estimate wind from waves by inverse Modeling	Natural Hazards, 49(2), 293-310
08	2009	Guven, A.	Linear genetic programming for time-series modelling of daily flow rate	Journal of Earth Syst. Sci., 118(2), 137-146

19	2010	Kambekar, A. R., Deo, M. C.	Wave simulation and forecasting using wind time history and data driven Methods	Ships and Offshore Structures
20	2010 a	Ghorbani, M. A. , Makarynskyy, O., Shiri, J., Makarynska, D.	Genetic Programming for Sea Level Predictions in an Island Environment	International Journal of Ocean and Climatic systems
21	2010 b	Ghorbani, M. A., Khatibi, R., Aytek, A., Makarynskyy, O., Shiri, J.	Sea water level forecasting using genetic programming and comparing the performance with Artificial Neural Networks	Computers and Geosciences
12	2012	Kambekar, A. R., Deo, M. C.	Wave Prediction Using Genetic Programming And Model Trees	Journal of Coastal Research, Doi: 10.2112/Jcoastres-D-10-00052.1, 28(1), 43-50

was made available by National Institute of Ocean Technology (NIOT) under the National Data Buoy Programme implemented by the Department of Ocean Development, Government of India from January 2000 to December 2003 (www.niot.res.in). The initial parameters selected for a GP run were as follows: initial population size = 500; mutation frequency = 95%; crossover frequency = 50%. The fitness criterion was the mean squared error.

When the similar work was also carried out using ANN it was found that GP produces results that are marginally more satisfactory than ANN. Another exercise was also carried out especially to estimate peaks by calibrating a separate model for high wave data which showed a marginal improvement in prediction of peaks. A similar exercise was carried out by [15], albeit in altogether different area of Gulf of Mexico near the USA coastline. Gaps in hourly significant wave height records at one location were filled by using the significant wave heights at surrounding 3 locations at same time instant and the soft tool of GP and ANN. In all data spanning over 4 years was used for the study. The exercise was carried out for 4 locations in the Gulf of Mexico. The data can be downloaded from www.ndbc.noaa.gov. The typical value of the population size was 500, number of generations 15 and number of tournaments 90,00,000. The mutation and the cross-over frequency also varied fordifferent testing exercises and it ranged from 20% to 80%. The fitness criterion was the mean squared error between actual observations and corresponding predictions.

The suitability of this approach was also tried for different gap lengths ranging from 1 day to 1 month and it was concluded on the basis of 3 error measures that the accuracy of gap filling decreases with increase in the gap length. The accuracy of the results were also judged by calculating statistical parameters of the wave records without gaps filled and with gaps filled using GP model. When the gap lengths did not exceed 1 or 5 days all the four statistics were faithfully reproduced. Compared to ANN GP produced marginally better results. In both the cases Linear Genetic Programming technique was employed.

In another earlier works of GP current predictions over a time step of twenty minutes, one hour, 3 hours, 6 hours, 12 hours and 24 hours at 2 locations in the tidal dominated area of the Gulf of Khambhat along west coast of India was carried out using two soft techniques of ANN and GP and 2 hard techniques of traditional harmonic analysis and ARIMA [16]. The work involved antecedent values of current only to forecast the current for various lead times at these locations. The fitness function selected was the mean square error, while the initial population size was 500, mutation frequency was 95%, and the crossover frequency was kept at 50%. The authors concluded that the model predictions were better for alongshore currents and small interval of times. For cross shore currents ARIMA performs better than ANN and GP even at longer prediction intervals. In general the three data driven techniques performed better than harmonic analysis. The new technique GP performed at par with ANN if not better. Perhaps the only drawback of the work was that the data (spanning over 7 months) is less than a year indicating that all possible variations in data set were not presented while calibrating the model making it susceptible when it is used at operational level.

Online wave forecasts over lead times of 3, 6, 12 and 24 hours were carried out at two locations in the gulf of Mexico using past values of wave heights (3 in number) and the soft computing technique of GP [17]. The data measured from 1999 to 2004 was available for free download on the web site of National Buoy Centre (http://www.ndbc.noaa.gov). The data belonged to the hourly wave heights measured over a period of 15 years with an extensive testing period of about 5 years which is the most in the papers reported till this time (with ANN as modeling tool). The locations chosen were differing to a large extent in that one was a deep water buoy and the other was a coastal buoy. The work was different from others in one aspect that monthly models were developed instead of routine yearly models. However any peculiar effect of this either good or bad on forecasting accuracy was not evident from the 3 error measures calculated. Though the results of GP were promising (high correlation coefficients for 3 and 6 hr forecast) the forecasting accuracy decreased for longer lead times of 12 hr and 24 hr. It was found that the results of GP were superior to ANN. For GP model the initial population size was 500 while the number of generations was 300. The mutation frequency was 90 percent while the cross over frequency was 50 percent. Values of these

control parameters were selected initially and thereafter varied in trials till the best fitness measures were produced. The fitness criterion was the mean squared error between the actual and the predicted value of the significant wave height. Another exercise on real time forecasting of waves for warning times up to 72 hours at three locations along the Indian coastline using alternative techniques of ANN, GP and MT was carried out by [18]. The data was measured from 1998 to 2004 by the national data buoy program (www.niot.res.in). Forecasting waves up to 72hr and that too with reasonable accuracy is itself a specialty of this work. The data had many missing values which were filled by using temporal as well as spatial correlation approaches. Both MT and GP results were competitive with that of the ANN forecasts and hence the choice of a model should depend on the convenience of the user. The selected tools were able to forecast satisfactorily even up to a high lead time of 72 hrs. The authors have rightly stated that this accuracy was possible in the moderate ocean environment around Indian coastline where the target waves were less than around 6 m and 2.5 m for the offshore and coastal stations respectively. The paper does not provide any information about the initial parameters chosen for implementing GP. The significant wave height and average wave period at the current and subsequent 24 hr lead time were predicted from continuous and past 24-hourly measurements of wind speeds and directions as well as two soft computing techniques of GP and MT [19]. The data collected at 8 locations in Arabian Sea and Indian Ocean (www.niot.res.in) was used to develop both hind-casting and forecasting models. Both the methods, GP and MT, performed satisfactorily in the given task of wind wave simulation as reflected in high values of the error statistics of R, R^2, CE and low values of MAE, RMSE and SI. This is noteworthy since MT is not purely non-linear like GP. Although the magnitudes of these statistics did not indicate a significant difference in the relative performance of GP and MT, qualitative scatter diagrams and time histories showed the tendency of MT to better estimate the higher waves. Forecasting at higher lead times were fairly accurate compared to the same at lower ones. In general the performance of wave period was less satisfactory than that of wave height and this can be expected in view of a highly varying nature of wave period values. For details regarding the initial GP parameters involved in calibration readers are referred to the original paper where an exhaustive list of parameters is given. Lately [12], extended their earlier work by forecasting Significant wave height and zero cross wave period over time intervals of 1 to 4 days using the current and previous values of wind velocity and wind direction at 2 locations around the Indian coastline. It was found out that best results were possible when the length of the input sequence matched with that of the output lead time. As observed earlier here also it was found that the accuracy of prediction decreases with increase in lead time. However the results were satisfactory for 4 days ahead predictions also. In general it was observed that results of MT were slightly inferior to that of GP. Separate models were also developed to account for the monsoon (rainfall season in India) which showed a considerable improvement over yearly models. The models calibrated at one location when applied for another nearby locations also shown satisfactory performance provided both sites have spatial homogeneity in terms of openness, long offshore distances and deep water conditions. This work used tree based GP where as earlier mentioned three works used Linear Genetic Programming.

GP was used to forecast sea levels averaged over 12 h and 24 h time intervals for time periods from 12 to 120 h ahead at the Cocos (Keeling) Islands in the Indian Ocean [20]. The model produced high quality predictions over all considered time periods. The presented results demonstrates the suitability of GP for learning the non-linear behavior of sea level variations in terms of the R^2(with values no lower than 0.968), MSE(with values generally smaller than 431) and MARE(no larger than 1.94%). This differs from earlier applications particularly for wave forecasting in that for forecasting of waves it was difficult to achieve higher order accuracy in terms of r, rmse and other error measures for as far as 24 hour forecast. Perhaps the recurring nature of sea water levels (the deterministic tidal component which is inherent in water level, is the reason behind this high level accuracy. In order to assess the ability of GP model relative to that of the ANN technique, a comparison was performed in terms of the above mentioned statistics. The developed GP model was found to perform better than the used ANNs. In the current work, the linear genetic programming approach was employed. The water level at Hillary's Boat Harbor, Australia was predicted three time steps ahead using time series averaged over 12hr, 24hr, 5 day and 10 day time interval and the soft tool of GP [21]. The results are compared with ANN. Total 12 years of data was used out of which 3 years of data is used for model validation. Tree based GP was used. The results of 12 hr averaged input data were found to be better than 24 hr averaged input data and in general the accuracy of prediction reduced for higher lead times. For both the cases GP results were better than ANN. For 5 day averaged inputs performance of GP was inferior to that of ANN though it improved for 10 day averaged inputs. It may be noted that the input data is averaged over 12hr, 24hr, 5days and 10 days which means there is possibility of loss of information which can be major draw back of this work. For both the above works the hourly sea-level records from a SEA-level Fine Resolutions Acoustic Measuring Equipment (SEA-FRAME) station were used. The information about initial parameters of GP is however not mentioned in both the works.

Estimation of wind speed and wind direction using the significant wave height, zero cross wave period, average wave period and the soft tools of ANN and GP was carried out at 5 locations around Indian coastline [22]. The paper has three folds in that in the first attempt both ANN and GP were tried for estimating the wind speed in which GP was found better and therefore in the second fold GP was only used to determine both wind speed and direction by calibrating the model by splitting of wind vector into two components. Two variants of GP, one based on Tree based approach and the other on Linear Genetic Programming were also tried though the accuracy of estimation for both the approaches was at par. In the third fold a network of wave buoys were formed and wind direction and wind speed at one location was estimated using the same at other locations. This was also done by combining data of all locations and making a regional model. All the attempts yielded highly satisfactory results as far as accuracy of estimation is considered. It was also confirmed that for estimation of only wind speed the non-splitting of wind velocity gives better results. Similarly wind speed and its directions were predicted for intervals of 3hr, 6hr, 9hr, 12hr and 24 hr at locations along the west coast of India using two soft computing techniques of ANN and GP and previous values of the same [23]. It was found that GP rivaled ANN predictions at all the cases and even bettered it particularly for open sea location. The results for prediction of wind speed and wind direction together were better when training of GP and ANN models was done on the basis of splitting of wind vector into two components along orthogonal directions although a separate model for wind speed alone was better (as shown by [22]). In general long interval predictions were less accurate compared to short interval predictions for both the techniques. Data for one location was for about 1.5 years while for the other location it was for 3 years. A discussion on appropriate use of statistical measures to assess the model accuracy was also presented. A similar work was carried out to estimate the wind speed at 5 locations around the Indian coastline using the wave parameters and 3 data driven techniques namely GP (program based- tree type), MT and another data driven tool of Locally weighted projection regression (LWPR) by [24]. All models showed tendency to underestimate higher values in given records. When all of the eight error statistics employed were viewed together, no single method appeared distinctly superior to others, but the use of an average evaluation index EI which they have suggested in this work gave equal weightage to each measure showed that the GP was more acceptable than other methods in carrying out the intended inverse modeling. Separate GP models were developed to estimate higher wind speeds that may be encountered in stormy conditions. At all the locations, these models indicated satisfactory performance of GP although with a fall in accuracy with increase in randomness. For all the above works the data was measured by national data buoy program of India (www.niot.res.in) however no mention is made about the initial parameters chosen for GP implementation.

The estimation of longshore sediment transport rate at an Indian location was carried out using GP and combined GP-ANN models [25]. The data was actually measured by one of the authors in his field study. The inputs were significant wave height, zero cross wave period, breaking wave height, breaking wave angle and surf zone width. The limitation of the work was the amount of data (81) used for training and testing of the models. The choice of control parameters was as follows: initial population size = 500; mutation frequency = 95%; crossover frequency = 50%. The initial trial with GP yielded reasonable results (r = 0.87). However by first training the ANN with same inputs and using the output as input for GP model yielded better results (r = 0.92). Thus the paper shows that combined ANN-GP model is more attractive than single GP model. It may be noted this is a kind of work done in the domain of Ocean Engineering wherein a different parameter (sediment transport rate) is modeled rather than the usual parameters of waves, periods etc. Another different work was carried out by [26], for prediction of scour depth due to ocean/lake waves around a pile/pier in medium dense silt and sand bed using Linear Genetic Programming and Adaptive Neuro-Fuzzy Inference system and measured laboratory data. For initial GP parameters readers are referred to actual paper where in an exhaustive list of parameters is provided. The study was carried out in both dimensional and non-dimensional form in which non-dimensional form yielded better results. The relative importance of input parameters on scour process was also investigated by first using all the influential parameters as inputs and then removing them one by one and observing the results. The drawback of the work is perhaps the small number of data used in model making (total 38 data, 28 of which is used for training the model) which may be impediment in operational use of this model. The results were found to be superior to ANFIS results.

In all the above cases where GP is compared with another data driven technique like ANN, MT or LWPR it was found that GP is superior to all of them in terms of accuracy of results. However it can be said that GP needs to be explored further particularly for prediction of extreme events like water levels, wave heights during hurricanes. A detailed study on effect of variation of GP control parameters like initial population, mutation, crossover percentage etc. on model accuracy is now need of the day. Similarly the critic on other approaches about decreasing forecasting accuracy with increase in the lead time seems to be true for GP as well. This needs more attention if GP is here to stay.

7. APPLICATIONS IN HYDROLOGY

Table 2 exhibits the applications of GP in Hydrology chronologically which are reviewed in this paper. The table also indicates that the applications of GP to the field of Hydrology started much earlier as compared to Ocean Engineering.

Table 2. Applications of GP in Hydrology

REF. NO.	YEAR	AUTHOR	TITLE OF PAPER	JOURNAL/PUBLICATION
27	1999	Savic A.D., Walters, G. A., Davidson J.W	A genetic Programming approach to rainfall-runoff modeling	Water Resources Management
28	1999	Drecourt J	Application of Neural Networks and Genetic Programming to Rainfall Runoff Modeling.	Danish Hydraulic Institute (Hydro-Informatics Techonologies - HIT)
29	2001	Whigham, P. A., Crapper, P. F.	Modeling rainfall runoff using Genetic Programming	Mathematical and Computer Modelling,
30	2001	Khu, S. T., Liong, S. U., Babovic, V., Madsen, H., Muttil, N.	Genetic Programming And Its Application In Real-Time Runoff Forecasting	Journal of American Water Resources Association

31	2002	Babovic, V., Keijzer, M.	Rainfall runoff modeling Based on Genetic programming	Nordic Hydrology
32	2007	Sivapragasam,C., Maheswaran, R., Venkatesh, V.	Genetic programming approach for flood routing in natural channels	Hydrological processes
33	2007	Parasuraman, K., Elshorbagy, A., Carey, S. K.	Modelling the dynamics of the evapotranspiration process using genetic Programming	Hydrological Sciences
34	2010	El. Baroudy, I., Elshorbagy, A., Carey, S. K., Giustolisi., O., Savic, D	Comparison of three data-driven techniques in modeling the evapotranspiration process	Journal of Hydroinformatics

13	2010	Londhe, S. N. and Charhate S. B.	Comparison of data driven modeling techniques for river flow forecasting	Hydrological sciences
35	2011	Azmathullah, MD., Ghani, A. AB., Leow, C. S., Chang., C. K., Zakaria, N. A.	Gene-Expression Programming for the Development of a Stage-Discharge Curve of the Pahang River	Water Resource Management

Genetic Programming is used in Hydrology (science of water) for various purposes such as modeling of phenomena like rainfall-runoff process, evapo-transpiration, flood routing, stage-discharge curve. The GP approach was applied to the flow prediction of the Kirkton catchment in Scotland (U.K.) [27]. The results obtained were compared to those attained using optimally calibrated conceptual models and an ANN. The data sets selected for the modeling process were rainfall, streamflow and Penman open water evaporation. The data used for calibration was of 610 days while that of validation was of 1705 days. The models were developed with preceding values of rainfall, evaporation and stream flow for predicting stream flow one time step ahead. Two conceptual models as well as ANN were employed for developing the stream flow forecasting model. It was observed that the rainfall data was the most influencing factor on the output. All models performed well in terms of forecasting accuracy with GP performing better. The paper does not give any details about the values of the parameters used for calibration of GP model. In another work one day ahead forecasting of runoff knowing the rainfall and runoff of the previous days and the soft computing tool of Linear Genetic Programming was carried out in Lindenborg catchment of Denmark by [28]. The models were developed for forecasting runoff as well as variation of runoff by using previous values of variation of discharge as input as well as previous values of discharge as input along with rainfall information. It was found that it was necessary to include information of discharge rather than variation of discharge. The model predicting discharge gave wrong local peaks in the low regime where as models predicting variation of discharge gave less wrong peaks in the low flow. Both the models had difficulty in predicting high peaks. The models were also developed using ANN. The author concluded that GP is more efficient in peak flow prediction where as ANNs were better in dealing with the noise. The author suggested specialized model for each type of flow to improve the accuracy at peak prediction. He also suggested coupling of black box models with gray models. No specific information is provided about the initial values of GP parameters. The rainfall-runoff relationship in two different catchments was discovered by [29] using GP. The results obtained with a deterministic lumped parameter model, based on the unit hydrograph approach were compared with those obtained using a stochastic machine learning model of GP. For the Welsh catchment in UK, the results between the two models were similar. Since rainfall and runoff were highly correlated, the deterministic assumption underlying the IHACRES model (deterministic) was satisfied. Therefore, IHACREX could achieve a satisfactory correlation between calibration and simulation data. The GP approach which did not require any causal relationships achieved similar results. The behavior of the studied Australian catchment is very different from the Welsh catchment. The runoff ratio was very low (7%), and hence, the a priori assumptions of IHACRES (and other deterministic models) were a poor representation of the real world. This was demonstrated by the inability of IHACREJS to use more than one season's data for calibration purposes and only able to use data from a high rainfall period. Since the GP approach did not make any assumptions about the underlying physical processes, calibration periods over more than one season could be used. These led to significantly improved generalizations for the modeled behavior of the catchment. In summary, either approach worked satisfactorily when rainfall and runoff were correlated. However, when this correlation was poor, the CFG-GP had some advantages because it did not assume any underlying relationships. This is particularly important when considering the modeling of environmental problems, where typically the relationships are nonlinear, and are often measured at a scale which does not match with conceptual or deterministic modeling assumptions. Readers are referred to original paper for details of parameters setting for evolving the rainfall-runoff model. In their work of GP in hydrology, [30] first used a simple example of the Bernoulli equation to illustrate how GP symbolically regresses or infers the relationship between the input and output variables. An important conclusion from this study was that non-dimensionalizing the variables prior to symbolic regression process significantly enhance the success of GSR (Genetic Symbolic Regression). GP was then applied to the problem of real-time runoff forecasting for the Orgeval catchment in France. GP functions as an error updating procedure complementing the rainfall-runoff model, MIKE11/ NAM. Ten storm events were used to infer the relationship between the NAM simulated runoff and the corresponding prediction error. That relationship was subsequently used for real-time forecasting of six storm events. The results indicated that the proposed methodology was able to forecast different storm events with great accuracy for different updating intervals. The forecast hydrograph performs well even for a long forecast horizon of up to nine hours. However, it was found that for practical applications in real-time runoff forecasting, the updating interval should be less than or equal to the time of concentration of the catchment. The results were also compared with two known updating methods such as the auto-regression and Kalman filter. Comparisons showed that the proposed scheme, NAM-GSR, is comparable to these methods for real time runoff forecasting. Readers are referred to original paper for details of initial values of various parameters used in calibrating the GP model. The rainfall-runoff models were created on the basis of data alone as well as in combination with conceptual models and Genetic Programming [31]. The study was carried out in Orgeval catchment of France having an area about 104 km^2 using hourly rainfall runoff data of 10 storms for calibration and 6 storms for testing the models. The models were calibrated to forecast the temporal difference between the current and future discharge rather than absolute value of discharge for the lead times of 1 to 12 hours. In fact the paper discusses the phase lag associated with temporal time series forecasting models and removal of it by forecasting the temporal difference. The results were superior to conceptual numerical model. The model was then calibrated using a hybrid method in that the surface runoff value was first forecasted by using a conceptual forecasting model and then using the simulation error and GP to forecast the stream flow. The hybrid models provided a many fold improvement over the raw GP models. The paper in our opinion serves as a basic paper in the field of application of GP in Hydrology and readers may read the paper in original for all details about the GP models developed. The details are not produced here to save the space. Linear Genetic Programming technique was used to predict daily river discharge one day ahead using previous values of the same at SchuylkillRiver at Berne, PA, USA [8]. Additionally the models were developed using multilayer perceprton as well as Generalized Regression Neural Networks (GRNN). The statistical ARMA method was also used to develop the stream flow forecasting model. The results showed that both LGP and NN techniques predicted the daily time series of discharge with quite good agreement as indicated by high value of coefficient of determination and low values of error measures with the observed data. LGP models generally predicted the maximum and minimum discharge values better than the NN models though LGP results were also far from accurate. The robustness of the developed models was tested by using applied data which was neither used in training or testing and the results were judged using Akaike Information Criterion (AIC). For LGP parameters readers are requested to refer the comprehensive list presented in the paper.

The potential of the GP-based model for flood routing between two river gauging stations on river Walla in USA was explored for single peaked as well as multi-peaked flood hydrographs by [32]. The accuracy of GP models was far superior than modified Muskingum method which is a traditional physics based hydrologic flood routing model which also showed time lag in predictions. The inputs were current and antecedent discharge at upstream station and antecedent discharge at downstream station while the output was current discharge at the downstream station. The LGP was employed for the flood routing exercise. The optimal GP parameters used in this study were: crossover rate, 0.9; mutation rate, 0.5; population size, 200; number of generations, 500; and functional set, i.e. simple arithmetic functions (plus, minus, multiply, divide).

The utility of genetic programming in modeling the eddy-covariance (EC) measured evapo-transpiration flux was investigated by [33]. The performance of the GP technique was compared with artificial neural network and Penman-Monteith model estimates. EC measured evapo-transpiration fluxes from two distinct case-studies with different climatic and topographic conditions were considered for the analysis and latent heat is modeled as a function of net radiation, ground temperature, air temperature, wind speed and relative humidity. Results from the study indicated that both data-driven models (ANN and GP) performed better than the Penman-Monteith method. However, the performance of the GP model is comparable with that of ANN models. One of the important advantages of employing GP to model evapo-transpiration process is that, unlike the ANN model, GP resulted in an explicit model structure that can be easily comprehended and adopted. Another advantage of GP over ANN was found that unlike ANN, GP can evolve its own model structure with relevant inputs reducing the tedious task of identifying optimal input combinations. This work was extended by [34] where in an additional data driven tool of Evolutionary Polynomial Regression was used to model the evapo-transpiration process. Additionally the effect of previous states of input variable (lags) on modeling the EC measured AET (actual evapo-transpiration) is investigated. The evapo-transpiration is estimated using the environmental variables such as net radiation (NR), ground temperature (GT), air temperature (AT), wind speed (WS) and relative humidity (RH). It has been found out that random search and evolutionary-based techniques, such as GP and EPR techniques, do not guarantee consistent performance in all case studies e.g. good and/or bad performance for modelling AET. The authors further stated that this may be due to the practical impossibility of conducting exhaustive search, i.e. searching the entire solution space, to reach the optimal model. The results of ANN, GP and EPR were mostly at par with each other though EPR models were easier to understand. Readers may refer the original papers for above two works for the values of GP parameters.

Recently the stage –discharge relationship for the Pahang River in Malaysia was modeled using Genetic Programming (GP) and Gene Expression Programming (GEP) by [35]. The data was provided by Malaysian Department of Irrigation and Drainage (DID). Gene Expression Programming is an extension of GP. GEP is a full-fledged genotype/phenotype system in which both are dealt with separately, whereas GP is a simple replicator system. Stage and discharge data from 2 years were used to compare the performance of the GP and GEP models against that of the more conventional (stage-rating curve) SRC and (Regression) REG approaches. The GEP model was found to be considerably better than the conventional SRC, REG and GP models. GEP was also relatively more successful than GP, especially in estimating large discharge values during flood events. For details of initial GP parameters the original paper may be referred. The paper elaborates the details of the Gene-expression programming, the new variant of GP.

Like applications in Ocean Engineering it can be said that there is a lot of scope for use of GP in the field of Hydrologic Engineering and more and more applications needs to be tried out.

8. APPLICATIONS IN HYDRAULICS

A few applications of GP in Hydraulic Engineering are also reported in reputed journals which are from open channel hydraulics. Various GP models were developed by [36] to predict velocities across a compound channel with vegetated floodplains. The velocity data was collected in a laboratory flume with steady flow and deep channel and relatively shallow vegetated floodplain on either side. The GP model was developed with all 12 variables in dimensional form depicted accurate results though the evolved equation was complex. The GP models were developed with dimensionless variables and separate for main channel and floodplain. Both the velocity prediction on flood plain and main channels showed good correlations with measured values. However the resulting expressions were complex. A dimensionally aware GP was then used to predict the velocity separately in main channel and flood plains. The performance of the symbolic expressions induced by the dimensionless GP for the floodplain and main channel was marginally better than those for the dimensionally aware GP. However, the expressions were more complex and not particularly useful for knowledge induction. The dimensionally aware GP was shown to hold more scientific information, as units of measurement were included, although it was also shown to be open ended in that it does not strictly adhere to the dimensional analysis framework, thereby allowing improved goodness-of-fit whilst yielding on goodness-of-dimension. The paper provides no information about the initial values of GP parameters used in evolving the GP model. GP was applied to the determination of the Chezy's roughness coefficient for corrugated channels in wake-interference flow, i.e. hyper-turbulent flow by [37]. The GP models were calibrated using the experimental data devised by carrying out experiments for 3 plastic corrugated pipes with variations of discharge and slope. GP quite easily and quickly supplied at least two good formulae that fit the experimental data better and are more parsimonious than the monomial formula (mathematical). Moreover, GP has supplied six parsimonious expressions (one or two constants compared to four for the monomial formula) for the Chezy's resistance coefficient, all confirming the dependencies on hydraulic radius, slope and roughness index. It can be said that the two new formulae for the Chezys resistance coefficient, derived from these GP formulae by means of 'mathematical/physical post-refinement', are suitable for explaining the effect of the macro-roughness elements, with respect to the behavior of the rough commercial channels and their traditional expressions for resistance coefficients. The work indicated that this approach, which combines data-mining techniques together with a theoretical understanding, provides very good results. It was also commented that strictly speaking, GP is a data-driven technique, but prior knowledge during the setting up of the evolutionary search and final physical post-refinement of the hypothesis should make it very close to a white box technique, especially when GP is used in scientific discovery problems. The initial model parameters can be found in the original paper. To save space the list is not provided here.

An alternative approach of GP was proposed in the estimation of relative scour depth using field data by [38]. The comparison between the GP model with ANN found that the GP model has good ability of forecasting the scour depth. The discharge intensity and height of fall were used as inputs to estimate scour depth below tail water. The predictive ability of this approach is however clouded by use of very small number of data (total 91 data sets) used for calibration and testing of the model. The values of initial model parameters can be referred from the original paper.

9. CASE STUDY I: SOFT COMPUTING APPROACH FOR REAL-TIME ESTIMATION OF MISSING WAVE HEIGHTS

The work dealt with application of GP to retrieve the missing/ lost wave data at a particular location using the wave heights at other locations in the region. Six regional networks (with buoys 42001, 42003, 42007, 42036, 42039,42040) were developed in the Gulf Of Mexico (Figure 2) around USA coastline to estimate the wave heights at a location using wave heights at other five locations in the network. The required data from these six buoys was measured by NationalDataBuoyCenter (NDBC, http://www.ndbc.noaa.gov) of National Oceanic and Atmospheric administration of USA (NOAA, http://www.noaa.gov). The common wave data at all the above six locations for the years 2002-2004 was used in the present work. The networks were developed by having one station as target location at a time and remaining five locations as inputs turn by turn. Approximately 70% of the total values were used to calibrate the model and the remaining was kept unseen for testing. While doing this a particular event which occurred during Hurricane Ivan in 2004 at buoy 42040 which involved a Significant Wave Height of 15.96 m was focused for studying the performance of developed models during extreme events. It is to be noted that the exercise was of estimation and not of forecasting for which both the tools did not performed well as noted in the section on applications of GP in Ocean Engineering.

Thus a network was developed with wave buoy 42040 as the target and buoys 42001, 42003, 42007, 42036, 42039 as inputs. Along with 42040 the other locations namely 42003, 42007, 42039 also experienced largest ever wave heights of 11.04, 9.09, 12.05 making the entire event a truly extra ordinary event having a return period of over 5000 years [39]. The initial parameters selected for a GP run were as follows: initial population size 500, mutation frequency 95%, and crossover frequency 50%. The fitness criterion was the mean squared error.

Additionally a three layer Feed Forward Neural Network was also developed for the same buoy network. The results were also compared with a large-scale continuous wave modeling /forecasting systems (NOAA's WAVEWATCH III model) which follows the approach of physics-based model. Though WAVEWATCH III is a continuous running forecasting model it was the only source of information for wave environment at a location and therefore in absence of any reliable observed data, these results were used for comparison. The GP model estimated a wave height of 13.67m as against 15.96 m as compared to 9.05m that of ANN model and 7.82m of WAVEWATCH III, which was an excellent result as far as GP approach is considered. Figure 3 shows the wave plot at 42040 in testing.

From results of all the models developed by both the approaches (ANN & GP), it was observed that all models performed reasonably well in testing as evident by wave height plots, scatter plots along with the correlation coefficient ranging from 0.85 to 0.98, MAE from 0.13 to 0.28, RMSE from 0.20 to 0.45 m and coefficient of efficiency from 0.67 and 0.96. When it was tried to remove 42001 from the network as it is away from the prevailing wind direction by training a separate GP model with 42003, 42007, 42036, and 42039 as 'input buoys' and 42040 as 'target buoy', though the value of correlation coefficient was increased, the peak prediction was not in a fair range of accuracy for extreme event of Hurricane Ivan. Due to better performance of the network with inclusion of buoy 42001 especially for extreme event, buoy 42001 was retained in the network. Also it was found that 42039 was a potential candidate for redeployment in any other suitable position outside the network as the buoy network developed for 42039, provided the wave heights using wave heights at other five locations in the network with the best accuracy achieved between all the networks (r = 0.98). Figure 4(a, b) shows the scatter plots for results of buoy

42039. Table 3 shows results reproduced from [6] giving the details of developed networks along with correlation coefficient between the model estimated and observed values for both GP and ANN models. In general it was shown that GP was superior to other soft tool of ANN and numerical model WAVEWATCH in retrieving the missing wave heights including the extreme events and in redeployment of buoy at other location outside the network.

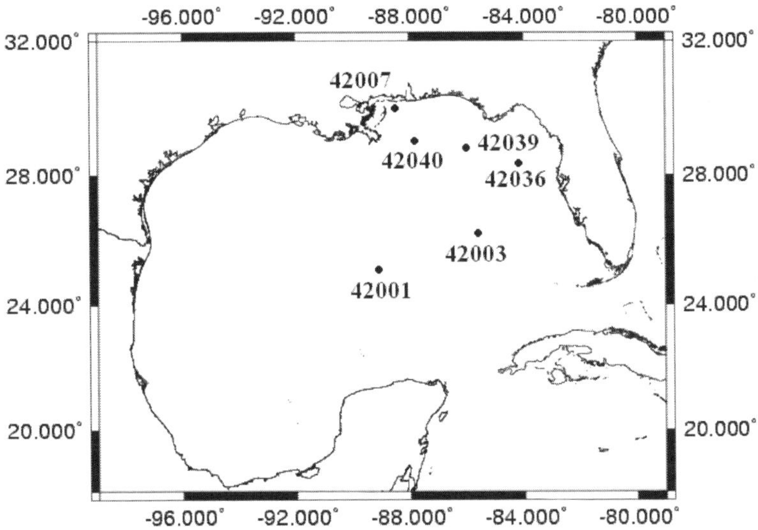

Figure 2. Study area and Buoy Locations (Ref: [6])

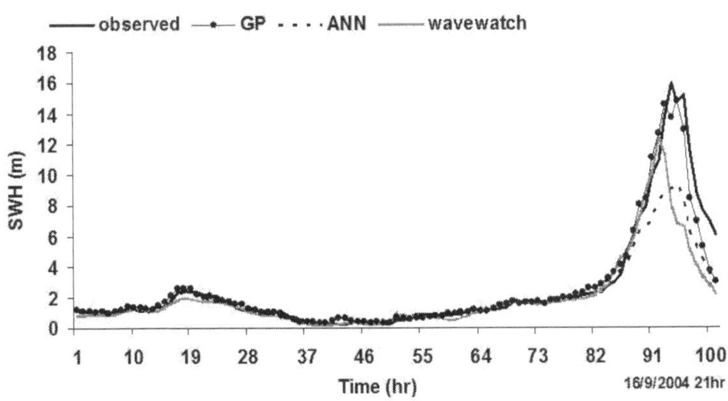

Figure 3. Wave height comparison at 42040 during Hurricane Ivan (Ref: [6])

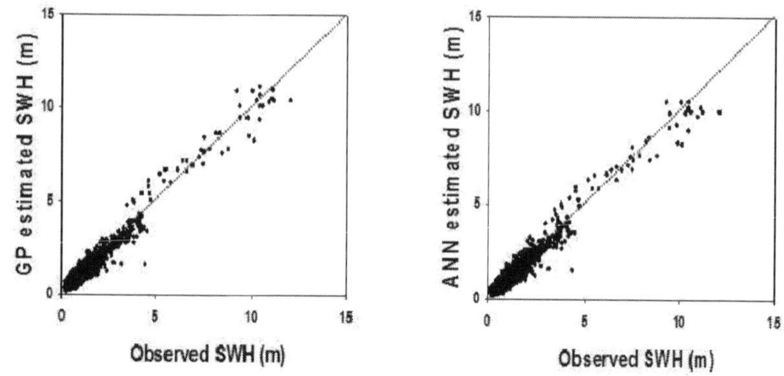

Figure 4. a. Scatter plot for buoy 42039 (GP approach); b. Scatter plot for buoy 42039 (ANN approach) (Ref: [6])

Table 3. Results of buoy networks [6]

network	Input buoys	Target buoy	r_{ANN}	r_{GP}
BN1	42003, 42007, 42036, 42039, 42040	42001	0.85	0.88
BN2	42001, 42007, 42036, 42039, 42040	42003	0.87	0.91
BN3	42001, 42003, 42036, 42039, 42040	42007	0.90	0.92
BN4	42001, 42003, 42007, 42039, 42040	42036	0.92	0.94
BN5	42001, 42003, 42007, 42036, 42040	42039	0.98	0.98
BN6	42001, 42003, 42007, 42036, 42039	42040	0.94	0.97

10. CASE STUDY II: COMPARISON OF DATA-DRIVEN MODELLING TECHNIQUES FOR RIVER FLOW FORECASTING

In the case study GP was used for prediction of average daily flow values one day in advance at two locations, Rajghat and Mandaleshwar, in the Narmada basin, India using the previous values of measured streamflows at these two locations. The observations of daily average stream flow values at both these stations for the years 1987–1997 were obtained from the Central Water Commission, Narmada Division, Bhopal, India. Considering the variations in daily stream flow values four separate models for the monsoon months of July, August, September and October were prepared along with the one separate but common model for the non monsoon months of November–June. Thus five models were developed in all for each station (total 10 models) to predict discharge at one day in advance. In a

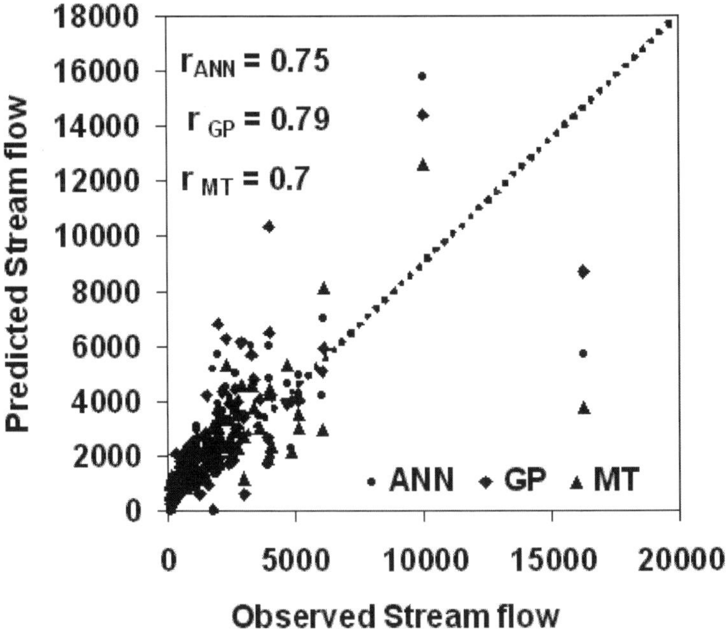

Figure 5. Scatter plot for RajJuly Model

view of fair judgment along with GP, ANN and Model trees approach was also employed to develop the models. The number of antecedent discharge values which were used for predicting discharge one day in advance was decided by carrying out the auto-correlation analysis.

The GP models were developed with major fitness function of mean squared error, initial population size of (2048), mutation frequency of (95%) and the cross-over frequency of (53%) with same data division for both ANN and GP models so that their results could be compared. All the developed forecasting models were tested for unseen inputs and their qualitative and quantitative performance was judged by means of correlation coefficient (r) between the observed and forecasted values along with root mean square error (RMSE) and plotting scatter plots between the same. Hydrographs were also plotted to visualize the behavior of the forecasting models particularly for extreme events (peaks).

After examining the results it was observed that for the location of Rajghat in the month of July, ANN model exhibited a reasonable performance in testing with an 'r' value of 0.75 between the observed and forecasted discharges whereas GP model had showed a better 'r' value of 0.78 with better performance for higher values of stream flow, though over-predicted in some instances. The MT model gave a lower 'r' value of 0.7 and prediction of MT model for high stream flows was poor as compared to ANN and GP models. The scatter plot (Fig. 5) between the observed and forecasted discharges confirmed this with a balanced scatter except at the high values of measured stream flows.

For the months of August and September, models showed similar performance with GP models performing better than their ANN and MT counterparts (r_{GP} = 0.75,r_{ANN} = 0.7, r_{MT} = 0.72 for Raj Aug and r_{GP} = 0.79,r_{ANN} = 0.76, r_{MT} = 0.78 for Raj Sept). For the October model, the predicted discharges in testing were highly in agreement with the observed values for both the models as shown by the discharge hydrograph (Fig. 6). The results were also supported by a high value of correlation coefficient (r = 0.92 for ANN and GP and r = 0.87 for MT) for all the three models in testing.

The Mandaleshwar models behaved in a similar fashion as that of the Rajghat models with correlation coefficients of $r > 0.7$ for all ANN, GP and MT models. For the month of August the performance of all models was reasonable with r values of 0.74, 0.78 and 0.71 for ANN, GP and MT models respectively. The other monthly models of ANN, GP and MT also performed well, with high correlation coefficients in testing ($r > 0.86$). It was again observed that GP models work better while predicting extreme events. The maximum observed discharge of 3790 m^3/s was predicted as 1742 m^3/s by the ANN model, 3342 m^3/s by the GP model and 1718 m^3/s by the MT model. Figure 7shows discharge hydrographs for the ManNov-June models. The RMSE values also showed a similar trend to that of the correlation coefficients.

Thus it was seen that the GP technique outperforms both ANN and MT in almost all the cases in terms of overall accuracy in prediction. The GP approach based on evolutionary principles has a completely different approach to the ANN technique in that it does not involve any transfer function, and evolves generations of "offspring" based on the "fitness criteria" and genetic operations; this seems to capture the underlying trends better than the ANN technique. Thus it can be said that ANN and MT perform almost equally but GP performed better than both of them where prediction accuracy in both normal and extreme events is concerned.

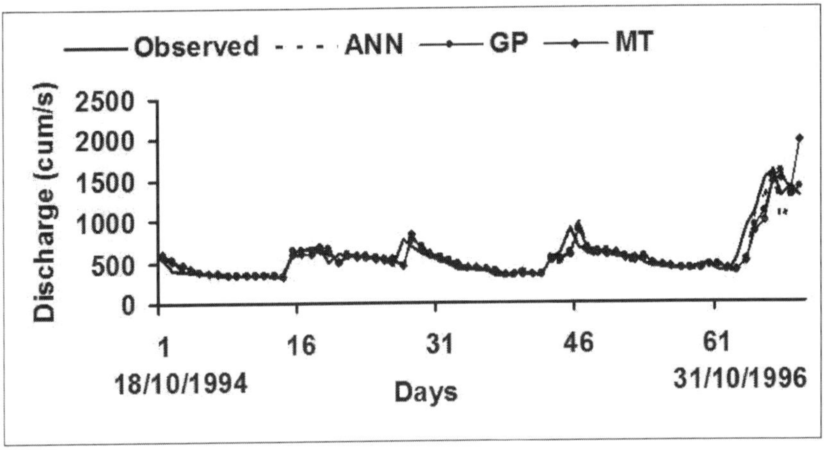

Figure 6. RajOct Model results [13]

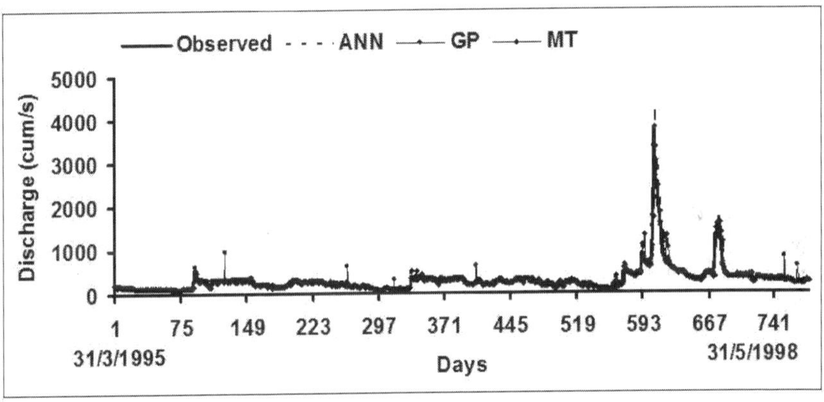

Figure 7. ManNovJune Model results [13]

11. Concluding remarks and future scope

Applications of GP for modeling water flows were discussed in the preceding sections of this chapter. It may be noted that every attempt is made to provide readers the details of GP techniques and their parameters employed in each work. However in view of keeping the length of the chapter in stipulated limits sometimes the readers are referred to the original paper. Details about the data are also provided at appropriate locations. Interested readers may further enquire the authors or download the data whenever possible from the web sites to perform the similar exercise. The applications were from three particular areas of water flows namely Ocean Engineering, Hydrology and Hydraulics. It was shown in all the applications for that modeling of natural random processes of complex underlying phenomenon the Genetic Programming can certainly be employed. The results of this technique were found to be superior than other contemporary soft computing techniques. However it was also seen that the tool is not explored to its full capacity by the research community in any of the above fields. The developed GP models also need to be applied at operational level. For this a partnership between the researchers and practitioners is necessary. The GP models can certainly work as supplementary tool if not as replacement techniques. It can be said that the early days of GP modeling are over and the tool needs to be used more judiciously for the problems worthy of its use. Otherwise a stage will be reached where in GP will be used because data is available. It's use is certainly for the phenomena which are difficult to explain and model. However if the technique is to stay here it needs to be explored further for more challenging problems like modeling of infiltration, high flood events, hurricane path, storm surge, tsunami water levels to name a few.

REFERENCES

1. L. Zadeh, 1994Fuzzy Logic, Neural Networks and Soft Computing. Communications of the ACM 37 (3), 77-84.
2. The ASCE Task Committee,2000Artificial neural networks in hydrology. I: preliminary concepts. J. Hydrol. Engg. ASCE 5(2). 115123
3. S. Maynard, 1975The Theory Of Evolution. Penguin. London.
4. V. Babovic, M. Keijzer, 2000Genetic programming as a model induction engine. Journal of Hydroinformatics. 2(1) 3561
5. J. Koza, 1992Genetic Programming: On the Programming of Computers by Means of Natural Selection. A Bradford Book. MIT Press.
6. S. Londhe, 2008Soft computing approach for real-time estimation of missing wave heights. Ocean Engineering. 35. 10801089
7. M. Brameier, 2004On linear genetic programming. Ph.D. thesis. University of Dortmund.
8. A. Guven, 2009Linear genetic programming for time-series modelling of daily flow rate. J. Earth Syst. Sci. 118(2). 137146

9. P. Jain, M. Deo, 2006Neural networks in ocean engineering. Int. Journal of Ships and Offshore Structures. 1. 2535
10. H. Maier, G. Dandy, 2000Neural networks for prediction and forecasting of water resources variables: a review of modelling issues and applications. Environ. Model. Soft. 15. 101124
11. C. Dawson, R. Wilby, 2001Hydrological modelling using artificial neural networks. Progr. Phys. Geogr. 25(1). 80108
12. A. Kambekar, M. Deo, 2012Wave Prediction Using Genetic Programming And Model Trees. Journal of Coastal Research. Doi:4350
13. S. Londhe, S. Charahate, 2010Comparison of data-driven modelling techniques for river flow Forecasting. Hydrological Sciences. 55(7). 11631173
14. R. Kalra, M. Deo, 2007Genetic Programming to retrieve missing informationin wave records along the west coast of India. Applied Ocean Research. 29. 99111
15. K. Ustoorikar, M. Deo, 2008Filling up Gaps in wave data with Genetic Programming. Marine Structures. 21. 177195
16. S. Charhate, M. Deo, Kumar. V. Sanil, 2007Soft and Hard Computing Approaches for Real Time Prediction of Coastal Currents in a Tide Dominated Area. Journal of Engineering for the Maritime Environment. Proceedings of the Institution of Mechanical Engineers, London, M4, 221:147 EOF163 EOF
17. S. Gaur, M. Deo, 2008Real time wave forecasting using genetic programming Ocean Engineering. 35. 11661175
18. P. Jain, M. Deo, 2008Artificial intelligence tools to forecast ocean waves in real time. The Open Ocean Engineering Journal. 1. 1321
19. A. Kambekar, M. Deo, 2010Wave simulation and forecasting using wind time history and data driven Methods. Ships and Offshore Structures. 5(3). 253266
20. M. Ghorbani, R. Khatibi, A. Aytek, O. Makarynskyy, J. Shiri, 2010aSea water level forecasting using genetic programming and comparing the performance with Artificial Neural Networks. Computers and Geosciences. 36. 620627
21. M. Ghorbani, O. Makarynskyy, J. Shiri, D. Makarynska, 2010bGenetic Programming for Sea Level Predictions in an Island Environment. International Journal of Ocean and Climatic systems. 1(1). 2735
22. S. Charhate, M. Deo, S. Londhe, 2008Inverse modeling to derive wind parameters from wave measurements. Applied Ocean Research.30. 120129
23. S. Charhate, M. Deo, S. Londhe, 2009Genetic programming for real time prediction of offshore wind. International Journal of Ships and Offshore Structures. 4(1). 7788

24. M. Daga, M. Deo, 2009Alternative data-driven methods to estimate wind from waves by inverse Modeling. Natural Hazards. 49(2). 293310
25. A. Singh, M. Deo, Kumar. V. Sanil, 2007Combined Neural network-genetic programming for sediment transport. Journal of Maritime Engineering,The Institution of Civil Engineers. Issue MAO. 17
26. A. Guven, Zakaria. N. Azmathulla, 2009Linear genetic programming for prediction of circular pile scour. Ocean Engineering. 36. 985991
27. D. Savic, G. Walters, J. Davidson, 1999A genetic Programming approach to rainfall-runoff modeling. Water Resources Management. 13. 219231
28. J. Drecourt, (199, of. Application, Networks. Neural, Programming. Genetic, Rainfall. to, Modeling. Runoff, Danish Hydraulic Institute (Hydro-Informatics Techonologies- HIT) June 1999. D2K-06991
29. P. Whigham, P. Crapper, 2001Modeling rainfall runoff using Genetic Programming. Mathematical and Computer Modelling. 33. 707721
30. S. Khu, S. Liong, V. Babovic, H. Madsen, N. Muttil, 2001Genetic Programming And Its Application In Real-Time Runoff Forecasting. J of American Water Resources Association. 37(2). 439450
31. V. Babovic, M. Keijzer, 2002Rainfall runoff modeling Based on Genetic programming. Nordic Hydrology. 33(5). 331346
32. C. Sivapragasam, R. Maheswaran, V. Venkatesh, 2007Genetic programming approach for flood routing in natural channels. Hydrological processes. 22. 623628
33. K. Parasuraman, A. Elshorbagy, K. Carey, 2007Modelling the dynamics of the evapotranspiration process using genetic Programming. Hydrological Sciences. 52(3). 563578
34. I. El Baroudy, A. Elshorbagy, S. Carey, O. Giustolisi, D. Savic, 2010Comparison of three data-driven techniques in modeling the evapotranspiration process. Journal of Hydroinformatics. 12.4. 365379
35. Ghani. A. Azmathullah, C. Leow, C. Chang, N. Zakaria, 2011Gene-Expression Programming for the Development of a Stage-Discharge Curve of the Pahang River. Water Resource Management. 25. 29012916
36. E. Harris, V. Babovic, R. Falconey, 2003Velocity Predictions in Compound Channels with Vegetated Floodplains using Genetic Programming. Int. J. River Basin Management. 1(2). 117123
37. O. Giustolisi, 2004Using genetic programming to determine Chezy's resistance coefficient in corrugated channels. Journal of Hydroinformatics. 6.3. 157173

38. Ghani. A. Azmathullah, N. Zakaria, S. Lai, C. Chang, C. Leow, 2008Genetic Programming to Predict Ski-Jump bucket Spillway Scour. Journal of Hydrodynamics. 20(4), 477-484
39. V. Panchang, D. Li, 2006Large waves in the Gulf of Mexico Caused by Hurricane Ivan. Bulletin of the American Meteorological Society.DOI:BAMS-87-4-481 EOF489 EOF

5
CHAPTER

AN ENHANCED GENETIC PROGRAMMING ALGORITHM FOR OPTIMAL CONTROLLER DESIGN

Rami A. Maher[1], Mohamed J. Mohamed[2]

[1]*Isra University, Amman, Jordan*

[2]*University of Technology, Baghdad, Iraq*

ABSTRACT

This paper proposes a Genetic Programming based algorithm that can be used to design optimal controllers. The proposed algorithm will be named a Multiple Basis Function Genetic Programming (MBFGP). Herein, the main ideas concerning the initial population, the tree structure, genetic operations, and other proposed non-genetic operations are discussed in details. An optimization algorithm called numeric constant mutation is embedded to strengthen the search for the optimal solutions. The results of solving the optimal control for linear as well as nonlinear systems show the feasibility and effectiveness of the proposed MBFGP as compared to the optimal solutions which are based on numerical methods. Furthermore, this algorithm enriches the set of suboptimal state feedback controllers to include controllers that have product time-state terms.

Keywords: Genetic Programming; Optimal Control; Nonlinear Control System

1. INTRODUCTION

Genetic Programming (GP) is a stochastic search method that inspired by the selection and the natural genetics. GP is characterized by its capability to evolve models (structure as well as parameters) for different kinds of problems in different scientific fields. However, GP in its basic standard form needs to be revised according to the applications nature and requirements. In order to increase the efficiency of GP to deal with optimal control problems, a set of syntactic rules are created to force all tree structures in the population such that the GP will evolve only solutions of desired form. These rules state for each node which terminal node and non-terminal node can be its children nodes while generating new trees and performing genetic operations. The idea of using constraint syntactic structure GP was suggested by Koza [1]. Then it was extended by Montana, who has developed the idea of strongly typed GP [2]. Further development was announced under what is known as a grammatical GP [3].

In many application areas, the GP is one of the powerful current soft computing algorithms [4-6]. It can solve different types of problems in control discipline. For instance, the GP is recently used to solve the well-known Hamilton-Jacobi-Bellman (HJB) equation. Joe Imae et al., in their works [7,8] showed how GP can be used to solve the HJB equation efficiently for linear and nonlinear control systems. The results of the used examples are coincident that based on the theoretical solutions. Enhancing the standard tree structure used in the GP algorithm by new thoughts, ideas, and tools represent a road map to get an efficient methodology for controller design for nonlinear dynamic systems.

2. THE PROPOSED MBFGP ALGORITHM

This paper proposes an approach to force GP tree structures to represent a certain random number of basis functions that are linear in parameters. The approach will be called MBFGP. In this way, the search space of all possible GP trees is reduced to a subspace of trees that satisfies the required data type constraints.

These constraints are defined before learning takes place, and they have an impact on the evolutionary process of the algorithm. Three considerations arise when GP is implemented with trees that have such constrained syntactic structures. These considerations are:

1) The initial population of the random individuals must be created such that every program in the population has the required syntactic structure.
2) When the genetic operations are performed, the required syntactic structure must be preserved so that the operations will always produce the offspring conforming to the syntactic structure.
3) The fitness measure must consider the syntactic structure.
4) The basic parts constituting of the MBFGP and other related details will be explained in the following subsections.

2.1. Representation

The structures of program trees in MBFGP are composed of a random number of linear and/or nonlinear basis functions (terms), which are forced to be linear in parameters. The MBFGP tree structure has a single root node, internal nodes, and leaf nodes. The general tree structure of MBFGP is divided into two main parts: the head part constructed from fixed (restricted to have specific locations in the tree) problem independent nodes set Σ, f or R and the tail part constructed from unfixed (freely to appear in the tree) problem dependent nodes set as shown in **Figure 1**.

The node Σ is restricted to appear only in the root of the tree structure, so this node will root every program tree. It allocates a space of a specified number N_b of arguments while it is created. However, not all of these arguments will be filled, but instead a random number of them in the range between 1 and N_b will be filled. The rest of the arguments is left empty. These empty argument spaces have an important role through the adaptation process of structures. They may be filled during the implementation of genetic operations on its tree structure.

This property gives the node Σ the ability to have been varying numbers of filled arguments through adaptation, and gives the overall structures high flexibility to adapt their size. The basis function node has two arguments of fixed type; it is also restricted to appear only as a child (argument) of the root node in every tree structure. The two arguments of this node carry different types of nodes. The first argument is restricted to carry only the numeric constant terminal node R, while the second argument may represent any unrestricted node from unfixed terminal and function sets. The R nodes represent the coefficients of the basis functions that are present in the tree structure. Each R node is restricted to appear only in the first argument of each basis function node. Finally, the unfixed node set represents all available functions and terminals that are chosen by the user to appear in the com-

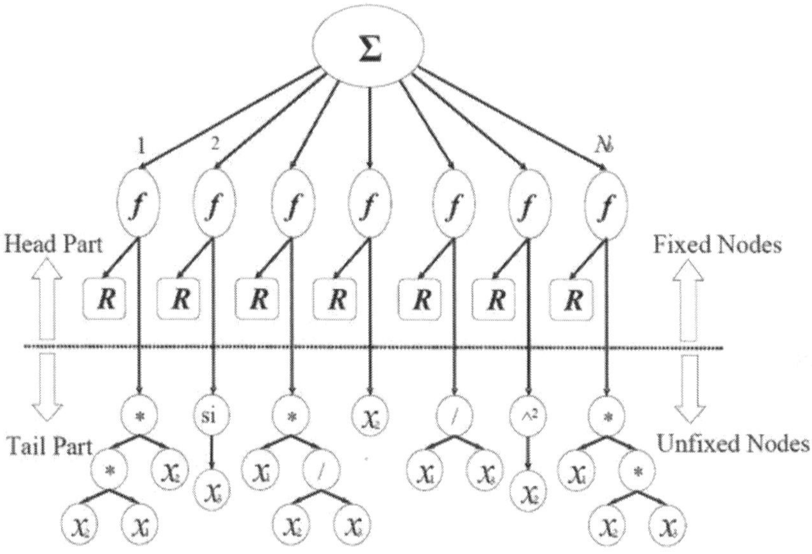

Figure 1. A general tree structure of MBFGP.

According to the set of specific rules that are defined to specify which terminals and functions are allowed to be child nodes of every function in the MBFGP tree structure, fixed sequence of nodes for each basis function will appear in the head part. On the other hand, in the tail part, the basis functions are completed freely without any restrictions on the sequence of nodes. Therefore, different basis functions in the tree structure can be obtained.

2.2. Initial Population

The initial population of random tree structures must be created using the syntactic rules of construction. The desired structure of the multiple basis functions can be created merely by restricting the choice of function for the root of the tree to node Σ. Then, using uniform random distribution, a random number is chosen in the range 1 to N_b. This random number specifies the number of arguments of the node Σ that is required to be filled. All branches of the node Σ are restricted to carry the basis function f nodes.

The first argument of each function node f is restricted to carry numeric constant terminal node R. The value for each created numeric constant terminal node is chosen randomly in a specified range (e.g., in range −10 to 10 with step size 0.001). The second argument is unrestricted. It can carry any available function from the set of the unfixed functions or any available terminal from the set of the unfixed terminals. The proceeding nodes in each branch are chosen randomly from the same unfixed function and terminal sets. The end of the tree structure is bounded by the parameter of maximum creation depth; this parameter is determined by the user.

2.3. Genetic Operations

The genetic operations, as is the case with the creation of initial population, must respect the syntactic rules to produce the correct offspring tree structure. The proposed genetic operations for MBFGP are described in what follows.

- Crossover Operation

Two types of crossover operation are implemented on MBFGP tree structures. These types are: the Internal Crossover Operation which occurs in the tail part of each parent tree structure. The operation starts by choosing randomly two parental trees from the population based on fitness measure. Choosing a crossover point in each parent is restricted to picking randomly a node from the tail part in order to preserve the required tree structure for the produced offspring. The simplest way to perform the restraining process is to exclude the fixed nodes (Σ, f and R) of the parental tree from being selected as a crossover point of either parent. This restraining secures that the crossover preserves the syntactic structure, and it will always produce the offspring tree structures. The second type is the External Crossover Operation, which occurs in the head part of the tree structure. In this type, two parental trees are selected randomly from the population based on fitness measure.

The number of existent basis functions in each parental tree is counted. Therefore, the syntactic rules enforce the crossover point in each parent to be one of the basis functions, which are selected randomly from the existent basis functions in the parental tree. Then, the swapping between these two selected basis functions is implemented to produce two new offspring.

- Mutation Operation

Different types of mutation operation are proposed. They are:

1) Swap operation, which is applied to the tail part of the parental tree structure only. The present unfixed nodes (functions and terminals) in the tail part of the selected parental tree structure are counted. One unfixed node is randomly selected from the tree structure. The number of arguments k_Y of the selection is checked. Another new node is chosen randomly with k_Y arguments from combined sets of unfixed function and terminal nodes. The new chosen node changes the existent node in the tree structure. If one considers the number of arguments of the terminal node is zero, another randomly chosen terminal node can swap the original terminal node.

2) Shrink operation, which is applied similarly as the swap operation. It begins by choosing randomly an unfixed function node and then the chosen function node is deleted and replaced with its child. If the deleted function node has a lot of children, one child among them is chosen randomly to take the place of its parent in the tree, and the rests of the children are deleted. This operation eventually leads to a lower depth of the overall tree.

3) Inverse shrink operation which has two modes of operations: the internal mode operates in the tail part, and the external mode operates in the head part. The internal operation will start by picking randomly an unfixed node. The sub-tree rooted at this node is stored and then deleted from the parental tree. Then, a new function node is chosen randomly from the available set of the unfixed function to take the place of the original unfixed node. The stored sub-tree is inserted back in the first argument of the new node of the unfixed function. If the new function node has more than one argument, randomly created sub-trees fill the remaining arguments. The depth of the created sub-trees is controlled by the parameter of maximum allowable depth. This operation eventually might lead to a higher depth of the overall tree. The external operation works such to increase the number of basis functions in the produced offspring. Nevertheless, the operation is ignored when the number of basis functions in the parental tree is equal to the maximum allowable number N_b. In this case, the offspring is an exact copy of the parent tree.

4) Branch operation which has also two modes of operation, internal and external. The former one works such to create randomly a sub-tree using available unfixed function and terminal sets with respect to the maximum allowable depth. Then, the new created sub-tree is inserted in the mutation point to produce a new offspring. A special case of this operation involves inserting a single terminal node at the selected mutation point. While the external operation works such to create a new subtree rooted with basis function node f. It is created with respect to the syntactic rules of construction, and it is inserted instead of a randomly deleted basis function to produce a new offspring.

- Additional Genetic Operations

Additional proposed operations that are used to vary and adapt the tree structures. They are:

1) Endowment operation: The name "Endowment" has been chosen to indicate the process of basis function endowment that occurs between two individuals. This operation starts by choosing randomly two parental individuals on the base of the fitness. The number of existent basis functions in each parent is counted. One basis function of the existent basis functions in each parent is chosen randomly. A copy of the selected basis function in the first parent is added to the basis functions in the second parent to produce the first offspring. While a copy of the selected basis function in the second parent is added to the basis functions in the first parent to produce the second offspring.
2) Delete operation, which is used to delete a basis function of the individual on the bases of the fitness value.
3) Merging operation: It edits and simplifies the individual tree structure during GP running. For example, if the tree has two or more basis functions with similar internal structure and contents, then this operator merges them in one basis function.

2.4. Enhancement Operations

A number of enhancement operations are proposed here. They are:

1) Nested function operation: It is responsible for solving the problem of the nested mathematical functions in the individual solutions. Every nested mathematical function node in the tree structure is deleted and

replaced by a new sub-tree, which is randomly created. This operator works on all the individuals in every generation.

2) Structural Sorting Operation: It emphasizes that the tree structure as well as the fitness of the individual is considered through implementing the sorting. The population of individuals is sorted first according to the fitness measure with the fittest at the top. Then it is starting from the best individual in the sorted population to pick the best individual and put it in a new list. The procedure proceeds to the less fit individual, if its tree structure and components are not picked before. This means that, any individual that has a structure with components being picked before is ignored, and thus each individual tree structure along with its components is picked only once. The new list of sorting will contain different sorted individuals. This structural sorting operation is based on fitness, and at the same time the sorted individuals are of different structures and components.

3) Enrichment Operation: In order not to discard too soon structures that may be valid, the operation uses first the proposed structural sorting operation. Then a specified number of the individuals is retained from the sorted population list. The proposed method feeds the next population by a number of trees that are different in structures and/or components. In this way, it increases the structural diversity in the subsequent generations.

4) Contribution Operation: It determines the contribution of each of the basis functions in the individual. It resolves the problem of poor diversity of the basis functions by deleting any basis function that has a trivial contribution in the fitness measure. The contribution operation is an effective method to determine which basis functions are significant in MBFGP, and are controlled by the frequency parameter F_{co}. It is either 1, 0, or an integer greater than one, thus the contribution operation is to be applied to every generation, to no generation or with a certain frequency respectively. In the Appendix, the operation algorithm is shown.

5) Numeric Constant Mutation: It is used, during the GP run, for the known reasons of replacing some of the numerical constant node values by new ones in the individual [6]. The proposed MBFGP here applies two proposed modes of mutating numeric constant node values. Before GP run, the user must specify the range and the resolution of the numeric constant node values (e.g., the range is −10 to 10 with resolution of 0.001). In this case, the algorithm avoids the use of default precision of the floating constant valid in the programming language. This gives the algorithm the ability to ignore the least

significant digits in the numeric constant value. The number of numeric constant nodes to be mutated in each individual is chosen randomly in the range 1 to n. For example, if the range is 1 to 3, then this will mean that moving in three dimensions on the cost surface of the numeric constant gives a good probability to climb out the local minimum or maximum. Then after the number of numeric constant nodes that will be mutated is determined, these numeric constants are chosen randomly in the tree. Each value of the numeric constant node is randomly chosen according to one of the following methods. The first method suggests that the new numeric constant values are chosen at random from a specific uniform distributed chosen range. The selection range for each numeric constant is specified as the old value of the numeric constant plus or minus a specified a percentage of the total allowed range. Therefore, it lets the mutation operation explore all the search space and avoid falling in local minimum or maximum. The second method suggests selecting the location of the digit to be mutated randomly. The new value of the numeric constant is equal to the old value plus or minus one for the selected digit. For example, if the old value is 3.791 and the least significant digit is chosen as the digit to be mutated, then the new value of the constant will be either 3.792 or 3.790 with equal probability. Therefore, the second method is useful for fine tuning where the need is only for small change in the numeric constant node values.

3. OPTIMAL CONTROL SOLUTION BASED MBFGP

As a first test of the proposed MBFGP, the design of controllers for nonlinear dynamic systems is introduced and compared to optimal control solutions. To emphasize the importance of using MBFGP, the systems are chosen such to have the only numerical solution and not a closedform one.

As it is known, with numerical methods, there are many difficulties concerning the accuracy and the convergence of the solution. In such circumstances, it is hoped that GP is a better alternative. Because not only a solution can be found, but also it will provide many possible solutions whose structures can be controlled by the designer. Therefore, based on the accuracy and the simplicity of the implementation, a choice of one solution can be decided later.

To illustrate the use of the MBFGP algorithm for solving optimal problems, three classical examples will be considered. The results are compared to that obtained by conventional optimal control theory.

Example 1

Consider the Van der Pol system given by

$$\begin{aligned} x_1'(t) &= \left(1 - x_2^2(t)\right)x_1(t) - x_2(t) + u(t), \quad & x_1(0) = 0 \\ x_2'(t) &= x_1(t), & x_2(0) = 3 \end{aligned} \tag{1}$$

It is required to determine the optimal control, which transfers the system to $x_1(10) = x_2(10) = 0$, while minimizing the performance index.

$$J = \int_0^{10} \left[x_1^2(t) + x_2^2(t) + u^2(t)\right] \mathrm{d}t \tag{2}$$

In [9], the method of the conjugate gradient is used to obtain the optimal control, where the optimum value is found to be approximately 21.4. However, when the method of control vector parameterization CVP is used, it is shown [10] that the optimum value is 21.4612, and the control law is

$$\overset{*}{u}_d(x_1, x_2) = -3.0912x_1 + 1.3495x_1x_2 - 0.299x_2 \tag{3}$$

The terminal values of the optimal trajectories are

$$\overset{*}{x}_1(10) = 1.353 \times 10^{-3}, \overset{*}{x}_2(10) = -1.047 \times 10^{-3}$$

The enhanced algorithm of MBFGP is now used to evolve optimal control laws. The MBFGP is enforced to evolve two forms of control laws. The first one is a function of the time and the system states $u_{GP}(x, t)$ while the second is a function of system states only $u_{GP}(x)$. In the first case, the unfixed terminal set is T = {x_1, x_2, t, one} while in the second case, the unfixed terminal set is T = {x_1, x_2, one}. The unfixed function set in both cases is F = {*, /, pow}. The fixed numeric constant node R is in the range −10 to 10 with a resolution of 0.001. A special integer numeric constant node R' is used to appear only in the power function using special structural constraint rules. The value of this type of numeric constant node is mutated by special type of mutation operation when the pow function is chosen in swap mutation operation. The integer range for R' node is −5 to 5. The fitness value is calculated discretely with 0.001 step size. At each step, the system equations are integrated numerically to obtain the instantaneous system states.

MBFGP control parameters are illustrated in **Table 1**, and the results are as follows:

$$u_{GP}(x,t) = -3.816x_1 - 0.218tx_2 + 1.056x_1x_2 - 0.445x_2 \tag{4}$$

The optimum value is 21.4335, and the terminal trajectory values are

$$\overset{*}{x}_1(10) = -6.065\times10^{-5}, \overset{*}{x}_2(10) = 5.232\times10^{-5}$$

Whereas,

$$u_{GP}(x) = -3.041x_1 + 1.273x_1x_2 - 0.328x_2 \tag{5}$$

The optimum value is 21.4572 and the terminal trajectory values are

$$\overset{*}{x}_1(10) = 1.311\times10^{-3}, \overset{*}{x}_2(10) = 7.463\times10^{-4}$$

Figure 2 shows the control actions of MBFGP and CVP approaches. As shown, they are all approximately the same. Although the first solution gives less minimal value of J*, the so close results address the second solution for the practical implementation. The most interesting results are that GP can result in different controller structures.

Table 1. GP control parameters (Example 1).

GP Control Parameter		MBFGP Algorithm
Population Size		200
Termination Criterion		300 Generations
Creation Probability		20%
Creation Type		Ramped-Half-and-Half
Crossover Probability	Internal	19%
	External	13%
Maximum Depth for Creation		5
Maximum Depth for Crossover		8
Selection Type		Tournament selection
Tournament Size		4
Swap Mutation Probability		8%
Shrink Mutation Probability		8%
Inverse Shrink Mutation Probability	Internal	4%
	External	4%
Branch Mutation Probability	Internal	4%
	External	4%
Probability of Delete Operation		8%
Probability of Endowment Operation		8%
Maximum Number of Basis Functions		7
Add Best Solutions to a New Generation		Yes
Number of Best Solutions Used in Enrichment		50
Use Contribution Operation		Yes
Frequency of Contribution Operation F_{co}		Each 3 generations
The Error Reduction Value ε		0.001
Use Merging Operation		Yes for all generations and all individuals
Number of Iterations Applying by Numeric Constant Mutation		10 iterations for each individual in the population, and additional 660 iterations for the elected individuals by the enrichment operation

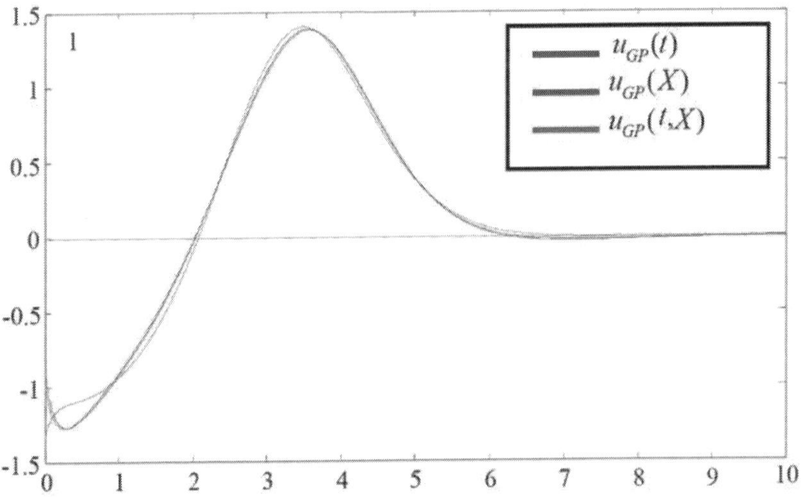

Figure 2. Optimal controls of MBFGP and CVP approach.

Example 2

Consider the following optimal control problem

$$x'(t) = -0.2x(t) + \tanh(u(t)), x(0) = 5 \tag{6}$$

It is required to find the optimal control law that minimizes the performance index

$$J = 10x^2(t_f) + \int_0^{0.5} \left[10x^2(t) + u^2(t)\right] dt \tag{7}$$

When the conjugate gradient method is used to solve this problem, it is found that within 17 iterations, the optimum value of the J(u) is 41.5953. Again, when CVP approach is used, the minimum return value J* is equal to 41.596 and the control law as a function of time is given by

$$\overset{*}{u}_d(t) = -2.591 + 1.406t + 3.329t^2 \tag{8}$$

The MBFGP algorithm combined with numeric constant mutation operation is proposed to evolve three control laws $u_{GP}(t)$, $u_{GP}(x)$, and $u_{GP}(t,x)$. These different functions of control laws can be obtained by enforcing the unfixed terminal sets in MBFGP algorithm to be T = {t, one}, T = {x, one} and T = {t, x, one} respectively.

The unfixed function set for all cases is F = {*, /, ^}. The ranges of the fixed numeric constant node R and the special integer numeric constant node Ŕ, are as in the previous example. The main MBFGP control parameters are also as shown in **Table 1**. The following three control laws are evolved in generations 399,245, and 282 respectively.

$$u_{GP}(t) = -10.621t^5 + 7.375t^3 + 1.873t - 2.615 \tag{9}$$

$$u_{GP}(x) = -0.04x^2 - 0.501x - 1.076 \tag{10}$$

$$u_{GP}(t,x) = -6.986t - 1.006x - 0.452tx - 0.93x^2t^3 + 2.433 \tag{11}$$

The final system state and optimal criterion for MBFGP and CVP method solutions are shown in**Table 2**. In fact, the control action and the state trajectory behavior of all solutions are almost the same.

The results again show that very near optimal solutions can be attained, even better than numerical methods. It is worth mentioning that for the exactly solved optimal problems, the enhanced proposed MBFGP algorithm can give the same results after enough generations [11].

Example 3

Consider the linear third order system [12]

$$\begin{aligned} x_1'(t) &= -x_1(t) + \frac{2}{\pi}\tan^{-1}(u(t)),\ x_1(0) = -0.6 \\ x_2'(t) &= x_1(t) - x_2(t),\ x_2(0) = -0.6 \\ x_3'(t) &= x_2(t) - x_3(t),\ x_3(0) = 4 \end{aligned} \qquad 12)$$

It is required to minimize the following optimal criterion

$$J(u) = \int_0^3 \left[(2x_2(t))^{20} + x_3^2(t) + 0.01u^2(t) \right] dt \tag{13}$$

The MBFGP combined with numeric constant mutation is proposed to evolve the optimal control laws. The MBFGP algorithm is enforced to evolve three control laws $u_{GP}(t)$, $u_{GP}(x)$, and $u_{GP}(t, x)$. The terminal sets for the three controllers are: T = {t, one}, T = {x_1, x_2, x_3, one}, and T = {x_1, x_2, x_3, t, one} respectively, while the function set in all cases is F = {*, /, ^}. The MBFGP is also initiated to similar setting as in the previous problems. The following three control laws are evolved in generations 94, 74, and 88 respectively.

$$u_{GP}(t) = -0.753t^3 + 5.748t^2 - 12.072t + 6.121$$

$$u_{GP}(X) = -0.482x_2 - 2.922x_3 + 5.943x_1x_2x_3 + 10x_2^2x_3 - 4.394x_1^2x_2^2x_3$$

$$u_{GP}(t, X) = -9.88x_1 - 0.538t + 8.469x_2^2 - 1.313x_3t^2 - 2.427x_3^2t^2 \tag{14}$$

Figures 3 and 4 show the plots of the system states and the optimal control respectively for all GP solutions.

Table 2. MBFGP and CVP method solutions.

Control law	Final state x_f	Optimal criterion J
$u_d(t)$	0.0417825	41.596
$u_{GP}(t)$	0.0354204	41.4707
$u_{GP}(x)$	0.0351676	41.4708
$u_{GP}(x, t)$	0.0354944	41.4705

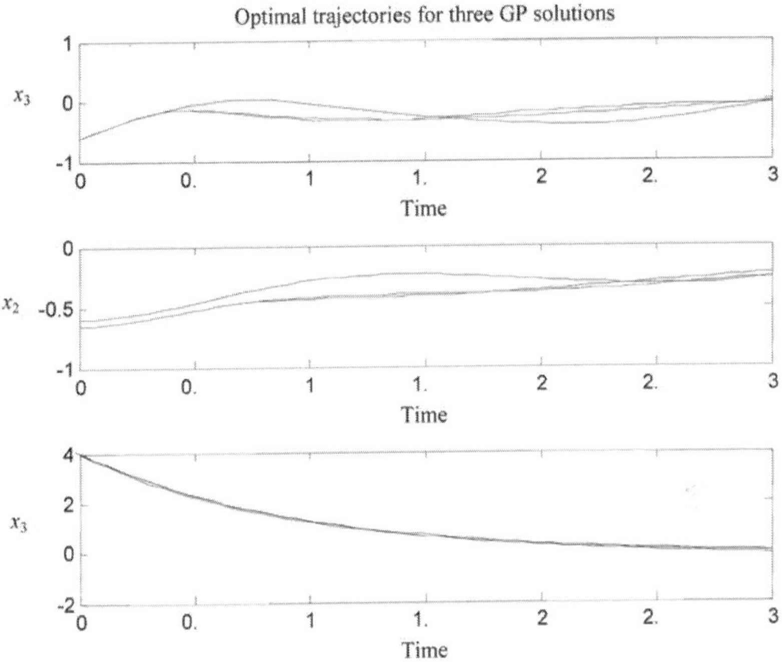

Figure 3. System states when GP solutions are applied.

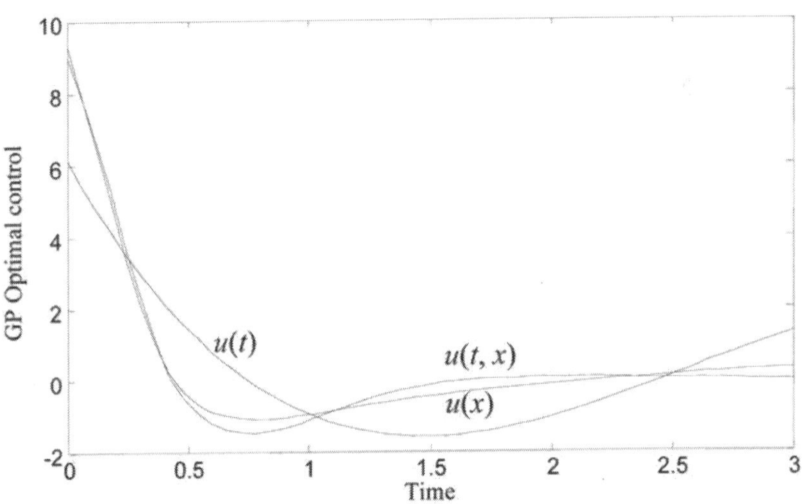

Figure 4. Optimal control u* for all GP solutions.

4. CONCLUSIONS

The standard GP algorithm is enhanced by creating a new tree structure. The crossover, the inverse shrink mutation, and the branch mutation operations are split into two operations (internal and external) with different probabilities.

Moreover, four new operations are added, the delete, contribution, merging and endowment operations, which are controlled by specific probabilities and special parameters. Therefore, a new algorithm named MBFGP is performed.

The MBFGP algorithm can be used efficiently to synthesize an optimal (or very near optimal) control law for linear as well as nonlinear systems. MBFGP algorithm deals with them all similarly without significant change. In addition, the MBFGP algorithm has the capability of determining beforehand the independent variables in the evolved optimal controller. The obtained results show that the MFBGP algorithm can evolve different controllers as many as the different terminal sets.

REFERENCES

1. J. R. Koza, "Genetic Programming: On the Programming of Computers by Means of Natural Selection," The MIT Press, Cambridge, 1992.
2. D. J. Montna, "Strongly Typed Genetic Programming," Evolutionary Computation, Vol. 3, No. 2, 1995, pp. 199- 230.
3. E. Hemberg, C. Gilligan, M. O'Neill and A. Brabazon, "A Grammatical Genetic Programming Approach to Modularity in Genetic Programming," Proceedings of the Tenth European Conference on Genetic Programming, Valencia, 11-13 April 2007.
4. I. G. Tsoulos and I. E. Lagaris, "Solving Differential Equations with Genetic Programming," Genetic Programming and Evolvable Machines, Vol. 7, No. 1, 2006, pp. 33-54.
5. C. Yuehui, Y. Ju, Y. Zhang and J. Dong, "Evolving Additive Tree Models for System Identification," International Journal of Computational Cognition, Vol. 3, No. 2, 2005, pp. 19-26.
6. J. Imae and J. Takahashi, "A Design Method for Nonlinear H_∞ Control Systems via Hamilton-Jacobi-Isaacs Equations: A

Genetic Programming Approach," Proceedings of 38th conference on Decision & Control, Phoenix, 7-10 December 1999.

7. J. Imae, et al., "Design of Nonlinear Control Systems by Means of Differential Genetic Programming," 43rd IEEE Conference, Atlantis, 14-17 December 2004.

8. M. Evett and T. Fernandez, "Numeric Mutation Improves the Discovery of Numeric Constants in Genetic Programming," Proceeding of the Third Annual Genetic Programming Conference, Madison, 22-25 July 1998, pp. 66- 71.

9. L. S. Lasdon, S. Mitter and A. Waren, "The Method of Conjugate Gradient for optimal Control Problems," IEEE Transactions on Automatic Control, Vol. AC-12, 1967.

10. A. M. Rami, "Optimization and Optimal Control, Lecture Notes," University of Technology, Baghdad, 1995-2003.

11. M. J. Mohamad, "A Proposed Genetic Programming Applied to Controller Design and System Identification," Ph.D. Thesis, University of Technology, Baghdad, 2008.

12. M. Noton, "Modern Control Engineering," Pergamon Press Inc., Oxford, 1972.

6 CHAPTER

PREDICTION OF CONCRETE FACED ROCK FILL DAMS SETTLEMENTS USING GENETIC PROGRAMMING ALGORITHM

Seyed Morteza Marandi, Seyed Mahmood VaeziNejad, Elyas Khavari

Civil Engineering Department, Shahid Bahonar University, Kerman, Iran

ABSTRACT

In the present study a Genetic Programing model (GP) proposed for the prediction of relative crest settlement of concrete faced rock fill dams. To this end information of 30 large dams constructed in seven countries across the world is gathered with their reported settlements. The results showed that the GP model is able to estimate the dam settlement properly based on four properties, void ratio of dam's body (e), height (H), vertical deformation modulus (E_v) and shape factor (Sc) of the dam. For verification of the model applicability, obtained results compared with other research methods such as Clements' formula and the finite element model. The comparison showed that in all cases the GP model led to be more accurate than those of performed in literature. Also a proper compatibility between the GP model and the finite element model was perceived.

Keywords: Concrete faced rock-fill dams; settlement; genetic programming algorithm; finite element model

1. INTRODUCTION

One of the most important reasons of dam failures is uncontrolled settlements. Especially in the case of earth dams due to weak compaction and the use of improper materials this may occur. Such phenomenon may lead to very huge economic costs and human casualties but it has not been studied completely yet.

In the last centuries various concrete faced rock-fill dams are designed and constructed in many countries across the world. Exclusively in the past decades, the designing process and their construction has been changed considerably [1]. Such phenomenon occurred specially for the concrete faced rock fill dams. Recent growing demands for taller and larger dams, has changed the fundamental rules dominant in their design. This has led to new theories on the basis of new methods of testing materials and new techniques for the analysis.

Basically deformation of a dam may happen in three steps or situations: during the construction, during the first impounding, and while servicing. There are two basic approaches found in the literature for the estimation of the crest and body settlement in dams: 1) Numerical methods such as the finite element method, finite difference method; and 2) Experimental methods.

Almost all methods exist for prediction of dam deformations cover only one or two steps of the three steps mentioned above. For example, finite element method is used for the analysis of dam deformation during construction and first impounding. While, experimental methods are used for estimation of dam deformation during construction and servicing [2].

Sowers et al. in 1965 gathered information of 14 dams without attention to their heights, methods used in their section design, material used in the dam body and their construction methods and draw a scatter chart for height of dams over logarithm of the time. While better methods of construction e.g. better compaction or better proofing decrease the amount of settlement, they indicated that the settlement is independent of all these factors [3].

Lawton and Lester (1964) used data of 11 dams where, their settlement were at least 0.02 percent of their heights and presented in a settlement equation. The equation used depends only on the height and is not related to the time needed for the settlement [4].

Soydemir and Kjaemsli (1979) combined displacement equations in respect to time and height and obtained a new equation for the displacement of dam in various time periods using 48 different dam settlements data [5].

In 1984 Clements studied on 68 earth dams with well compacted poured concrete deck. He determined limits on the maximum and minimum of crest settlements and made a comparison between Soydemir and Kjaemsli method and real measured values in the field. The results showed that the method may have big errors (correlation about 0.247 to 0.897) in the estimation. Clements also suggested new deformation graphs for constructed dams which can be used in design and estimation of settlements [6].

Pinto and Marques Filho in 1998 presented a simple way for an approximate estimation of concrete faced rock-fill dams (CFRD) deformations. Their investigation showed that the void ratio and downstream valley shape have the most important effect on the deformation modulus1 of under construction dams. Accordingly for narrow valleys whose shape factors are less than 3.5, the effect of valley shape is higher than those with bigger shape factors2 (SF > 4). This means in wider hills the void ratio is more effective [8]. They also presented the following equation for the vertical deformation modulus.

$$E_v = H \times h \times \frac{\gamma}{1000 \times S} \quad (1)$$

where E_v is vertical deformation modulus, H is embankment height above a determined point in meters, h is embankment height below a determined point, γ is embankment density in KN/m^3 and s is the settlement of specified point in meter [9].

The Finite element method is a new method in comparison with the other methods used in the literature. Its reliability is highly dependent on the selected constitutive model for materials and an appropriate meshing which best cover the real environment. Kovacevic (1994), Duncan (1992, 1996) are the first investigators who used the finite element methods for the study of rock-fill embankment deformations during dam construction and the first impounding. They discussed on the analysis methods, limitations and combining different stress-strain models and their errors. Based on Duncan's studies, a good correlation exists between the estimated and observed values [10-12].

Frequently, the estimation of dam properties is based on the experiments of previously constructed dams. There is much information published for estimation of concrete faced rock-fill dams. However these papers are written on the basis of limited information and in almost all cases concentrated on one or two of the effective parameters on rock modulus of elasticity or measured deformation. To overcome these limitations and present a simpler method, genetic programming algorithm which is of interest of various engineering fields can be aproposed method for the prediction of dam crests deformations. Due to high complexity and the presence of different variables in the soil responses, the genetic programming with a perfect training algorithm is extended. However, the authors could not find any data obtained for estimation of crest settlement of concrete faced rock-fill dams using GP algorithm in literature. In this paper an investigation is carried out on the deformation behavior of concrete faced rock-fill dams using GP modeling. For this purpose, documents from 30 information bases and from 7 countries across the world are used. The studies are concentrated on four effective parameters for prediction of dam crest settlement. These parameters are: void ratio of dam's body (e), height of dam (H), vertical deformation modulus (E_v) and shape factor of the dam (SF). For training of the model, 67 percent of information (information of 21 dams out of 30 dams) is randomly selected and 33 percent of the rest (information of 9 dams) is used for dam prediction testing. To verify the suggested model with other methods in literature, the prediction results obtained for concrete faced rock-fill dams is compared with the Clement method.

2. BEHAVIOR CHARACTERISTICS OF CONCRETE FACED ROCK-FILL DAMS (CFRDS)

Due to the better performance and lower costs, construction of the concrete faced rock-fill dams (CFRDs) have been used wide spread since 4 decades ago. The CFRDs have become more common than rock-fill dams with clayey cores. Experience showed that even though these types of dams are economical and reliable, but in most cases the concrete decks are exposed to failure, damage and settlement. **Table 1** shows performance and structural properties of CFRDs used in the present study [13].

Clements studied on the real settlements of 68 earth dams after construction and compared the results with the estimated values derived from the following equation:

$$S = aH^b \tag{2}$$

where S is the crest settlement in meters, H is the height of dam in meters, a and b are experimental constants of the equation. The constants values are given in **Table 2**.

Table 3 shows the measured values of the crest settlements of 35 dams in the fields and estimated values using Clements experimental equation for period of 10 years after construction. Statistical analysis between these two type of data shows that there is a weak correlation of $R^2 = 0.201$ between the results. Therefore, it seems the Clements method is very conservative.

3. THE GENETIC PROGRAMING (GP) MODEL

3.1. Structure of the GP SDEL

In the recent years, the GP algorithm which is inspired by the nature and is based on the Darwin' theory of evolution has been used for various purposes [7-14]. In 1992, John Koza used this algorithm as a specialization of the genetic algorithm (GA) with a difference that programs are replaced with individuals and establishes branches of a tree. Random changes are happened via replacement of the operators in the programs, changing value of a knot or replacement of the branches of the trees with each other [15,16]. **Figure 1** shows three examples of GPs as trees.

The main characteristic of the GP algorithms is that they need a large population with thousands or even millions of individuals. Therefore, these algorithms are usually very slow and because of working on the basis of trees, more individuals in the population, more efficient and faster algorithms are obtained [14]. However, in general case, attaining a desired fitness value is very time consuming, but this is not very horrific because with one time of running the algorithm, a model attains which could be used simply for the problem. Another special characteristic of the GP is that, the answer is a model instead of a value which may be nonlinear. In addition to these aspects, in the standard form of GA, the lengths of chromosomes are constant, but in the GP algorithm these lengths might be variable. In the GP algorithm the first step is to make the first generation by creation of random programs. Each program has a fitness value that determines the chance of the program in the creation of the next generation. In the GP algorithms, two main operators which are necessary to make the next generations are crossover and mutation.

Table 1. Performance and structural properties of CRFDs [13].

No.	Dam	Country	Year	Height (m)	Shape factor (A/H^2)	Void ratio	EV (MPa)	After impounding		
								Time (year)	Crest set. (m)	Crest set. (%)
1	Cethana	Australia	1971	110	2.5	0.26	140	30	0.176	0.160
2	Alto Anchicaya	Colombia	1974	140	1.1	0.22	145	10	0.173	0.124
3	Golillas	Colombia	1978	127	0.9	0.24	155	7	0.057	0.045
4	Sugaroaf	Australia	1979	85	11.5	0.302	55	16.2	0.207	0.244
5	Foz do Areia	Brazil	1980	160	5.4	0.33	47	20	0.210	0.131
6	Mackintosh	Australia	1981	75	4.9	0.24	45	19	0.235	0.313
7	Mangrove creek	Australia	1981	80	4.5	0.26	75	4	0.084	0.105
8	Tullabardine	Australia	1982	26	8.1	0.23	90	12.8	0.019	0.076
9	Murchison	Australia	1982	94	1.9	0.234	190	18	0.082	0.087
10	Bastyan	Australia	1983	75	3.4	0.23	160	9	0.053	0.071
11	Salvajina	Colombia	1983	154	2.4	0.21	205	7.5	0.090	0.061
12	KhaoLaem	Thailand	1984	113	11	0.29	59	14	0.187	0.165
13	Shiroro	Nigeria	1984	125	4.2	0.2	76	1.8	0.166	0.133
14	Kotmale	Sri Langka	1984	90	7.4	0.27	50	-	0.150	0.167
15	Dongbok	Korea	1985	44.7	3.5	0.27	26	7	0.043	0.096

16	Lower Pieman	Australia	1986	122	2.5	0.24	160	15	0.221	0.181
17	Pyonghwa (1st)	Korea	1988	80	7.1	0.4	71	5	1.168	1.460
18	Chengbing	China	1989	74.6	2.8	0.277	100	10	0.100	0.130
19	White Spur	Australia	1989	43	2.3	0.215	180	5.9	0.058	0.135
20	Xibeikou	China	1989	95	3.3	0.284	80	6	0.061	0.064
21	Crotty	Australia	1990	83	1.9	0.20	375	9	0.056	0.067
22	Segredo	Brazil	1993	145	4.1	0.37	45	8	0.229	0.158
23	Aguamilpa	Mexico	1993	187	3.9	0.18	190	7	0.340	0.182
24	Xingo	Brazil	1994	150	6.0	0.28	34	6	0.931	0.621
25	Wananxi	China	1995	93.8	2.0	0.257	100	-	0.336	0.358
26	Buan	Korea	1996	50	7.3	0.25	25	11	0.204	0.408
27	Tianshenqiao	China	2000	178	4.9	0.31	45	1.5	1.060	0.596
28	Ita	Brazil	2000	125	7.0	0.308	48	3	0.600	0.480
29	Yongdam	Korea	2001	70	8.8	0.32	52	6	0.123	0.176
30	Miryang	Korea	2001	89	6.8	0.18	90	6	0.088	0.099
31	Namgang	Korea	2001	34	36.2	0.27	47	6	0.013	0.038
32	Sancheong (L)	Korea	2002	70.9	6.3	0.27	83	6	0.087	0.122
33	Sancheong (U)	Korea	2002	86.9	3.1	0.27	92	6	0.300	0.345
34	Jangheung	Korea	2005	53	10.7	0.28	34	1	0.015	0.028
35	Daegok	Korea	2005	52	3.7	0.25	154	1	0.019	0.037

Table 2. Constants values of a and b [6].

Constants	*Initial impounding*	*After 10 years*
a	0.0002	14×10^{-7}
b	1.1	2.6

Table 3. Comparison of measured and estimated settlements values [13].

No.	Dam	Measured crest set. (m)	Estimated Crest set. Clements theory (10 years service)
1	Cethana	0.176	0.284
2	Alto Anchicaya	0.173	0.532
3	Golillas	0.057	0.413
4	Sugaroaf	0.207	0.145
5	Foz do Areia	0.210	0.753
6	Mackintosh	0.235	0.105
7	Tullabardine	0.019	0.007
8	Murchison	0.082	0.189
9	Bastyan	0.053	0.105
10	Salvajina	0.09	0.682
11	KhaoLaem	0.187	0.305
12	Shiroro	0.166	0.396
13	Kotmale	0.150	0.169
14	Dongbok	0.043	0.027
15	Lower Pieman	0.221	0.372

16	Pyonghwa (1st)	1.168	0.124
17	Chengbing	0.100	0.104
18	White Spur	0.058	0.025
19	Xibeikou	0.061	0.194
20	Crotty	0.056	0.137
21	Segredo	0.229	0.583
22	Aguamilpa	0.340	1.130
23	Xingo	0.931	0.637
24	Wananxi	0.336	0.188
25	Buan	0.204	0.037
26	Yongdam	0.123	0.088
27	Miryang	0.088	0.164
28	Namgang	0.013	0.013
29	Sancheong (L)	0.087	0.091
30	Sancheong (U)	0.300	0.154
Coefficient of correlation	1.000	0.201	

In the crossover process, a child program is made by changing the random parts of two selected parents. As shown in **Figure 2**, point C of the parent 1 and point D of the parent 2 are selected for the crossover process, and then the outcome children of such process are drawn. The mutation process in which, a child program is modified by altering a randomly selected part, is a guarantee for the existence of versatility in the population of a generation. An example of such process is shown in **Figure 3** where, the mutation has been done in point C. A schematic flowchart for the creation of the generations in the GP algorithm is shown in **Figure 4**. At the present study, a GP model is proposed for the prediction of concrete faced rock fill dams settlements considering different variables that affect the results and the domain in which these variables changes. It is noteworthy that using the GP algorithms does not guarantee obtaining the most optimum result but it allows achieving an approvable result in a reasonable calculating time.

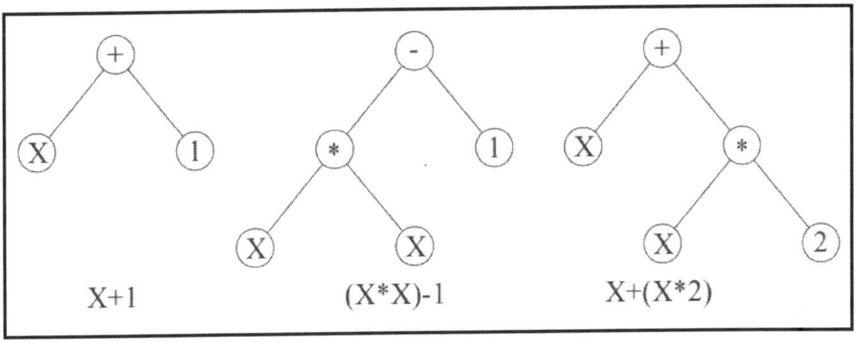

Figure 1. Examples of trees in the GP algorithm structure.

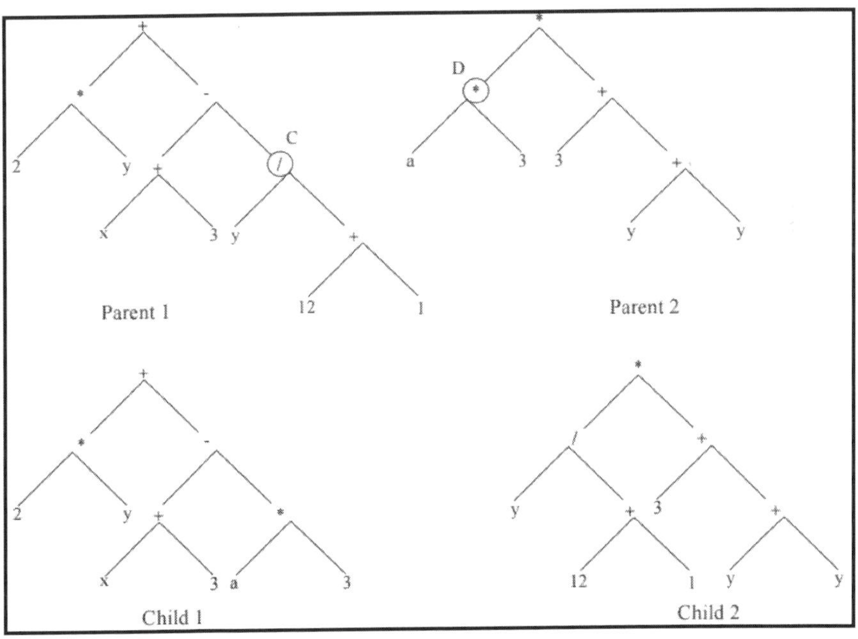

Figure 2. Example of crossover process.

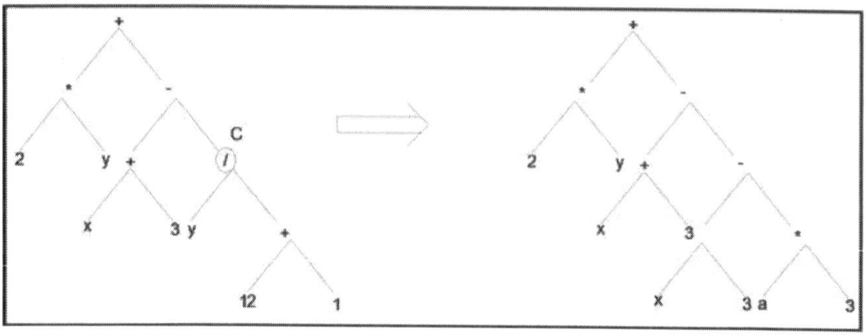

Figure 3. Example of mutation process.

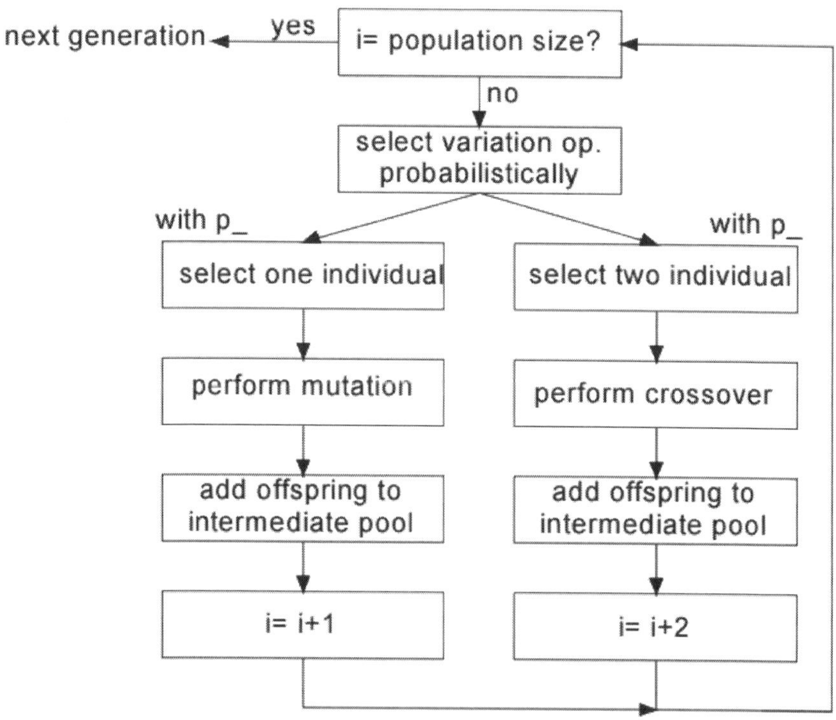

Figure 4. A schematic flowchart for the creation of generations in the GP algorithm.

3.2. Initial Information for the GP Model

Paying attention to the information in **Table 1**, it can be seen that big differences exist between the times when settlements are measured. It is also perceived that the settlement would reach to a moderately persistent amount about 6 years after construction of the CFRs, so information of settlement before this age is not invokable. According to this, information of 5 dams includes Mangrove Greek, Tianshengiao, Ita, Janheung and Daegok has been ignored and information of 30 other dams has been used. The range of changes in the height and length of these dams are 26 - 187 m and 110 - 1168 m respectively. The input variables which are used for the prediction of the settlement are shape factor (SF), void ratio (e), height (H) and vertical deformation modulus (E_v) of dams. **Table 4** shows the range at which these input parameters changes.

3.3. The GP Model for the Prediction of Dams Crest Settlements

A GP model is constructed on the basis of 67 percent of the all existing data (information of 21 dams of all 30 dams). The remaining information (the remaining nine dams) has been used for testing the model. The overall characteristics of the algorithm are presented in **Table 5**.

After training and using the above information, the model is finalized as follows:

$$\text{Settlement} = R^* \times R \tag{3}$$

where R and R^* are functions of the parametersas follows:

$$R = D^* / \cos\left(\cos\left(\ln(Sc - H)/\cos\left(\cos(66 \times Sc)\right)\right)\right)$$

$$R^* = \left[I^* \times e \times \left(\ln[Sc - H]/\ln[Sc - H]\right)/384\right]$$

$$A = \cos\left[\frac{\ln[0.2837 - H] \times 0.1435}{\cos(\cos(H \times \ln[H]))}\right]$$

$$B = \cos\left(\cos\left(\ln\left[13 - \frac{20}{A}\right]\right)\right) \Big/ 0.1367$$

$$C = \left[20/\cos(\ln[H])\right.$$
$$\left. -\left(11 \times Sc \times \ln\left[Sc - 11 \times \ln(Sc - H)\verb|^|2\right]\right)\right]$$
$$\times \ln(-0.0136 + 3.1416i) \times (E_V - 2.4849)$$

$$D = \ln\left[E_V - 11.02 \times \left(\ln\left[\cos(C) - H\right]\right) \times \ln[Sc - H]\right]$$

$$E = \ln\left[\frac{20}{\cos(\ln[H])} - \left(11 \times Sc \times \frac{D}{B}\right)\right]$$

$$F = \left[E_V - (E) \times \left(\ln[12 - H]/\cos(\cos(66 \times Sc))\right) \times 11\right]$$

$$G = \cos G$$
$$= \cos\left(\cos\left(\ln\left[13 - \left(20/\cos(\cos(11 \times Sc))\right)/0.1367\right]\right)\right)$$

$$I = 11 \times (F/G) \times ScJ$$
$$= 20/\cos\left(\ln\left[\cos(107.138 \times Sc) - H\right]/0.9983\right)K$$
$$= \left(20/\cos\left(\ln\left[\cos(11 \times (I - G)) - H\right]\right)/0.9983\right)A^*$$
$$= \ln\left[11 \times \left(E_V - \left(\ln(Sc - H)\right)^2\right)\right]$$

$$B^* = \left(20/\cos(\ln[H])\right) - \left(11 \times Sc \times \left(A^*/0.6805\right)\right)$$

$$M = \ln\left[E_V - 11 \times \left(\ln(Sc - H)\right) \times \left(\ln(L/0.9983)\right)\right]$$

$$N = 0.0.78 \times \left(\left[\ln(0.2837 - H) / \cos(\cos(1.792 \times H \times Sc)) \right] / 0.543 \right)$$

$$O = \cos\left(\cos\left(\ln\left[13 - (20/\cos(N))\right]/0.1367\right)\right)$$

$$C^{*} = \ln\left[(20/\cos(\ln[H])) - 11 \times Sc \times (M/O)\right]$$

$$P = \ln\left[E_V - 11 \times \left(\ln(12 - H)/\cos(\cos(66 \times Sc))\right) \times C^{*}\right]$$

$$Q = \cos\left(\cos\left(\ln\left[13 - (20/\cos(\cos(11 \times H)))\right]/0.1367\right)\right)$$

$$D^{*} = \ln\left[K - 11 \times Sc \times (P/Q)\right]$$

$$S = \ln\left[\left(\ln[12 - H]/\cos(\cos(66 \times Sc))\right) - 11 \times Sc \times \ln[Sc - H]\right]$$

$$T = \cos\left(\cos\left(\left(\ln\left[13 - (\ln[12 - H]/0.5735)\right]\right)/e\right)\right)$$

$$U = 20/[Sc \times S/T]$$

$$E^{*} = \ln\left[13 - \left(\ln[12 - H]/\cos(\cos(66 \times Sc))\right)\right]$$

$$V = \ln\left[E_V - 11 \times Sc^2\right]/\cos\left(\cos\left(E^{*}/16\right)\right)$$

$$W = \ln\left[\cos(198 \times (U - V \times H \times Sc)) - H\right]$$

$$F^{*} = \ln[Sc - H]/\cos(\cos(66 \times Sc))$$

$$X = W \Big/ \cos\left(\cos\left(13 \times \cos\left(\cos\left(F^{*}\right)\right)\right)\right)$$

$$Y = Sc \times \left(\ln\left[E_V - 11 \times X \times \ln[Sc - H] \right] / \cos\left(\cos\left(E_V\right)\right) \right)$$

$$Z = \ln\left[\left(\cos\left(\ln[0.96 - H] / \left((0.5402 + 3.1416i) \times Y \right) \right) \right) \right.$$
$$\left. -96 \times Sc \right]$$

$$G^* = Z / \cos\left(\cos\left(\ln[Sc - H] / c \right) \right)$$

$$H^* = e \times \left(\ln[Sc - H] / \cos\left(\cos\left(6 \times Sc \times \ln[Sc - H] \right) \right) \right) / 48$$

$$Cc = G^* \times$$
$$\left[H^* \times \left(\ln[0.2837 - H] / \cos\left(\cos\left(11 \times H \right) \right) \right) / 4.344 \right]$$

$$I^* = \left(\left(\ln[Sc - H] / \cos(CC) \right) / \cos\left(\cos\left(77 \times Sc \right) \right) \right)$$

Table 4. Range of input parameters changes.

Input variable	Range were considered
Dam height (H)	26 - 187 (m)
Void ratio (e)	0.17 - 0.4
Vertical deformation modulus after construction (E_V)	25 - 375 (MPa)
Shape coefficient (Sc)	0 - 34.6

Table 5. The overall characteristics of the GP algorithm.

Parameters	Properties
Functions	+, −, *, /, sin, cos, tan, $\log_e$
Population size	301
Tree initialization method	Ramped half and half
maximum number of generations	240
Genetic operators	Crossover, mutation
Measuring fitness	Raw fitness

The number of knots in the model is 701 and its depth is 50. The results indicate that; there is a good agreement between the results and measured settlements with correlation factor of 0.98, and a proper performance for the model in the testing stage is achieved.

4. THE VERIFICATION OF THE TRAINED MODEL

With training the model, and to demonstrate the efficiency of the algorithm for the prediction of the CFRDs settlements, information of 9 dams is used for the testing. To verify the trained model, the results obtained are compared with the findings of the Clements method. The reliability of the model and predicted values for the crest settlement obtained in the present work and the ones obtained by the Clements method is shown in **Figure 5**.

Table 6 shows the mean, standard deviation and the minimum least square error values between the measured values (using Clements model) and those obtained by present GP model. The results indicate that; even though the statistical analysis is derived from a limited set of information, however the performance of the present GP model is better in comparison with the Clements model. Due to the lack of physical model for testing and measurement of the crest settlement and for complex phenomena, it seems that; the presented GP algorithm has the capability for prediction of dam crest settlement.

5. COMPARISON BETWEEN THE GP AND FINITE ELEMENT MODELS

To evaluate and compare the results obtained by the GP and finite element models, the Daegok earth dam is modeled using the presented GP model and PLAXIS method. Daegok dam is a CFRD type dam with 52 m in height. The dam crest length and width are 190 m and 9.5 m respectively. The total volume of its body is 479 m^3. The slope of the upstream face is 1V:1.4H, and for the downstream face is 1V:1.8H. The details of the dam section and construction procedures are shown in **Figure 6** and **Table 7** [9]. Tables 8 and 9 present the overall specifications of soils used in the dam model. Due to using rock material in the dam body, a hardening hyperbolic soil model is used for the analysis. It is assumed that the soil is homogenous in all cases. **Table 8** describes the common properties of the Mohr-Coulomb and hardening models, while **Table 9** contains complementary parameters belong only to the hardening model.

There are 14 computing phases in the Plaxis model. The first phase is considered for applying initial stresses. Due to slope existence, the gravity loading method is used. The other 13 phases are considered for modeling of the layered soils and three impounding steps of 15, 30 and 40 meters levels. Using this model, the long term settlement for the dam crest is 7.9 cm, while the dam settlement at the end period of construction is about 3 cm, which is shown in **Figure 7**. Using equation (1), for a point located near the dam crest, the vertical deformation modulus (E_v) is determined 138.8 MPa at the end of construction period as follow:

$$E_v = \frac{4\times48\times21.5}{1000\times29.75\times10^{-3}} = 138.8 \text{ MPa} \approx 140 \text{ MPa} \tag{4}$$

At this stage, using Equation (3) and the values of e = 0.25, H = 52 m, S_c = 3.7, and E_v = 140 MPa, the dam crest settlement is predicted by the GP model, which is equal to 7.8 cm. This finding is very close to the ones obtained by the finite element method. The results confirm the liability of the presented GP model.

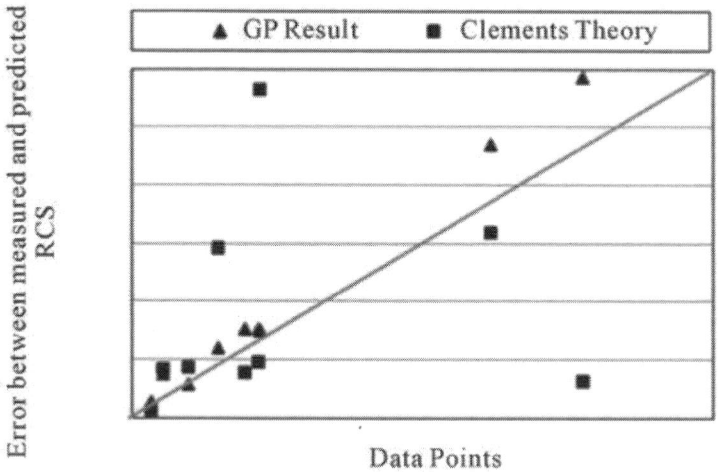

Figure 5. The results of present GP model in comparison with the Clements model.

Table 6. Statistical comparison between the present GP model and Clements model.

Model	RMSE	Absolute average error	Absolute standard deviation error
The present GP model	0.132	0.082	0.109
Clements theory	0.307	0.15	0.285

Table 7. The construction time-table of Daegok Dam [9].

Main construction process	
Period	**Explanation**
2001.9 - 2002.4	Completion of dam embankment (52 m) for 8 month
2002.4 - 2003.3	Stabilizing period and shotcrete on upstream slope for 12 months
2003.3 - 2003.5	Construction of the face deck, 3 months
2004.11	Beginning of impoundment

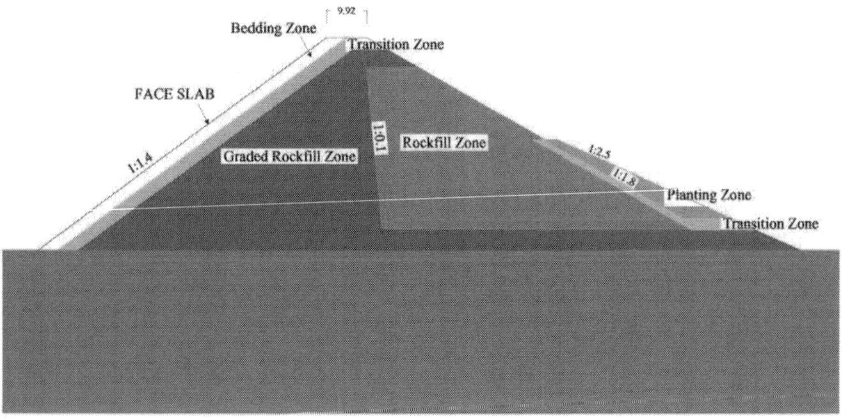

Figure 6. The Daegok dam cross section.

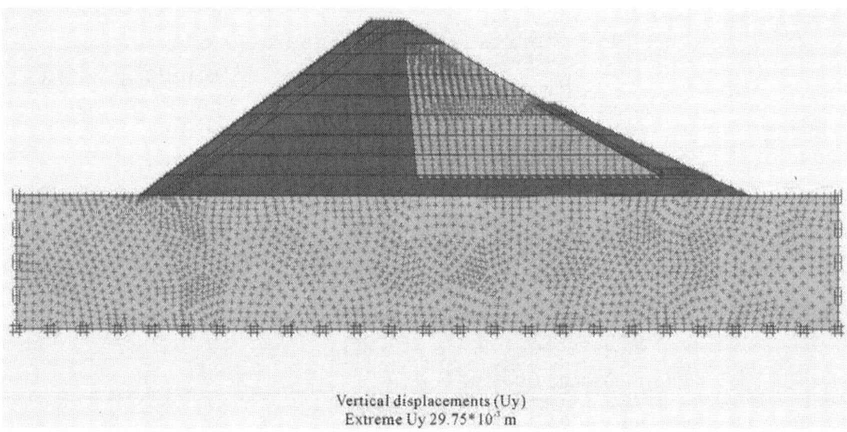

Figure 7. The crest settlement after dam construction.

Table 8. Properties of soil in the hardening and Mohr-Coulomb models.

Soil	Model	γ (kN/m^3)	Young's modulus (kN/m^2)	Poisson's ratio	Cohesion (kN/m^2)	Friction angle	Void ratio
Face bedding	Mohr-Coulomb	22.7	3×10^4	0.35	0	45	0.30
Face slab	Mohr-Coulomb	22.0	2×10^7	0.30	150	27	0.50
Foundation	Mohr-Coulomb	22.0	2×10^7	0.30	150	27	0.50
Graded rock-fill	Hardening model	21.5	-	0.30	0	45	0.25
Planting	Mohr-Coulomb	18.0	3×10^4	0.35	1	35	0.30
Rock-fill	Hardening model	20.3	-	0.30	0	39	0.25
Transition	Mohr-Coulomb	21.5	3×10^4	0.30	0	45	0.30

Table 9. Special properties for the soil hardening model.

Soil	E_{ur}^{ref} (kN/m^2)	E_{oed}^{ref} (kN/m^2)	E_{50}^{ref} (kN/m^2)
Graded rock-fill	1.3×10^6	5.5×10^5	6×10^5
Rock-fill	1.3×10^6	5.5×10^5	6×10^5

6. CONCLUSIONS

In the present study which focused on the prediction of earth dam crest settlement using the genetic program ming model the following conclusions are made:

1) The results obtained by the GP model is in agree with the ones calculated through the experimental measurements.
2) The GP model, which is based on four characteristics of: E_v, H, e, and Sc has the best applicability and is in contrast with conventional methods such as Clements method, which only uses the H parameter for estimation of the crest settlement.
3) The results obtained by the GP model have a good compatibility with the finite element modeling.
4) The GP model is a trained model, and is capable of calculating the dam crest settlement without using any field laboratory tests.
5) The GP model can be used for complex problems, where rock-fill with various settlement aspects are involved.
6) Even though, the GP model is derived from a limited set of information and is not necessarily the most perfect one, however, the performance of this model is better in comparison with the conventional models such as: the Clements model.
7) The main weakness of the GP modeling is the time consuming and the needs for a huge population, but when the model is trained, many complex aspects can be predicted.

REFERENCES

1. G. Hunter and R. Fell, "The Deformation Behavior of Rokfill," Uniciv. Report No. 405, The University of New South Wales, Sydney, 2002.
2. F. Saboya, R. Barosa and A. Vasconcelos, "The Influence of the Left Abutment Geometry on the Behaviour of Xingo Rock-Fill Dam," Proceedings of the International Symposium on Concrete Faced Rock-Fill Dams, Beijing, 18 September 2000, pp. 565-572.
3. G. F. Sowers, R. C. Williams and T. S. Wallace, "Compressibliity of Broken Rock and the Settlement of Rockfills," Proceedings of the 6th International Conference on Soil Mechanics and Foundation Engineering, Toronto, Vol. 2, 1965, pp. 561-565.
4. F. L. Lawton and M. D. Lester, "Settlement of Rockfill Dams," Proceedings of the 8th International Congress on Large Dams, Edinburgh, Vol. 3, 1964, pp. 599-613.
5. C. Soydemir and B. Kjaernsli, "Deformations of Membrane-Faced Rockfill Dams," Proceedings of the 7th European Conference on Soil Mechanics and Foundation Engineering, Brighton, Vol. 3, 1979, pp. 281-284.
6. R. P. Clements, "Post-Construction Deformation of Rockfill Dams," Journal of Geotechnical Engineering, Vol. 110, No. 7, 1984, pp. 821-840.
7. M. D. Fitzpatrick, B. A. Cole, F. L. Kinstler and B. P. Knoop, "Design of Concrete-Faced Rockfill Dams," In: J. B. Cooke and J. L. Shererd, Eds., Concrete Face Rockfill Dams-Design, Construction, and Performance, 1985, pp. 410-434.
8. N. L. S. Pinto and P. L. M. Filho, "Estimating the Maximum Face Slab Deflection in CFRDs," Hydropower & Dams, Vol. 5, No. 6, 1998, pp. 28-30.
9. P. Han-Gyu, S. Min-Woo, K. Yong-Soeng and L. HeiuDae, "Settlement Behavior Characteristics of CFRD in Construction Period-Case of Daegok Dam," Journal of the KGS, Vol. 21, No. 7, 2005, pp. 91-105.
10. N. Kovacevic, "Numerical Analyses of Rockfill Dams, Cut Slopes and Road Embankments," Ph.D. Thesis, Imperial College of Science, Technology and Medicine, London, 1994.

11. J. M. Duncan, "State of the Art: Static Stability and Deformation Analysis," ASCE Geotechnical Special Publication, Vol. 1, No. 31, 1992, pp. 222-266.

12. J. M. Duncan, "State of the Art: Limit Equilibrium and Finite-Element Analysis of Slopes," ASC.E Journal of Geotechnical Engineering, Vol. 122, No. 7, 1996, pp. 577-595.

13. Y. S. Kim and B. T. Kim, "Prediction of Relative Crest Settlement of Concrete-Faced Rockfill Dams Analyzed Using an Artificial Neural Network Model," Computers and Geotechnics, Vol. 35, No. 1, 2008, pp. 313-322.

14. Y. Zhang and S. Bhattacharyya, "Genetic Programming in Classifying Large-Scale Data: An Ensemble Method," Information Sciences, Vol. 163, No. 1-3, 2004, pp. 85- 101.

15. J. R. Koza, "Genetic Programming: On the Programming of Computers by Means of Natural Selection," 6th Printing, Massachusetts Institute of Technology, Cambridge, 1998.

16. J. R. Koza, M. A. Keane, M. J. Streeter, J. Matthew, W. Mydlowec, J. Yu and G. Lanza, "Genetic Programming IV: Routine Human-Competitive Machine Intelligence," Springer, New York, 2005.

7

CHAPTER

THREE-OBJECTIVE PROGRAMMING WITH CONTINUOUS VARIABLE GENETIC ALGORITHM

Adugna Fita

Department of Mathematics, Adama Science and Technology University, Adama, Ethiopia

ABSTRACT

The subject area of multiobjective optimization deals with the investigation of optimization problems that possess more than one objective function. Usually, there does not exist a single solution that optimizes all functions simultaneously; quite the contrary, we have solution set that is called nondominated set and elements of this set are usually infinite. It is from this set decision made by taking elements of nondominated set as alternatives, which is given by analysts. Since it is important for the decision maker to obtain as much information as possible about this set, our research objective is to determine a well-defined and meaningful approximation of the solution set for linear and nonlinear three objective optimization problems. In this paper a continuous variable genetic algorithm is used to find approximate near optimal solution set. Objective functions are considered as fitness function without modification. Initial solution was generated within box constraint and solutions will be kept in feasible region during mutation and recombination.

Keywords: Chromosome, Crossover, Heuristics, Mutation, Optimization, Population, Ranking, Genetic Algorithms, Multi-Objective, Pareto Optimal Solutions, Parent Selection

1. INTRODUCTION AND BACKGROUNDS

Three-objectives programming problem is special cases of multicriteria optimization problem with three objectives. Multiobjective optimization examines problems featuring several different objective functions which have to be considered simultaneously. Usually these objectives are also competing with each other which aggravates the situation. For instance, a fundamental challenge in portfolio management is to maximize the rate of return while reducing the risk involved in the investment(s) at the same time. In general there does not exist a single solution that optimizes all functions of the problem at once. Thus, a selection of alternatives, so-called nondominated set and elements of this set are usually infinite. It is from this set decision made by taking elements of nondominated set as alternatives, which is given by analysts. But practically extraction of nondominated solutions and setting fitness function are difficult.

Typically, the set of efficient solutions is very large and the different solutions are incomparable with each other with respect to the employed ordering concept. The reason for the incomparability is that we utilize partial orders in vector spaces rather than total orders.

In order to solve our decision making problem by some systems analytical methods, we usually require that degrees of objectives be represented in numerical terms, which may be of multiple kinds even for one objective. In order to exclude subjective value judgment at this stage, we restrict these numerical terms to physical measures (for example money, weight, length, and time).

As a performance index, for the objective Y_i an objective function $f_i : X \to \mathrm{R}^1$ is introduced. Where R^1 denotes one dimensional Euclidean space. The value $f_i(x)$ indicates how much impact is given on objective Y_i by performing an alternative x. In this paper we assume that a smaller value for each objective function is preferred to large one [1] .

Now we can formulate our decision making problems as a Multiobjective optimization problem:

$$\begin{array}{ll} f_1(x) \to \text{Min/Max} & \\ f_2(x) \to \text{Min/Max} & \text{Over, } x \in X. \\ \vdots & \\ f_p(x) \to \text{Min/Max} & \end{array} \tag{1.1}$$

where:

$$X = \{x \in R^n : g_j(x) \le 0, j = 1, 2, \ldots, m, x \ge 0\} \tag{1.2}$$

$$Y = \{y \in R^p : y_1 = f_1(x), y_2 = f_2(x), \ldots, y_p = f_p(x), x \in X\} \tag{1.3}$$

In some cases, some of the objective functions are required to be maintained under given levels prior to minimizing other objective functions. Denoting these objective functions by $g_j(x)$, we require that

$$g_j(x) \le 0, \quad j = 1, 2, \ldots, m \tag{1.4}$$

Such a function $g_j(x)$ is generally called a constraint function. According to the situation, we consider either the problem (1.1) itself or (1.1) accompanied by the constraint conditions (1.4).

Of course, an equality constraint $h_k(x) = 0$ can be embedded within two inequalities $h_k(x) \le 0$ and $-h_k(x) \le 0$, and hence, it does not appear explicitly in this paper.

We call the set of alternatives X the feasible set of the problem. The space containing the feasible set is said to be a decision space, whereas the space that contains the image of the feasible set $Y = f(X)$ is referred to as criterion space [2] .

Unlike the traditional mathematical programming with a single objective function, an optimal solution in the sense of one that minimizes all the objective function simultaneously does not necessarily exist in multiobjective optimization problem, and hence, we are in trouble of conflicts among objectives in decision making; the final decision should be made by taking the total balance of objectives into account [3] .

Scalarization approach is one of the solution methods in multiobjective programming that is studied by different scholars. In solving scalarized problems which are obtained by weighting sum of objective functions to single objective, each substitute problem is characterized by a unique weighting parameter vector, the entries of which are the specific weights for the individual objective functions [1] [4] . A fundamental challenge lies in the selection of the "right" weighting parameters that lead to different optimal solutions that subsequently constitute meaningful approximations of the efficient sets.

Vector evaluated genetic algorithm (VEGA) Schaffer (1985) presents one of the first treatments of multi-ob- jective genetic algorithms, although he only considers unconstrained problems [5] . The general idea behind Schaffer's approach, called the vector evaluated genetic algorithm (VEGA), involves producing smaller subsets of the original population, or sub-populations, within a given generation, [6] [7] . One sub-population is created by evaluating one objective function at a time rather than aggregating all of the functions.

The process is based on the idea that the minimum of a single objective function is a Pareto optimal point (assuming the minimum is unique). However, considering only one objective function at a time is comparable to setting all but one of the weights to zero, Goldberg (1989), and Fonseca and Fleming (1993) provide detailed explanations and critiques of Schaffer's ideas. A class of alternatives to VEGA involves giving each member of a population a rank based on whether or not it is dominated (Goldberg 1989; Fonseca and Fleming 1993); Fitness then is based on a design's rank within a population.

Ishibuchi and Murata (1996), and Murata et al. (1996) use a procedure called an elitist strategy, which functions independent of rank. As with the Pareto-set filter, two sets of solutions are stored: a current population and a tentative set of non-dominated solutions, which is an approximate Pareto set [8] . With each generation, all points in the current population that are not dominated by any points in the tentative set are added to the set and dominated points in the set are discarded. After crossover and mutation operations are applied, a user's specified number of points from the tentative set is reintroduced into the current population. These points are called elite points. In addition, the k solutions with the best values for each objective function can be regarded as elite points and preserved for the next generation (Murata et al. 1996).

Two points, called candidate points, are randomly selected from the current population and compute for survival in the next generation [9] . A separate set of points called a tournament set or comparison set is also randomly compiled. The candidate points are then compared with each member of the tournament set.

If there is only one candidate that is non-dominated relative to the tournament set, that candidate is selected to be in the next generation. However, if there is no preference between candidates, or when there is a tie, fitness sharing is used to select a candidate. The user specifies the size of the tournament set as a percentage of the total population.

Consequently, the size of the tournament set imposes the degree of difficulty in surviving, which is called the domination pressure. An insufficient number of Pareto optimal points will be found if the tournament size is too small, and premature convergence may result if the tournament size is too large [7] [10] .

Fitness sharing is a common niche technique the basic idea of which is to penalize the fitness of points in crowded areas, thus reducing the probability of their survival to the next generation [11] ; Deb 1989; Srinivas and [12] . The fitness of a given point is divided by a constant that is proportional to the number of other points within a specified distance in the criterion space. In this way, the fitness of all the points in a niche is shared in some sense, thus the term "fitness sharing" [7] .

Different techniques are discussed that serve as potential issues in a genetic multi-objective optimization algorithm. In accordance with much of the literature on multi-objective genetic algorithms, constraints are not addressed directly. It is assumed that a penalty approach is used to treat constraints and external penalty function is used in this paper as seen in Figure 1. But those approaches are difficult to model the fitness function that best evaluates the solution (chromosomes) for further selections and keeping those solutions in feasible region during mutation and recombination [13] .

In this paper objective function and variables are taken without modification and continuous variable genetic algorithm is used. Variables are considered in box constraint and initial solution will be generated within box constraint and will keep in feasible region during mutation and recombination.

2. PREFERENCE ORDERS AND DOMINATION STRUCTURES

Preference Orders represents the preference attitude of the decision maker in the objective space. Ranking of objectives with multiple attributes or solving the multi-dimensional problem

It is usually represented by a binary relation. For a given pair, y^1 and y^2:

- y^1 is preferred to y^2, denoted by $y^1 > y^2$.
- y^1 is less preferred to y^2, denote by $y^1 < y^2$.
- y^1 is equally preferred to y^2, denoted $y^1 \sim y^2$.

The preference relation between y^1 and y^2 is no related, denote by $y^1||y^2$.

Since ordering in objective space is incomplete (i.e. a partial ordering) which are not directly comparable with each other the problem has more than one solution there does not necessarily exist a solution that is best with respect to all objectives because of conflict among objectives [1] [3] [14] .

There usually exist a set of solutions; nondominated or efficient or Pareto optimal solutions. An alternative is Pareto optimal or non-dominated, if it is: best in at least one criterion (better than any other alternative); or equal to the best in at least one criterion without being worse in all other criteria. For minimization problem decision vector X_1 is preferred to X_2:

If $f_i(X_1) \le f_i(X_2)$ and $f_i(X_1) < f_i(X_2)$ for at least one i, for $i = 1, 2, \ldots, m.$ [15]

Pareto optimal solutions form (possibly nonconvex and non-connected) Pareto optimal set as seen inFigure 1, Figure 2. But for linear problems where the objective and constraint are linear the Pareto optimal solutions set is convex as seen in Figure 3. In the case of Figure 2, Figure 4 the non dominated red region is not necessarily convex as the problem are non linear.

In [1] Pareto optimal solution(s) exist if the objective functions are lower semi continuous and the feasible region is nonempty and compact. In some literatures, non dominated set of solution are found on closure (boundary) of the feasible surface which is clearly seen in Figures 4-6.

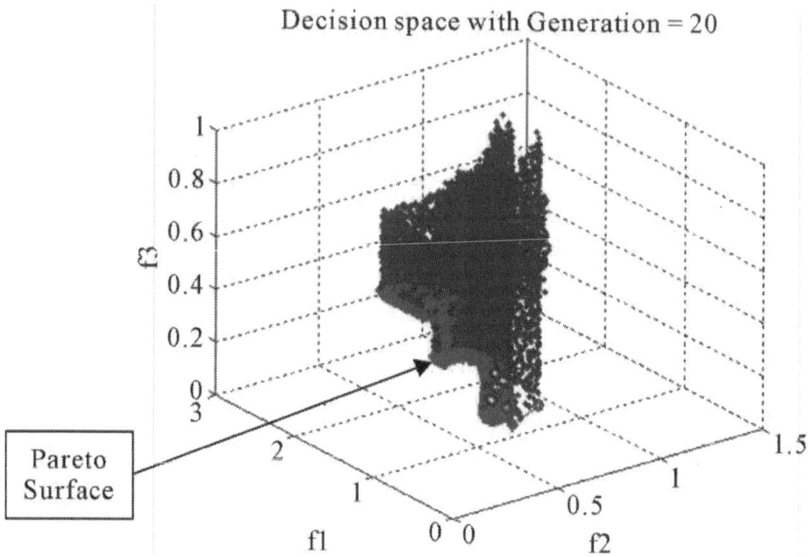

Figure 1. Simulation results.

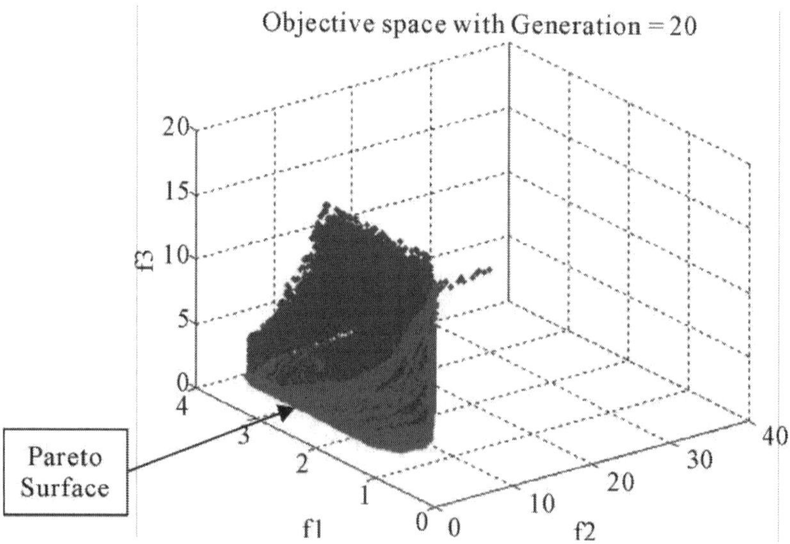

Figure 2. Simulation results.

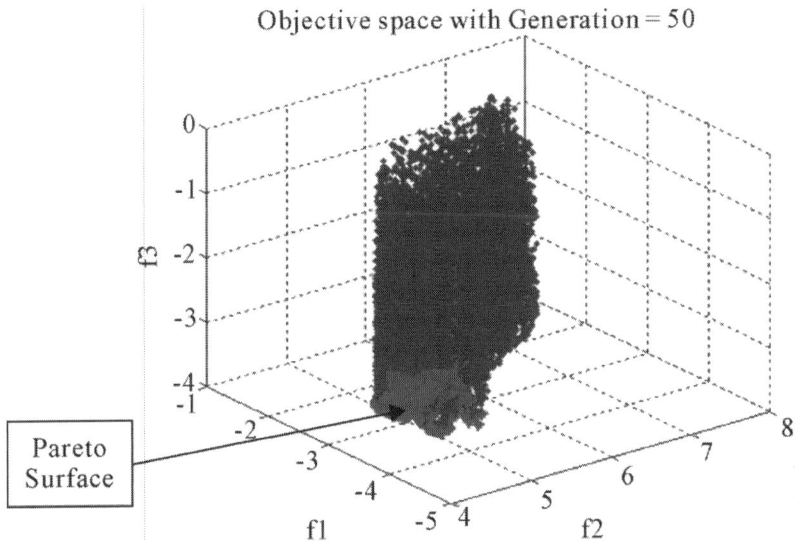

Figure 3. Simulation results.

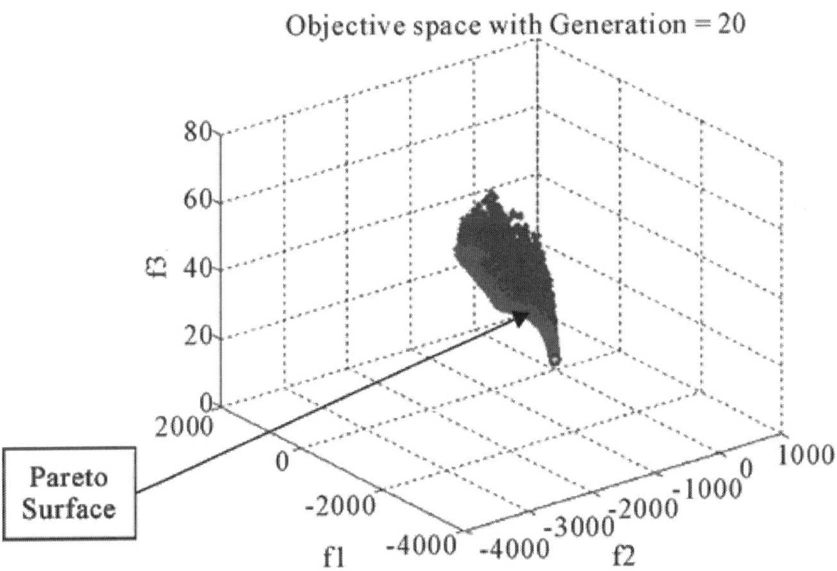

Figure 4. Simulation results.

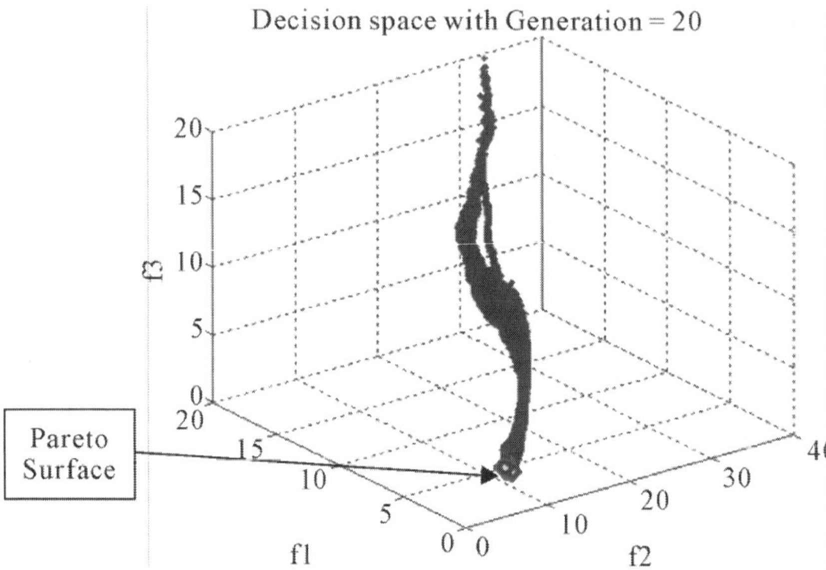

Figure 5. Simulation results.

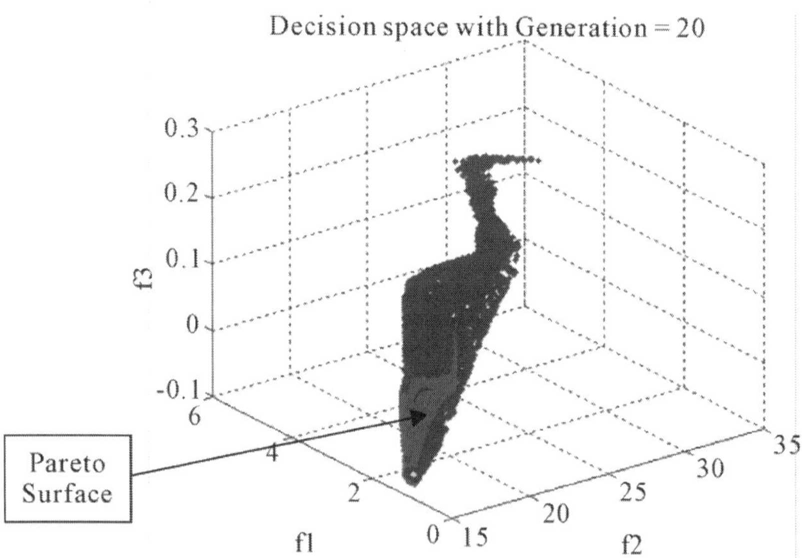

Figure 6. Simulation results.

Almost in all Figures the red surface is nondominated solutions while the blue region is feasible solution but dominated by objective values on red surfaces.

Even though, the existence of efficient solution is mathematically proved under some conditions such as the convexity, connectedness, and compactness of feasible region and lower semi continuity of objectives functions. But practical estimation of efficient set is very difficult [13] .

Therefore, in the next chapter one of a global search heuristics which find the true or approximate of near optimal solutions to problems is discussed. This method is less susceptible to the connectivity and convexity of feasible set (search space) Figure 1, Figure 6. In addition to this continuity and differentiability of objective functions does not require.

3. CONTINUOUS VARIABLE GENETIC ALGORITHM

3.1. Introduction

Genetic algorithms is a class of probabilistic optimization algorithms inspired by the biological evolution process uses concepts of "Natural Selection" and "Genetic Inheritance" (Darwin 1859) originally developed by John Holland [16] [17] . Particularly well suited for hard problems where little is known about the underlying search space.

The specific mechanics of the algorithms involve the language of microbiology and, in developing new potential solutions, through genetic operations. A population represents a group of potential solution points. A generation represents an algorithmic iteration. A chromosome is comparable to a design point, and a gene is comparable to a component of the design vector. Genetic algorithms are theoretically and empirically proven to provide robust search in complex phases with the above features.

Many search techniques required auxiliary information in order to work properly. For e.g. Gradient techniques need derivative in order to chain the current peak and other procedures like greedy technique requires access to most tabular parameters whereas genetic algorithms do not require all these auxiliary information. GA is blind to perform an effective search for better and better structures they only require objective function values associated with the individual strings.

A genetic algorithm (or GA) is categorized as global search heuristics used in computing to find true or approximate solutions to optimization problems.

3.2. Initialization of GA with Real Valued Variables

Initially many individual solutions are randomly generated to form an initial population. The population size depends on the nature of the problem, but typically contains several hundreds or thousands of possible solutions.

Commonly, the population is generated randomly, covering the entire range of possible solutions (the search space).

To begin the GA, we define an initial population of N_{pop} chromosomes. A matrix represents the population with each row in the matrix being a 1 × N_{var} array (chromosome) of continuous values. Given an initial population of N_{pop} chromosomes, the full matrix of $N_{pop} \times N_{var}$ random values is generated by:

$$pop = rand\left(N_{pop}, N_{var}\right)$$

If variables are normalized to have values between 0 and 1, If not the range of values is between X_{lb} and X_{ub}, then the unnormalized values are given by:

$$X = \left(X_{ub} - X_{lb}\right)X_{norm} + X_{lb}$$

where X_{lb}: lowest number in the variable range;

X_{ub}: highest number in the variable range;

X_{norm}: normalized value of variable [17] .

But one can generate an initial feasible solution from search space simply as,

for $i = 1 : N_{pop}$ $pop(i,:) = \left(X_{ub} - X_{lb}\right) \cdot rand(1, nvar) + X_{lb};$ % generate real valued population matrix end; this generates $N_{pop} \times N_{var}$ population matrix.

3.3. Evaluation (Fitness Function)

Fitness values are derived from the objective function values through a scaling or ranking function. Note that for multiobjective functions, the fitness of a particular individual is a function of a vector of objective function values. Multiobjective problems are characterized by having no single unique solution, but a family of equally fit solutions with different values of decision variables.

Therefore, care should be taken to adopt some mechanism to ensure that the population is able to evolve the set of Pareto optimal solutions.

Fitness function measures the goodness of the individual, expressed as the probability that the organism will live another cycle (generation). It is also the basis for the natural selection simulation better solutions have a better chance to be the next generation. In many GA algorithm fitness function is modeled according to the problem, but in this paper we use objective functions as fitness function.

$\text{Cost} = f(\text{chromosome})$ that means

$$\text{Cost1} = f(X_1 \quad X_2 \quad X_3 \quad X_4 \quad \cdots \quad X_{nvar})$$

$$\text{Cost2} = f(X_1 \quad X_2 \quad X_3 \quad X_4 \quad \cdots \quad X_{nvar})$$

$$\text{Cost3} = f(X_1 \quad X_2 \quad X_3 \quad X_4 \quad \cdots \quad X_{nvar})\cdots$$

Sorting cost according to cost1

[f1, ind1] = sort (fout(:,1)); sorts objective function values

f2 = fout (ind1, 2);

[f2, ind2] = sort (fout(:,2));

f3 = fout(ind2, 3);

Chro = Chro (ind2,:); Sort the chro using induces

assign chrom on Pareto front cost = rank = 1

rank = rank + 1 and so on.

Replicate this chromosomes to get full number of population.

3.4. Parent Selection

During each successive generation, a proportion of the existing population is selected to breed a new generation.

Individual solutions are selected through a fitness-based process, where fitter solutions (as measured by a fitness function) are typically more likely to be selected. Certain selection methods rate the fitness of each solution and preferentially select the best solutions. Other methods rate only a random sample of the population, as this process may be very time-consuming.

Most functions are stochastic and designed so that a small proportion of less fit solutions are selected. This helps keep the diversity of the population large, preventing premature convergence on poor solutions. Popular and well-studied selection methods include roulette wheel selection and tournament selection and rank based selections [18] .

3.4.1. Roulette Wheel Selection

In roulette wheel selection, individuals are given a probability of being selected that is directly proportionate to their fitness. Two individuals are then chosen randomly based on these probabilities and produce offspring.

Roulette Wheel's Selection Pseudo Code:

```
        for all members of population
        sum = fitness of individuals;
        end for
for all members of population
probability = sum of probabilities + (fitness/sum)
        sum of probabilities = probability
        end for
        loop until new population is full ;do this twice
        number = Random between 0 and 1
                for all members of population
        if number > probability but less than next probability then you
        have been selected
                        end for; end
```

create offspring

end loop

3.4.2. Tournament-Based Selection

For K less than or equal to the number of population, extract K individuals from the population randomly make them play a "tournament", where the probability for an individual to win is generally proportional to its fitness.

$$M = \text{ceil}\left(\left(\text{pop size} - \text{keep}\right)/2\right); \text{number of mating}$$

$$\text{Picks} = \text{ceil}\left(\text{keep} \cdot \text{rand}\left(K, M\right)\right);$$

Repeat M time. The parameter for tournament selection is the tournament size Tour.

Tour takes values ranging from 2 to N_{pop} (number of individuals in population). Selection intensity increases with Tournament size.

3.5. Reproduction

The next step is to generate a second generation population of solutions from those selected through genetic operators: crossover (also called recombination), and mutation.

For each new solution to be produced, a pair of "parent" solutions is selected for breeding from the pool selected previously.

By producing a "child" solution using the above methods of crossover and mutation, a new solution is created which typically shares many of the characteristics of its "parents". New parents are selected for each child, and the process continues until a new population of solutions of appropriate size is generated. These processes ultimately result in the next generation population of chromosomes that is different from the initial generation.

Generally the average fitness will have increased by this procedure for the population, since only the best organisms from the first generation are selected for breeding, along with a small proportion of less fit solutions, for reasons already mentioned above.

3.5.1. Crossover

The most common type is single point crossover. In single point crossover, you choose a locus at which you swap the remaining alleles from one parent to the other. This is complex and is best understood visually.

As you can see, the children take one section of the chromosome from each parent.

The point at which the chromosome is broken depends on the randomly selected crossover point.

This particular method is called single point crossover because only one crossover point exists. Sometimes only child 1 or child 2 is created, but oftentimes both offspring are created and put into the new population.

Crossover does not always occur, however. Sometimes, based on a set probability, no crossover occurs and the parents are copied directly to the new population.

1) Crossover (Real Valued Recombination)

Recombination produces new individuals in combining the information contained in the parents

The simplest methods choose one or more points in the chromosome to mark as the crossover points.

Some of Real valued recombination (crossover).

- Discrete recombination
- Intermediate recombination
- Line recombination

Real valued recombination: a method only applicable to real variables (and not binary variables).

The variable values of the offspring's are chosen somewhere around and between the variable values of the parents as:

offspring = $parent_1 + \lambda(parent_2 - parent_1)$ is convex combination of parents.

where $\lambda \varepsilon [-d, 1+d]$.

In intermediate recombination $d = 0$,

for extended intermediate recombination $d > 0$.

A good choice is d = 0.25. (in some literature)

Randomly selecting crossover point:

α = roundup (rand × Nvar)

We'll let

$$\text{parent}_1 = [X_{m1} \quad X_{m2} \quad X_{m3} \quad \cdots \quad X_{m\alpha} \quad \cdots \quad X_{mNvar}]$$

$$\text{parent}_2 = [X_{d1} \quad X_{d2} \quad X_{d3} \quad \cdots \quad X_{d\alpha} \quad \cdots \quad X_{dNvar}]$$

where: the m and d subscripts discriminate between the mom and the dad parent. Then the selected variables are combined to form new variables that will appear in the children:

$$X_{\text{new}1} = X_{m\alpha} - \lambda[X_{m\alpha} - X_{d\alpha}]$$

$$X_{\text{new}2} = X_{d\alpha} + \lambda[X_{m\alpha} - X_{d\alpha}]$$

where λ is also a random value between 0 and 1

The final step is:

$$\text{Offspring}_1 = [X_{m1} \quad X_{m2} \quad X_{m3} \quad \cdots \quad X_{\text{new}1} \quad \cdots \quad X_{mNvar}]$$

$$\text{Offspring}_2 = [X_{d1} \quad X_{d2} \quad X_{d3} \quad \cdots \quad X_{\text{new}2} \quad \cdots \quad X_{dNvar}]$$

3.5.2. Mutation

After selection and crossover, you now have a new population full of individuals. Some are directly copied, and others are produced by crossover [19] . In order to ensure that the individuals are not all exactly or the same, you allow for a small chance of mutation. You loop through all the alleles of all the individuals, and if that allele is selected for mutation, you can either change it by a small amount or replace it with a new value. The probability of mutation is usually small. Mutation is, however, vital to ensuring genetic diversity within the population. We force the routine to explore other areas of the cost surface by randomly introducing changes, or mutations, in some of the variables. We chose a mutation rate, [19].

$$\text{Nmut} = \text{ceil}\left(\text{popsize} \cdot Nvar \cdot \text{mutrate}\right);$$

Randomly choose rows and columns of the variables to be mutated.

$$mcol = \text{ceil}\left(\text{rand}\left(1, Nmut\right) \cdot Nvar\right);$$

A mutated variable is replaced by a new random number.

For Example

$$mrow = \begin{bmatrix} 4 & 5 & 7 & 7 \end{bmatrix}$$

$$mcol = \begin{bmatrix} 2 & 2 & 1 & 5 \end{bmatrix}$$

The first random pair is (4, 2).

Thus the value in row 4 and column 2 of the population matrix is replaced.

By $\text{mean}\left(\left[X_{ub} - X_{lb}\right]\right) \cdot \text{rand}\left(1, Nmut\right) + \text{mean}\left(\left[X_{lb}\right]\right)$

3.6. Elitism

With crossover and mutation taking place, there is a high risk that the optimum solution could be lost as there is no guarantee that these operators will preserve the fittest string. To counteract this, elitist preservation is used. Elitism is the name of the method that first copies the best chromosome (or few best chromosomes) to the new population. In an elitist model, the best individual from a population is saved before any of these operations take place. Elitism can rapidly increase the performance of GA, because it prevents a loss of the best found solution [20].

In this paper chromosome on Pareto front is used as elite children and not participate in mutation operations.

3.7. Parameters of Genetic Algorithm

Crossover probability: how often crossover will be performed. If there is no crossover, offspring are exact copies of parents. If there is crossover, offspring are made from parts of both parent's chromosome. If crossover probability is 100%, then all offspring are made by crossover. If it is 0%, whole new generation is made from exact copies of chromosomes from old population. Crossover is made in hope that new chromosomes will contain good parts of old chromosomes and therefore the new chromosomes will be better [19] .

Mutation probability: the probability of mutation is normally low because a high mutation rate would destroy fit strings and degenerate the genetic algorithm into a random search. Mutation probability value in some literature is around 0.1% to 0.01% are common. If mutation is performed, one or more parts of a chromosome are changed. If mutation probability is 100%, whole chromosome is changed, if it is 0%, nothing is changed. Mutation generally prevents the GA from falling into local extremes.

Population size: how many chromosomes are in population (in one generation). If there are too few chromosomes, GA has few possibilities to perform crossover and only a small part of search space is explored. On the other hand, if there are too many chromosomes, GA slows down. Research shows that after some limit (which depends mainly on encoding and the problem) it is not useful to use very large populations because it does not solve the problem faster than moderate sized populations.

3.8. Termination Conditions

Commonly, the algorithm terminates when either a maximum number of generations has been produced, or a satisfactory fitness level has been reached for the population. If the algorithm has terminated due to a maximum number of generations, a satisfactory solution may or may not have been reached. Thus generational process is repeated until a termination condition has been reached.

Common terminating conditions can be:

- A solution is found that satisfies minimum criteria
- Fixed number of generations reached
- Manual inspection
- Any Combinations of the above

4. TEST FUNCTIONS

Three-objective test functions for the Simulation of the algorithm. the red surface is non dominated solutions while the blue region is feasible solutions which is domenated by points on red surface.

1) (Problem from Kalyanmoy Deb 2001)

$$\text{Min } f_1 = 1 + (x_1 - 1)^5$$

$$\text{Min } f_2 = x_2$$

$$\text{Min } f_3 = x_3$$

s.t. $x_3^2 + \left(1 + (x_1 - 1)^5\right)^2 - 0.5 \geq 0;$

$$x_3^2 + x_2^2 - 0.5 \geq 0;$$

$$ub = [2,1,1]; \; lb = [0,0,0];$$

2) (Adugna, 2014) [19] .

$$\text{Min } f_1 = x_1;$$

$$\text{Min } f_2 = \frac{(x_2 + 2)}{x_1}$$

$$\text{Min } f_3 = x_1^2 + X_2;$$

s.t. $ub = [4,3]; lb = [0.1,1];$

3) Unconstrained linear minimization (Adugna, 2014) [19]

$$\text{Min } f_1 = x_1 - 3x_2;$$

$$\text{Min } f_2 = 3x_1 + x_2$$

$$\text{Min } f_3 = x_3 - 2x_2;$$

s.t. $ub = [2,2,2];\; lb = [1,1,0];$

4) Comet problem (Problem from Deb 2001)

$$\text{Min } f_1 = (1 + x_3)\cdot\left((x_1)^3 \cdot (x_2)^2 - 10x_1 - 4x_2\right);$$

$$\text{Min } f_2 = (1 + x_3)\cdot\left((x_2)^3 \cdot (x_2)^2 - 10x_1 + 4x_2\right);$$

$$\text{Min } f_3 = 3\cdot(1 + x_3)\cdot(x_1)^2;$$

s.t $ub = [3.5,2,1];\; lb = [1,-2,0];$

5)

$$\text{Min } f_1 = x_1^2 + (x_2 - 1)^2$$

$$\text{Min } f_2 = x_1^2 + (x_2 + 1)^2 + 1$$

$$\text{Min } f_3 = (x_1 - 1)^2 + x_2^2 + 2$$

s.t. $ub = [4,3];\; lb = [0,1]$

6) (Problem from R. Viennet, C Fonteix, and I. Marc.1996) [21] .

$$\text{Min } f_1 = 0.5\left(x_1^2 + x_2^2\right) + \sin\left(x_1^2 + x_2^2\right)$$

$$\text{Min } f_2 = \frac{(3x_1 - 2x_2 + 4)^2}{8} + \frac{(x_1 - x_2 + 1)^2}{27} + 15;$$

$$\text{Min } f_3 = 1/\left(x_1^2 + x_2^2 + 1\right) - 1.1e^{\left(x_1^2 - x_2^2\right)};$$

s.t. $ub = [2, 2.5];\ lb = [-1.8, -1];$

5. DISCUSSIONS AND CONCLUSIONS

Many search techniques required auxiliary information in order to work properly. For example Gradient techniques need derivative in order to minimize/maximize a given objective where as genetic algorithms do not require all these auxiliary information. GA uses probabilistic transition rules to guide their search towards regions of search space with likely improvement. It is also better than other optimization algorithm when domain knowledge is scarce or expert knowledge is difficult to encode to narrow the search space and bad proposals do not affect the end solution (independent of initial feasible solution).

In general, multi-objective optimization requires more computational effort than single-objective optimization.

Genetic algorithms require several heuristic parameters and this process is not necessarily straightforward; it may require significant experience in selection. However, genetic multi-objective algorithms are relatively easy to use then other evolutionary algorithm.

In this paper algorithm is tested with linear, non-linear three objective functions and with constrained objectives functions after external penalty is carefully selected and the Simulation results from test functions show that the performance is quite satisfactory. The result on the approximation of the test function described in this paper is still preliminary. Further work should be carried out to check the conjectures on multiobjective optimization problems with a higher design space.

REFERENCES

1. Sawaragi, Y., Nakayama, H. and Tanino, T. (1985) Theory of Multiobjective Optimization. Academic Press, Waltham.
2. Steuer, R.E. (1986) Multiple Criteria: Theory, Computation and Application. John Wiley & Sons, New York.
3. Ehrgott, M. (2005) Multicriteria Optimization. Springer, New York.
4. Eichfelder, G. (2008) Vector Optimization. Springer, Berlin Heidelberg.
5. Schaffer, J.D., Ed. (1989) Advances in Genetic Programming. Proceedings of the Third International Conference on Genetic Algorithms, Morgan Kaufmann, Burlington.
6. Coley, D.A. (1999) An Introduction to Genetic Algorithms for Scientists and Engineers. World Scientific Publishing Co. Pte. Ltd., River Edge.
7. Deb, K., Agrawal, S., Pratap, A. and Meyarivan, T. (2000) A Fast Elitist Non-Dominated Sorting Genetic Algorithm for Multi-Objective Optimization: NSGA-II. Proceedings of the Parallel Problem Solving from Nature VI Conference, 849-858.
8. Fonseca, C.M. and Fleming, P.J. (1995) An Overview of Evolutionary Algorithms in Multiobjective Optimization. Evolutionary Computation Journal, 3, 1-16.
9. Knowles, J.D. and Corne, D.W. (1999) The Pareto Archived Evolution Strategy: A New Baseline Algorithm for Multiobjective Optimization. Proceedings of the 1999 Congress on Evolutionary Computation, Washington DC, 06 Jul-09 Jul 1999.
10. Bot, R.I., Grad, S.-M. and Wanka, G. (2009) Duality in Vector Optimization. Springer-Verlag, Berlin Heidelberg.
11. Goldberg, D.E. (1989) Genetic Algorithms in Search, Optimization, and Machine Learning. Addison-Wesley, Boston.

12. Deb, K. (2001) Multi-Objective Optimization Using Evolutionary Algorithms. Wiley, Hoboken.

13. Sivanandam, S.N. and Deepa, S.N. (2008) Introduction to Genetic Algorithms. Springer-Verlag, Berlin Heidelberg.

14. Semu, M. (2003) On Cone D.C Optimization and Conjugate Duality. Chinese Annals of Mathematics, 24, 521-528.

15. Goh, C.J. and Yang, X.Q. (2002) Duality in Optimization and Variational Inequalities. Taylor and Francis, New York.

16. Holland, J.H. (1975) Adaptation in Natural and Artificial Systems. University of Michigan Press, Ann Arbor. (2nd Edition, MIT Press, 1992.)

17. Haupt, R.L. (2004) Sue Ellen Haupt: Practical Genetic Algorithms. 2nd Edition, John Wiley & Sons, Inc., Hoboken.

18. Koza, J.R. (1992) Genetic Programming. Massachusetts Institute of Technology, Cambridge.

19. Fita, A. (2014) Multiobjective Programming with Continuous Genetic Algorithm. International Journal of Scientific & Technology Research, 3, 135-149.

20. Ikeda, K., Kita, H. and Kobayashi, S. (2001) Failure of Pareto-Based MOEAs: Does Nondominated Really Mean Near to Optimal. Proceedings of the Congress on Evolutionary Computation, 2, 957-962.

21. Viennet, R., Fonteix, C. and Marc, I. (1996) Multicriteria Optimization Using a Genetic Algorithm for Determining a Pareto Set. International Journal of Systems Science, 27, 255-260.

22. http://www.matworks.com

8

CHAPTER

INTER-COMPARISON OF AN EVOLUTIONARY PROGRAMMING MODEL OF SUSPENDED SEDIMENT TIME-SERIES WITH OTHER LOCAL MODELS

M. A. Ghorbani[1], H. Asadi[1], P. Yousefi[1] and R. Khatibi[2]

[1] *University of Tabriz, East Azerbaijan, Iran*

[2] *Consultant Mathematical Modeller, Swindon, Wilts., UK*

1. INTRODUCTION

The experience of applying evolutionary computing to time series describing local physical problems has benefited the modelling culture by showing that many different mathematical formulae can be produced to describe the same problem. This experience brings into the focus the roles of pluralism in the modelling culture as opposed to searching for the best model, where physical problems provide relevance and context to the choice of modelling techniques. Both of these roles are often overlooked and do not directly influence research agenda. Although the focus of this paper is on evolutionary computing, it also promotes a pluralistic modelling culture by studying other modelling techniques, as well as by keeping the role of physical problems in the foreground.

Estimating suspended sediment loads is a problem of practical importance and includes such problems as changing courses in rivers, loss of fertile soil, filling reservoirs and impacts on water quality. The study of these problems in the short-run are referred to as sediment transport and erosion for those in the long-run. Past empirical capabilities remain invaluable but are not sufficient on their own as management and engineering solutions often require an insight into the problem. Empirical knowledge has been incorporated into the body of distributed modelling techniques giving rise to sophisticated modelling software tools but their applications require a great deal of resources. There remains a category of problems, often referred to as time series analysis, which uses the sequences of time variations and predicts the future values. This category of models provides useful information to management of local problems. For instance, such models may be used to schedule dredging requirements or other maintenance activities. Time series analysis is developing into local management tools and it is a focus of this chapter.

The aim of this chapter is to predict suspended sediment load of a river into the future. Besides the traditional empirical Sediment Rating Curve (SRC), there are several strategies for analysing such time series and *evolutionary computing* is one of Artificial Intelligence (AI) approaches, which broadly include capabilities for searching and recognising patterns among others. This chapter also employs Artificial Neural Network (ANN), which is another AI approach. Yet another strategy is to regard time series as outcomes of many random drivers and this assumption is supported by a whole body of probabilistic approaches, where this chapter uses Multi-Linear Regression (MLR) analysis to model the same data. Over the past few decades, research has increasingly focused on the application of deterministic chaos (or chaos theory or dynamic systems) showing that many of apparently randomly varying system behaviours can be explained by deterministic chaos. The concept behind this modelling strategy is that the particular data can largely be explained by deterministic behaviour, where in time the system evolves asymptotically towards an *attractor*. Its random-looking variations are assumed to be an internal feature of the system and depending on its initial conditions, its state under a certain range may become highly erratic but with a predictable behaviour. Evidently, none of these strategies are identical and different models rarely produce identical results. This chapter therefore compares the performance of these modelling strategies for solving an engineering problem.

The study employs 26 years of the Mississippi River data recorded at Tarbert + RR Landings and involve both flows and suspended sediment load. The river discharges about 200 million metric tons of suspended sediment per year to the Gulf of Mexico, where it ranks about sixth in the world today.

2. LITERATURE REVIEW

Sediment Rating Curve (SRC) is an empirical approach used by practitioners in the engineering studies of sediment and erosion problems. The log linear rating curve method has been used widely andSivakumar and Wallender (2005) outline the many flaws associated with this technique, including the lack of fit due to missing variables (e.g. Miller, 1951), retransformation bias (e.g. Ferguson, 1986), and non-normality of the error distribution (e.g. Thomas, 1988). According to Sivakumar and Wallender (2005), the technique has been modified including, among others, use of separate curves for different seasons (Miller, 1951), stratifying the data according to the magnitude of flow and applying a separate curve for each stratum (Glysson, 1987), and use of a single multivariate model instead of multiple rating curves (Cohn *et al.*, 1992). Sivakumarand Wallender (2005) argue that there is not a simple (and universal) 'water discharge-suspended sediment concentration-suspended sediment load' relationship. A brief overview of past studies is as follows.

Kisi, et al (2008) review the application of ANN and neuro-fuzzy techniques to time series analysis of sediment loads at various timescales, uncertainty in the data. Variations of these techniques have also been reported by Jain (2001), Tayfur (2002), Cigizoglu (2004), Kisi (2004), Raghuwanshi*et al.* (2006),Cigizoglu& Kisi (2006). Other studies on the application of ANN to suspended sediment include that by Wang et al (2008), who applied ANN to derive the coefficients of regression analysis for their SRC model.

Aytek and Kishi (2008) used the GP approach to model suspended sediment for two stations on the Tongue River in Montana, USA, andindicate that the GP formulation performs quite well compared to sediment rating curves and multi linear regression models.

Chaotic signals have also been identified in time series of suspended sediment loads by Sivakumar and Jayawardena (2002, 2003), Farmer and Sidorowich, 1987). The outcomes revealed the usefulness of these methods towards an effective prediction capability.

Overall, a general understanding of the analysis of suspended sediment load is yet to emerge and one way to gain an insight into the problem is to carry out inter-comparison studies of the performance of a host of models applied to diversity of rivers of different shapes and sizes.

3. STUDY AREA AND DATA

3.1. Understanding the Problem

Sediment transport is concerned with entrained soil materials carried in water by erosion on the catchment and within channels. Sediment particles are categorised as follows (i) the saltation load (not discussed here); (ii) bedload (not discussed here) and (iii) suspended load including clay (< $62\mu m$ in particle diameter), silt and sand. Suspended load (both as "fine-grained sediment" and "wash load") is directly a result of the turbulence in water and forms a large proportion of the transported load, where the turbulence is a measure of the energy in the water to carry the load.

Sediment discharge is a measure of the mass rate of sediment transport at any point in space and time and determines whether the load is being transported or deposited. The whole process comprises soil erosion, sediment transport and sediment yield, where the deposited load delivered to a point in the catchment is referred to as sediment yield and is expressed as tons per unit area of the basin per year, measured at a point. Estimation of sediment yield (and soil erosion) is essential for management but these and mathematical models are used to gain an insight into the underlying processes. Sediment yield is estimated by (i) direct measurement, (ii) using local time series models to predict future states; (iii) using mathematical models to study jointly both erosion and sediment processes.

Suspended sediment forms most of the transported load and can be affected by many parameters including rainfall, land use pattern, slope, soil characteristics, e.g. soil moisture content but their considerations lead to distributed models, which are complex. Recorded suspended sediment derives distributed models by serving them as boundary conditions or input sources but their inherent information is not tapped on. There is a case for local models to study the information contained in recorded sediment loads alone in terms of flow and sediment hydrographs. This chapter is concerned with the study of the suspended load of a river, as discussed below.

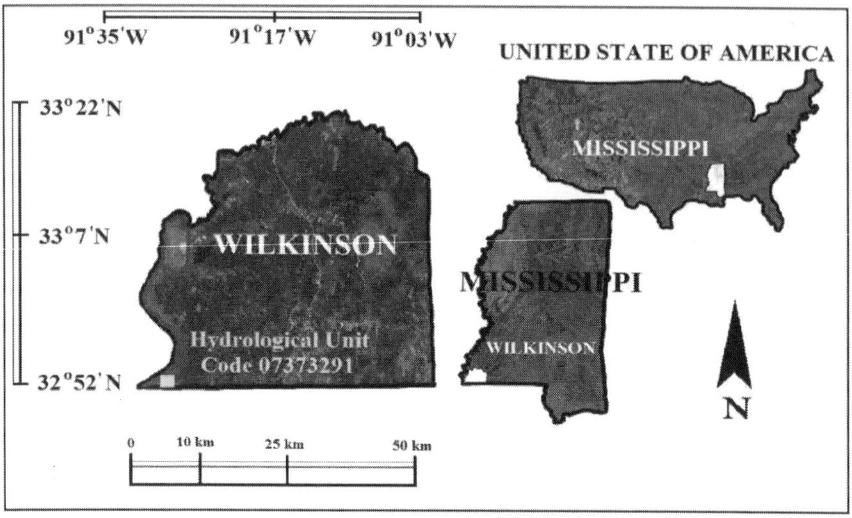

Figure 1. Mississippi River Station at Tarbert + RR Landings (http://pubs.usgs.gov/circ/circ1133/geosetting.html).

3.2. Study Area

The flow–sediment time series data of a Mississippi river Station is used in the study, the location of which is shown in Figure 1. The gauge is situated at Tarbert + RR Landings, LA (USGS Station no. 07373291, latitude 30°57′40″, longitude 91°39′52″) and it is operated by the US Geological Survey (USGS) – the location map is shown in Figure 1. The Mississippi River discharges an average of about 200 million metric tons of suspended sediment per year to the Gulf of Mexico and to the ocean.

3.3. Review of Data Records

Daily suspended sediment measurements for the above station have been made available by the USGS from April 1949. The data used herein span over a period of about 26 years (amounting to 9496 datapoints) starting on October 1, 1949. Figures 2 show the variation of the daily suspended sediment and stream flow series observed at the above station.

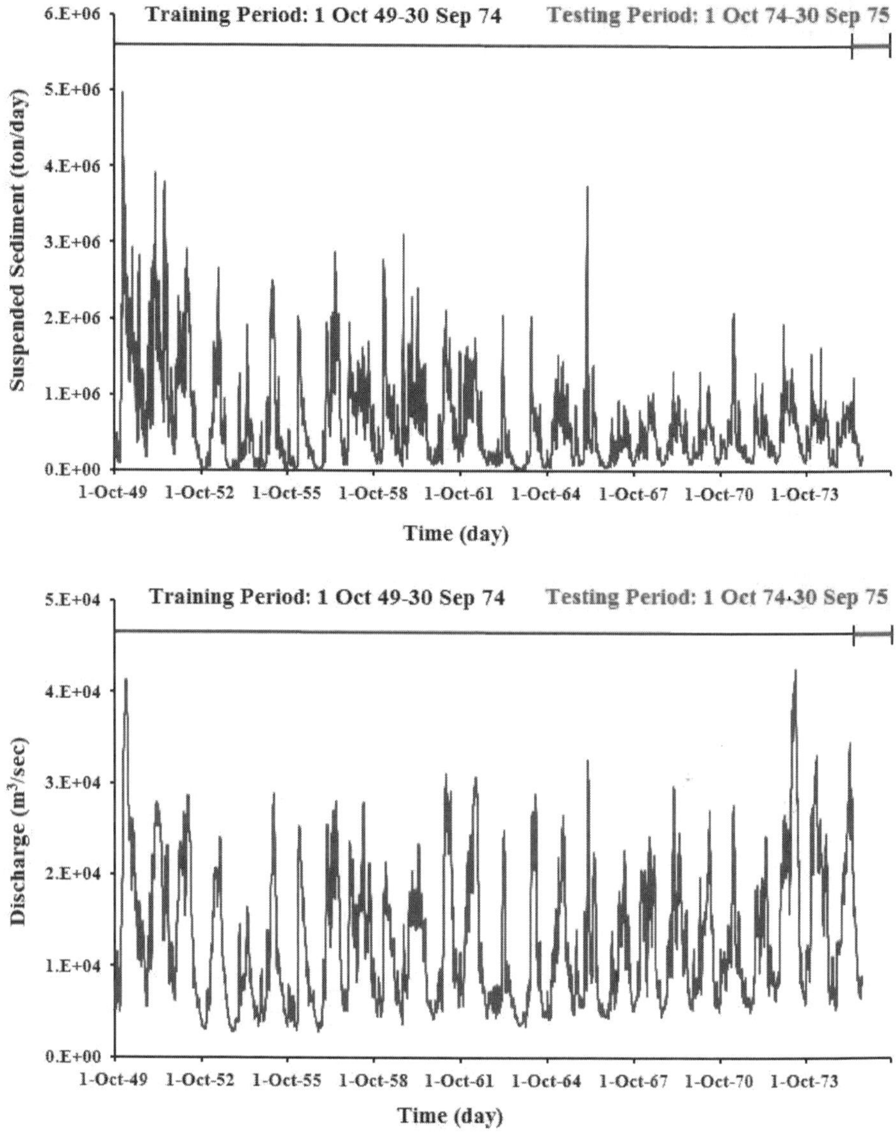

Figure 2. Variation of Daily Suspended Sediment and Flow Data in the Mississippi River Basin

Of the 26 water-years of the data sample of daily records of flow and suspended sediment (9496 datapoints), the first 25 water years of data (9131 datapoints) were used to train the models and the remaining 365 datapoints of daily records were used for testing. The statistical parameters of stream flow and sediment concentration data are shown in Table 1. These results show that the overall contribution of the datapoints in the test period is average; its individual characteristics in terms of kurtosis show the annual hydrographs to be less peaked and more flat but at the same time, the suspended sediment load during the year is significantly high. Thus, the minimum values during this year were significantly above the average but persistent and though less dynamic.

TABLE 1.

Statistical Parameters for Dataset from the Mississippi River Basin

Table 1. Statistical Parameters for Dataset from the Mississippi River Basin

Data Type	Training set		Testing set		All Dataset	
	Suspended Sediment (ton/day)	*Discharge (m^3/sec)*	*Suspended Sediment* (ton/day)	*Discharge (m^3/sec)*	*Suspended Sediment (ton/day)*	*Discharge (m^3/sec)*
Datapoints	9131	9131	365	365	9496	9496
Mean	6.37E5	1.27E4	4.52E5	1.58E4	6.30E5	1.28E4
St dev	6.30E5	7.60E3	2.53E5	7.80E3	6.21E5	7.60E3
Max	4.97E6	4.25E4	1.22E6	3.45E4	4.97E6	4.25E4
Min.	4.00E3	2.80E3	6.70E4	5.40E3	4.00E3	2.80E3
CV	1.0	0.60	0.56	0.49	0.99	0.59
Skew	1.78	0.95	0.10	0.51	1.82	0.93
Kurt	3.98	0.34	-0.98	-0.85	4.20	0.27

*Data = Number of Data; Std = Standard Deviation; Max = Maximum Value; Min = Minimum Value; CV = Coefficient of Variation; Skew = Skewness; Kurt = Kurtosis

3.4. Overview of the Models

The sediment rating curve method is the traditional method for converting measured flows to predict suspended sediment load and this paper aims to test the performance of evolutionary computing models but uses a host of other techniques for the inter-comparison purpose. These models are outlined in this section but evolutionary computing is explained in more detail. Their underlying notion is that past values contain a sufficient amount of information to predict the future values and a systematic way of representing this notion is purported in Table 2 in terms of a selection of models. These models, in essence, are reminiscent of regression analysis but GEP, ANN and MLR models approach the problem in their own individual ways to unearth the structure of the information inherent in time series. Notably, the SRC model is expressed by Model 1 and the deterministic chaos model is expressed by Model 0. These models will all be evaluated by using coefficient of Correlation (CC), Relative Absolute Errors (RAE) and Root Mean Square Errors (RMSE).

Table 2. Modelling Structures of the Selected Modelling Techniques

Model	Input variables	Output variables	The Structure
Model 0	$S_{t-1}, S_{t-2}...$	S_t	Chaos
Model 1	Q_t	S_t	ANN, SRC
Model 2	Q_t , S_{t-1}	S_t	GEP, ANN, MLR
Model 3	Q_t ,Q_{t-1}	S_t	GEP, ANN, MLR
Model 4	Q_t , Q_{t-1} , S_{t-1}	S_t	GEP, ANN, MLR
Model 5	Q_t,Q_{t-1},Q_{t-2}	S_t	GEP, ANN, MLR
Model 6	Q_t,Q_{t-1},Q_{t-2},S_{t-1}	S_t	GEP, ANN, MLR

Where Qt and St represent respectively flow and suspended sediment load at day t.

3.4.1. Sediment Rating Curve

Sediment rating-curve is a flux-averaged relationship between suspended sediment, *S*, and water discharge, *Q*, expressed as a power law in the form of: S=aQb, where *a* and *b* are coefficients. Values of *a* and *b* for a particular stream are determined from data via a linear regression between (log *S*) and (log *Q*). The SRC model is represented in terms of Model 1 in Table 2. For more critical views on this model, references may be made Kisi (2005) and Walling (1977), among others.

3.4.2. Evolutionary Computing

Evolutionary computing techniques apply optimisation algorithms as a tool to facilitate the mimicking of natural selection. A building block approach to generalised evolution driven by natural selection is yet to be presented, although Khatibi (2011) has outlined a rationale for it. Traditional understanding of natural selection for biological species is well developed, according to which the process takes place at the gene level of all individuals of all species carrying hereditary material for reproduction by inheriting from their parents and by passing on a range of their characteristics to their offspring. The process of reproduction is never a perfect copying process, as mutation may occur from time to time in biological reproductions involving the random process of reshuffling the genes during sexual reproduction. The paper assumes preliminary knowledge on genes, chromosomes, gene pool, DNA and RNA, where the environment also has a role to play. The environment for the production of proteins and sexual reproduction is different than the outer environment for the performance of the individual entities supported by the proteins or produced by sexual reproduction. The outer environment is characterised by (i) being limited in resources, (ii) having no foresight, (iii) organisms tend to produce more offspring than can be supported, a process that is driven by positive feedback loops, and (iv) there is a process of competition and selection. Some of these details are normally overlooked or simplified in evolutionary computing and therefore the paper stresses the point that natural selection takes place at the gene level and this is not directly applicable to that at the social level.

Facts on natural selection are overwhelming but there are myths as well, e.g. the myth of "the survival of the fittest" and this term is widely used in evolutionary computing. Although the fittest has a selective advantage to survive, this is not a guarantee for the survival in the natural world. An overview of the dynamics of natural selection in an environment is that (i) the environment can only support a maximum population of certain size, but there is also a lower size at the critical mass below which a population is at risk of losing its viability; (ii) there is a process of reproduction, during which natural selection operates at the gene level, although there are further processes operating at the individual levels beyond the direct reach of natural selection (e.g. interactions among the individuals catered for by other mechanisms or each individual is under selection pressure by the environment); (iii) the process of reproduction is associated with mutation, which gives rise to the production of gene pools.

A great deal of the above overview has been adopted in evolutionary computing, the history of which goes back to the 1960s when Rechenberg (1973) introduced evolution strategies. The variants of this approach include genetic algorithm (Holland, 1975), evolutionary programming (Fogel et al, 1966), genetic programming (Koza, 1992) and Gene Expression Programming (GEP), Ferreira (2001a). This paper uses the latter approach, which in a simple term is a variation of GP but each of these techniques have differences with one another. These techniques have the capability forderiving a set of mathematical expressions to describe therelationship between the independent and dependent variables using such functions as mutation, recombination(or crossover) and evolution.

This chapter is concerned with GEP and one of the important preliminary decisions in its implementations is to establish the models represented in Table 2 (Models 2-6). There is no prior knowledge of the appropriateness of any of these models and therefore this is normally fixed in a preliminary modelling task through a trial-and-error procedure. Whichever the model choice (Model 2 – Model 6 or similar other ones), each implementation of GEP builds up the model in terms of the values of the coefficients (referred to as terminals) and the operations (functions) through the procedure broadly outlined in Figure 3.

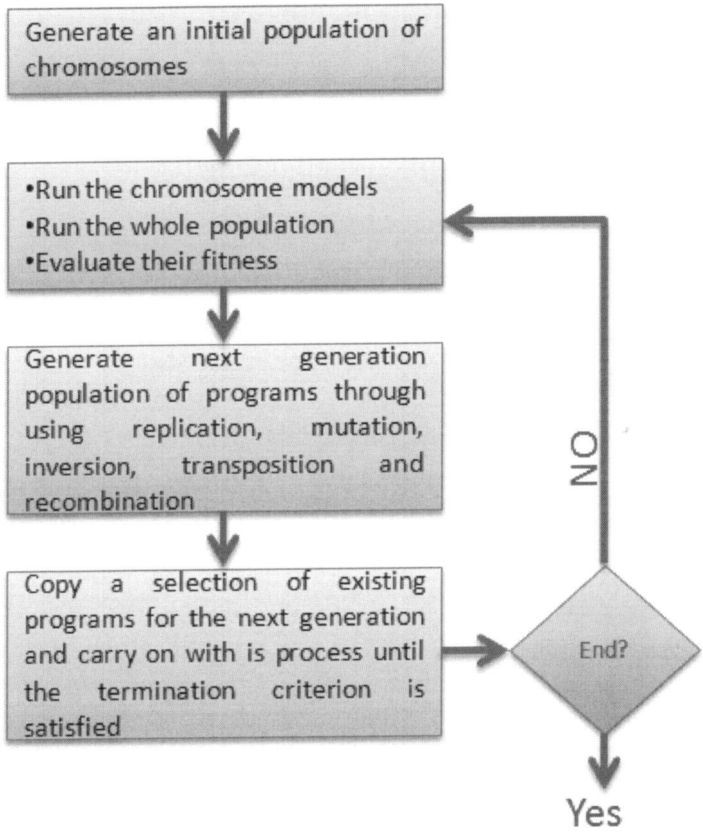

Figure 3. Simplified Outline of Implementation of Evolutionary Programming Models

The working of a gene expression program depicted in Figure 3 is outlined as follows. A chromosome in GEP is composed of genes and each gene is composed of (i) terminals and (ii) functions. The gene structures and chromosomes in GEP are illustrated for the solution that is obtained for the dataset used in this study (see Section 4.2). The terminals as their names suggest are composed of constants and variables and the functions comprise mathematical operations, as shown by (4.a)-(4.f).

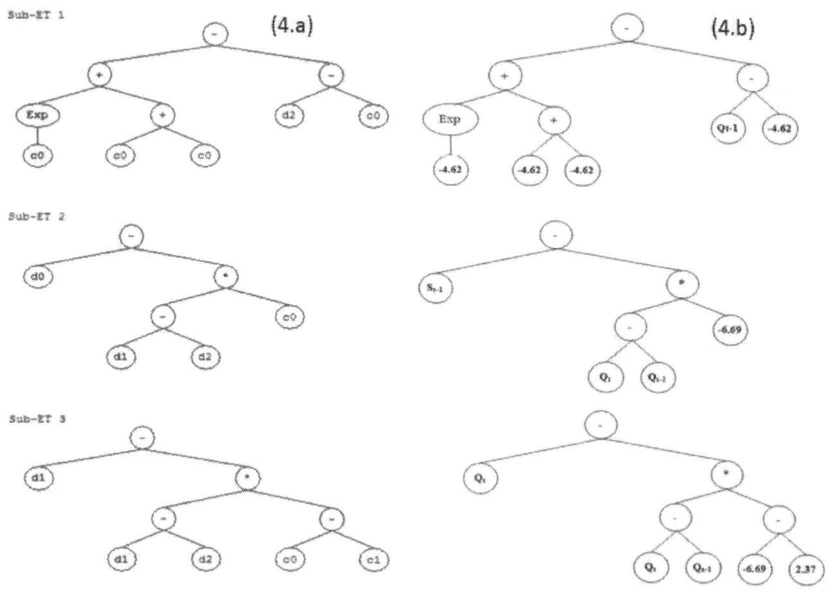

Figure 4. Expression Trees – (a) typical expression tree; (b) the selected GEP model in this study

As the term terminal suggests, it comprises a set of values at the tail-ends of the genes of the chromosomes and these are made meaningful by the functions making up the other component of the genes of the chromosomes. In GEP, these are represented by a bilingual notation called Karva language of (i) genetic codes, which are not deemed necessary for a description here and (ii) expression trees (or parse trees), as illustrated by Figure 4.a and the recommended solution is shown in Figure 4.b, which is transcribed by Equation (4) in Section 4.2. The initial chromosomes of the initial population are no different than the solution shown in Figure 4.b but their difference is that the composition of each of the initial chromosomes is selected often in random and then GEP is expected to improve them through evolution by the strategy of selections, replication and mutation but there are other facilities that not mentioned facilitating a more robust solution and these include inversion, transposition and recombination. The improvements are carried out through selection from one generation to another and this is why this modelling strategy is called evolutionary computation. The main strength of this approach is that it does not set up any system of equation to predict the future but it evaluates the fitness of each chromosome and selects from those a new population with better performance traits.

The GEP employed in this study is based on evolving computer programs of different sizes and shapes encoded in linear chromosomes of fixed lengths, Ferreira, 2001a; Ferreira, (2001b). The chromosomes are composed of multiple genes, each gene encoding a smaller subprogram. Furthermore, the structural and functional organisation of the linear chromosomes allows the unconstrained operation of important genetic functions, such as mutation, transposition and recombination.It has been reported that GEP is 100-10,000 times more efficient than GP systems (Ferreira, 2001a; Ferreira, 2001b) for a number of reasons, including: (i) the chromosomes are simple entities: linear, compact, relatively small, easy to manipulate genetically (replicate, mutate, recombine, etc); (ii) the parse trees or expression trees are exclusively the expression of their respective chromosomes; they are entities upon which selection acts, and according to fitness, they are selected to reproduce with modification.

3.4.3. Artificial Neural Networks (Anns)

Whilst evolutionary programming emulates the working of Nature, ANNs emulate the workings of neurons in the brain. Both the brain and ANNs are parallel information processing systems consisting of a set of neurons or nodes arranged in layers but this is where the parallel ends. The actual process of information processing in the brain is a topical research issue but the drivers of ANNs are polynomial algebra and there is no evidence that the brains of humans, monkeys or any other animals employ algebraic computations such as optimisation methods. Although there is a great incentive to understand the working of the brain, it is not imperative to be constrained by it and the use of algebra in ANNs is not criticised here but awareness is raised as these two processes are not identical.

The ANN theory has been described in many books, including the text by Rumelhart et al. (1986). The application of ANNs has been the subject of a large number of papers that have appeared in the recent literature. There are various implementations of ANNs but the type used in this study is a Multi-Layer feedforward Perceptron (MLP) trained with the use of back propagation learning algorithm with the following functions: (i) the input layer accepts the data, (ii) intermediate layer processes them, and (iii) the output layer displays the resultant outputs. The number of hidden layers is decided in a preliminary modelling process by finding the most efficient number of layers through a trial-and-error procedure. Each neuron in a layer is connected to all the neurons of the next layer, and the neurons in one layer are not connected among themselves. All the nodes within a layer act synchronously.

This study implements the ANN models in terms of Models 1-6 of Table 2 and Figure 5 shows one of the implementation selected. For each of these models, the data passing through the connections from one neuron to another are multiplied by weights that control the strength of a passing signal. When these weights are modified, the data transferred through the network changes; consequently, the network output also changes. The signal emanating from the output node(s) is the network's solution to the input problem.

In the back-propagation algorithm, a set of inputs and outputs is selected from the training set and the network calculates the output based on the inputs. This output is subtracted from the actual output to find the output-layer error. The error is back propagated through the network, and the weights are suitably adjusted. This process continues for the number of prescribed sweeps or until a prescribed error tolerance is reached. The mean square error over the training samples is the typical objective function to be minimized. After training is complete, the ANN performance is validated. Depending on the outcome, either the ANN has to be retrained or it can be implemented for its intended use.

3.4.4. Multi Linear Regression (Mlr)

An overview of the data presented in Figure 2 invokes the thought that other than the annual trend within the data, the underlying process is probably random and a more rational way of explaining the data would be through probabilistic approaches. One such method applied to the selected data is the Multi-Linear Regression (MLR) model. It fits a linear combination of the components of a multiple signals x (e.g. recorded flows and suspended sediment timeseries as defined by the Models 2-6 in Table 2) to a single output signal y, as defined by (1.a) (e.g. predicted suspended sediment load) and returns the residual, r, i.e. the difference signal, as defined by (1.b):

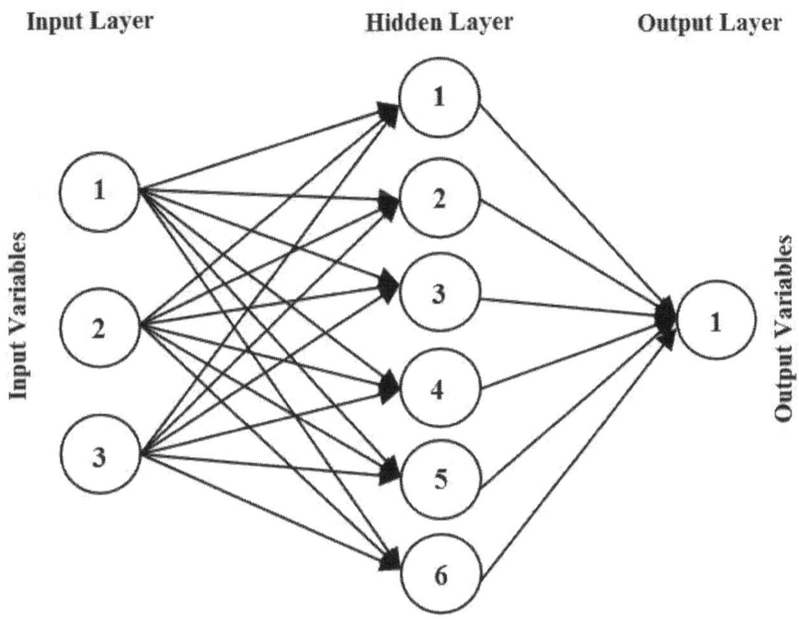

Figure 5. Implementation of the ANN Models and its Various Layers

$$y = b + \sum_{i=0}^{N} a_i x_i \tag{1a}$$

$$r = y - a_1 x_1 - a_2 x_2 - \ldots - b \tag{1b}$$

Where xi is defined in Table 2 in terms of various models and ai values are called regression coefficients, which are estimated by using the least square or any other similar method. In this study, the coefficients of the regressions were determined using the least square method.

3.4.5. Chaos Theory

A cursory view of the suspended sediment record of the Mississippi River in Figure 2 provides no clue to a strategy for its underlying patterns, if any, although annual trend superimposed on random variation may be an immediate reaction of a hydrologist. Another strategy to explore such possible patterns is through the application of chaos theory, more specifically through the "phase-space diagram" as shown in Figure 6 for this river data. A point in the phase-space represents the state of the system at a given time. The narrow dark band in the figure signifies strong determinism but its scattered band signifies the presence of noise and therefore there is a possibility to explain this set of data by chaos theory. The dark band signifies convergence of the trajectories of the phase-space with a fractal dimension towards the attractor of the data, where the dynamics of the system can be reduced to a set of deterministic laws to enable the prediction of its future states.

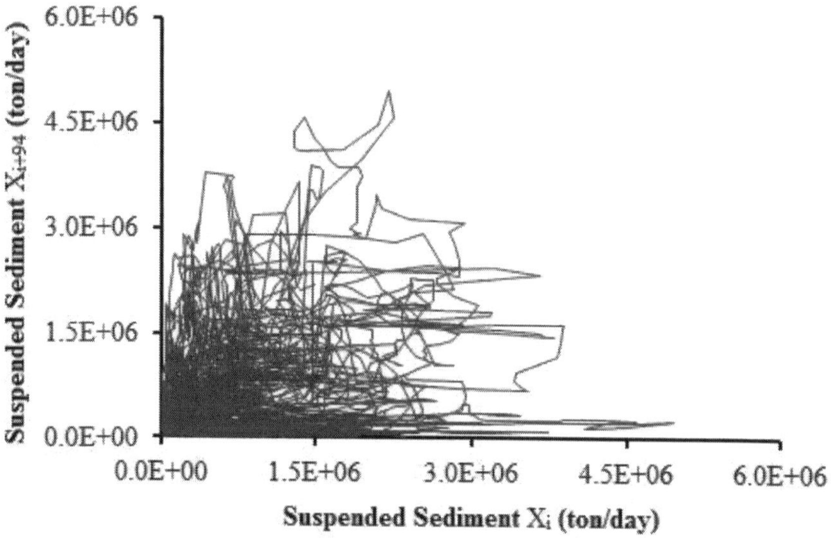

Figure 6. Phase-space Diagram of Daily Suspended Sediment Data in the Mississippi River Basin

Chaos theory is a method of nonlinear time series analysis and involves a host of methods, essentially based on the phase-space reconstruction of a process, from scalar or multivariate measurements of physical observables. This method is implemented in terms of Model 0 of Table 2. It is largely based on the representation of the underlying dynamics through reconstruction of phase-space, originally given by Takens, 1981. It is implemented in terms of two parameters of delay time and embedding dimension, according to which given a set of physical variables and an analytical model describing their interactions, the dynamics of the system can be represented geometrically by a single point moving on a trajectory, where each of its points corresponds to a state of the system. The phase-space diagram is essentially a co-ordinate system, whose coordinates represent the variables necessary to completely describe the state of the system at any moment.

One difficulty in its construction is that in most practical situations, information on every variable influencing the system may not be available. However, a time series of a single variable may be available, which may allow the construction of a (pseudo) phase-space. The idea behind such a reconstruction is that a non-linear system is characterized by self-interaction, and a time series of a single variable can carry the information about the dynamics of the entire multi-variable system. The trajectories of the phase-space diagram describe the evolution of the system from some initial state, and hence represent the history of the system.

This paper applies chaos theory to analyse the suspended sediment load of the Mississippi River data in a similar fashion to the other modelling strategies described above. It uses the local prediction method for training and testing, as outlined below, but it is a traditional practice to apply several methods to build evidence for the existence of chaotic signals in a particular data. These techniques employ the delay-embedding parameters of τ and m, which are unknown a-priori. The following methods are used in this chapter:

1. Average Mutual Information (AMI) is used to estimate τ; and the minimization of the False Nearest Neighbours to do that of the optimal values for the embedding dimension, m.

AMI (Fraser and Swinney, 1986) defines how the measurements $X(t)$ at time t are related, from an information theoretic point of view, to measurements $X(t+\tau)$ at time $t+\tau$. The average mutual information is defined as:

$$I(\tau) = \sum_{X(i),X(i+\tau)} P(X(i),X(i+\tau)) \log\left[\frac{P(X(i),X(i+\tau))}{P(X(i))P(X(i+\tau))}\right] \quad (2a)$$

where *i* is total number of samples. P(X(i)) and P(X(i+τ)) are marginal probabilities for measurements X(i) and X(i+τ) , respectively, whereas P(X(i)) , P(X(i+τ)) is their joint probability. The optimal delay time τ minimises the function I(τ) *for* t=τ , X(i+τ) adds the maximum information on X(i).

The False Nearest Neighbours procedure (Kennel et al., 1992) is a method to obtain the optimum embedding dimension for phase-space reconstruction. By checking the neighbourhood of points embedded in projection manifolds of increasing dimension, the algorithm eliminates 'false Neighbours': This means that points apparently lying close together due to projection are separated in higher embedding dimensions. when the ratio between the number of false neighbours at the dimension m +1 and m is below a given threshold, generally smaller than 5%, each m'>m+1 is an optimal embedding. A poor reconstruction of few embedding states with several components is obtained if m' is too large and the next analyses should not be performed.

1. Correlation Dimension (CD) method: is a nonlinear measure of the correlation between pairs lying on the attractor. For time series whose underlying dynamics is chaotic, the correlation dimension gets a finite fractional value, whereas for stochastic systems it is infinite. For an m -dimensional phase-space, the correlation function Cm(r) is defined as the fraction of states closer than r (Grassberger and Procaccia, 1983; Theiler, 1986):

$$C(r) = \lim_{N\to\infty} \frac{2}{N(N-1)} \sum_{i,j=1}^{N} H(r - |Y_i - Y_j|) \quad (2b)$$

Where H is the Heaviside step function, Y⃗ iis the ith state vector, and N is the number of points on the reconstructed attractor. The number w is called Theiler window and it is the correction needed to avoid spurious results due to temporal correlations instead of dynamical ones. For stochastic time series Cm(r)∝rm holds, whereas for chaotic time series the correlation function scales with r as:

$$C_m(r) \propto r^{D_2} \tag{2c}$$

where D2, correlation exponent, quantifies the degrees of freedom of the process, and defined by:

$$D_2 = \lim_{r \to 0} \frac{\ln C(r)}{\ln r} \tag{2d}$$

and can be reliably estimated as the slope in the lnCm(r) vs. ln(r) plot.

2. Local Prediction Model: The author's implementation of the local prediction method for deterministic chaos is details in Khatibi et al (2011) but the overview is that a correct phase-space reconstruction in a dimension m facilitates an interpretation of the underlying dynamics in the form of an m-dimensional map, fT, according to

$$Y_{j+T} = f_T(Y_j) \tag{2e}$$

whereYj and Yj+T are vectors of dimension m, describing the state of the system at times j (i.e. the current state) and j+T (i.e. the future state), respectively. The problem then is to find an appropriate expression for fT (i.e. FT). Local approximation entails the subdivision of the fT domain into many subsets (neighbourhoods), each of which identifies some approximations FT valid only in that same subset. In other words, the dynamics of the system is described step-by-step locally in the phase-space. In this m-dimensional space, prediction is performed by estimating the change of Xi with time, which are observed values of discrete scalar timeseries, with delay coordinates in the m-dimensional phase space. The relation between the points Xt and Xt+p (the behaviour at a future time p on the attractor) is approximated by function F as:

$$X_{t+p} \cong F(X_t)$$

(2f)

In this prediction method, the change of Xt with time on the attractor is assumed the same as those of nearby points,

(XTh,h=1,2,...,n). Herein, Xt+p is determined by the dth order polynomial F(Xt)as follows (Itoh, 1995):

$$x_{t+p} \cong f_0 + \sum_{k_1=0}^{m-1} f_{1k_1} X_{t-k_1\tau} + \sum_{\substack{k_2=k_1 \\ k_1=0}}^{m-1} f_{2k_1k_2} X_{t-k\tau_1} X_{t-k_2\tau} + \dots + \sum_{\substack{k_d=k_{d-1} \\ \vdots \\ k_2=k_1 \\ k_1=0}}^{m-1} f_{dk_1k_2\dots k_d} X_{t-k_1\tau} X_{t-k_2\tau} \dots X_{t-k_d\tau}$$

(2g)

Using n of XTh and XTh+p for which the values are already known, the coefficients, f, are determined by solution of the following equation:

$$X \cong Af$$

(2h)

where

$$X = (X_{T_{1+p}}, X_{T_{2+p}}, \dots, X_{T_{n+p}})$$

(2i)

and

$$f = (f_0, f_{10}, f_{11}, \dots, f_{1(m-1)}, f_{200}, \dots, f_{d(m-1)(m-1)\dots(m-1)})$$

(2j)

and A is the n×(m+d)!/m!d! Jacobian matrix which in its explicit form is:

$$A = \begin{bmatrix} 1 & X_{T_1} & X_{T_{1-\tau}} & \cdots & X_{T_{1-(m-1)\tau}} & X_{T_1}^2 & \cdots & X_{T_{1-(m-1)\tau}}^d \\ 1 & X_{T_2} & X_{T_{2-\tau}} & \cdots & X_{T_{2-(m-1)\tau}} & X_{T_2}^2 & \cdots & X_{T_{2-(m-1)\tau}}^d \\ \vdots & & & \vdots & & \vdots & & \vdots \\ 1 & X_{T_n} & X_{T_{n-\tau}} & \cdots & X_{T_{n-(m-1)\tau}} & X_{T_n}^2 & \cdots & X_{T_{n-(m-1)\tau}}^d \end{bmatrix}$$

(2K)

In order to obtain a stable solution, the number of rows in the Jacobian matrix A must satisfy:

$$n \geq \frac{(m+d)!}{m!d!} \tag{21}$$

As stated by Porporato and Ridolfi (1997), even though F-values are first degree polynomials, the prediction is nonlinear, because during the prediction procedure every point x(t) belongs to a different neighbourhood and is therefore defined by different expressions for f (Koçak,1997).

4. SETTING UP MODELS AND PRELIMINARY RESULTS

4.1. Performance of Sediment Rating Curve

The SRC model was implemented by using a simple least squares method leading to

$$S=13.2Q^{1.14} \tag{22}$$

The performance of this model is summarised in Table 3 and shown in Figure 7.Evidently, its performance is poor and the concern raised in the literature on this model is confirmed. This is a sufficient justification to search for reliable models.

Table 3. Statistical Performance of the Sediment Rating Curve for the Training and Test Periods

Model Input	Training			Testing		
	CC	MAE	RMSE	CC	MAE	RMSE
Model 1: Q_t	0.76	2.62E5	4.11E5	0.82	3.89E5	4.86E5

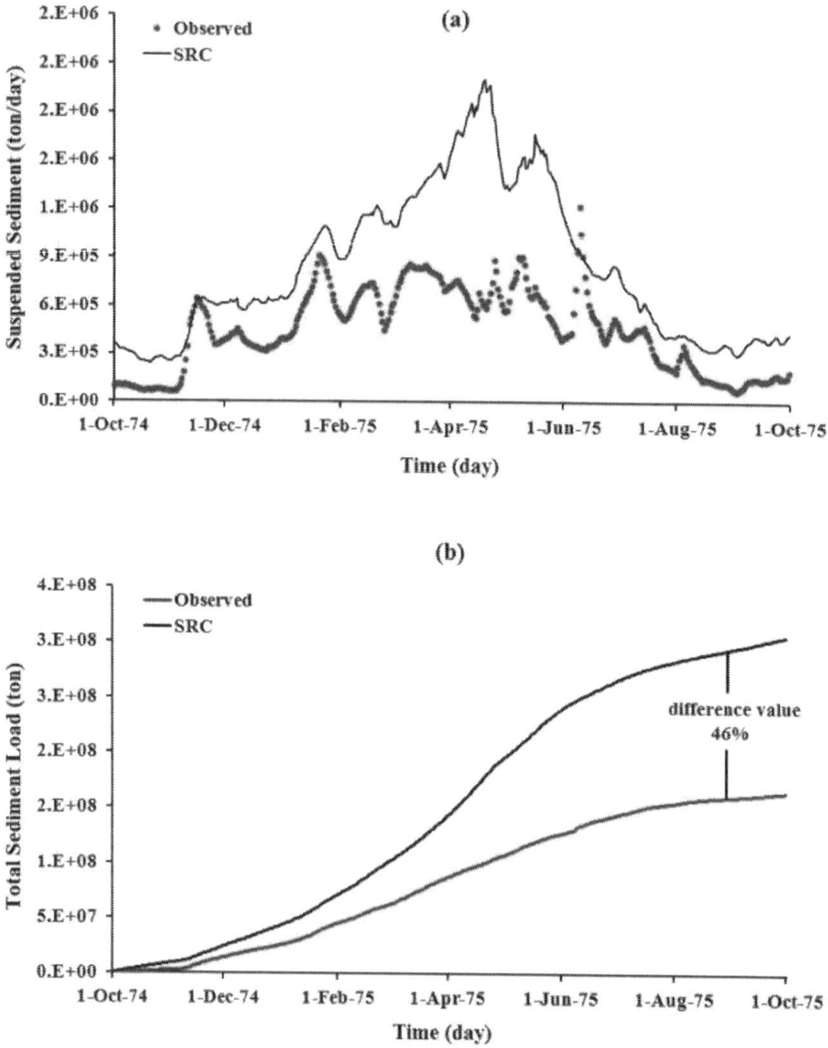

Figure 7. Comparison of Observed Suspended Sediment with that Modelled by SRC; (a) hydrograph, (b) cumulative values

4.2. Implementation of Gep

The preliminary investigation for the construction of a relationship between flows and suspended sediment in GEP requires: (i) the setting of the functions, as discussed below; (ii) the fitness function; and (iii) a range of other parameters, but the default values, given in Table 11, were sufficient in this study. The following functions were investigated:

$$\{+,-,\times\} \tag{4a}$$

$$\{+,-,\times,\ x\} \tag{4b}$$

$$\{+,-,\times,\ x^2\} \tag{4c}$$

$$\{+,-,\times,\ x^3\} \tag{4d}$$

$$\{+,-,\times,\ e^x\} \tag{4e}$$

$$\{+,-,\times,\ \ln(x)\} \tag{4f}$$

The performance of each function was investigated in terms of CC, MAE, and RMSE and the results are shown in Table 4.a for the training periods. The results show that (i) the model performances are more sensitive to the choice of independent variables than the function choices; (ii) the models not including suspended sediment time series perform poorly; and (iii) the model performance is not overly sensitive to the choice of the function. Appendix I, Table 11 specifies the fitness function to be Root Relative Squared Errors (RRSE).

The performance of the GEP model is presented in Table 4.b, according to which there is not much to differences between performances of a number of the alternative models but (4.e) is selected in this study for the prediction purposes (its expression tree is given in Figure 4) and given below.

$$S_t = S_{t-1} + 16.77Q_t - 16.77Q_{t-1} - 13.87 \tag{5}$$

Table 4. a. Statistical Performance of a Selection of Functions for the Training Period

Model		Q_t	Q_t, S_{t-1}	Q_t, Q_{t-1}	Q_t, Q_{t-1}, S_{t-1}	Q_t, Q_{t-1}, Q_{t-2}	$Q_t, Q_{t-1}, Q_{t-2}, S_{t-1}$
4.a):	CC	0.77	0.99	0.78	0.99	0.78	0.99
{+,-,×}	MAE	2.79E5	3.88E4	2.78E5	3.25E4	2.79E5	3.37E4
	RMSE	4.13E5	8.43E4	4.07E5	7.74E4	4.05E5	7.98E4
(4.b):	CC	0.77	0.99	0.77	0.99	0.77	0.99
{+,-,×, x}	MAE	2.82E05	3.87E04	2.81E05	3.80E04	2.78E05	3.27E04
	RMSE	4.15E05	8.42E04	4.14E05	8.36E04	4.10E05	7.75E04
(4.c):	CC	0.77	0.99	0.78	0.99	0.78	0.99
{+,-,×, x^2}	MAE	2.82E05	3.89E04	2.78E05	3.25E04	2.76E05	3.45E04
	RMSE	4.15E05	8.43E04	4.08E05	7.74E04	4.05E05	8.02E04

(4.d): {+,-,×,x^3}	**CC**	0.77	0.99	0.77	0.99	0.77	0.99
	MAE	2.43E5	3.89E4	2.76E5	3.21E4	2.76E5	3.41E4
	RMSE	4.05E5	8.43E4	4.12E5	7.76E4	4.13E5	8.03E4
(4.e): {+,-,×,e^x}	**CC**	0.77	0.99	0.77	0.99	0.77	0.99
	MAE	2.81E5	3.88E4	2.81E5	3.56E4	2.42E5	3.64E4
	RMSE	4.15E5	8.43E4	4.14E5	8.16E4	4.00E5	8.23E4
(4.f): {+,-,×,ln(x)}	**CC**	0.76	0.99	0.76	0.99	0.78	0.99
	MAE	2.56E5	3.89E4	2.64E5	3.25E4	2.60E5	3.21E4
	RMSE	4.09E5	8.42E4	4.10E5	7.72E4	4.02E5	7.72E4

Table 4 b. Statistical analysis of the estimated values for the test period

Model		Q_t	Q_t , S_{t-1}	Q_t ,Q_{t-1}	Q_t , Q_{t-1} , S_{t-1}	Q_t,Q_{t-1},Q_{t-2}	Q_t,Q_{t-1},Q_{t-2},S_{t-1}
(4.a): {+,-,×}	**CC**	0.83	0.99	0.84	0.99	0.84	0.99
	MAE	3.99E5	2.34E4	4.01E5	2.32E4	4.08E5	2.08E4
	RMSE	4.72E5	3.87E4	4.73E5	4.06E4	4.79E5	3.75E4
(4.b) {+,-,×,x}	**CC**	0.83	0.99	0.84	0.99	0.84	0.99
	MAE	3.99E05	2.33E04	4.01E05	2.28E04	3.96E05	2.34E04
	RMSE	4.69E05	3.87E04	4.70E05	3.08E04	4.65E05	4.04E04
(4.c) {+,-,×,x^2}	**CC**	0.83	0.99	0.84	0.99	0.84	0.99
	MAE	4.00E05	2.35E04	4.01E05	2.32E04	3.79E05	2.31E04
	RMSE	4.69E05	3.86E04	4.71E05	4.06E04	4.67E05	3.96E04

(4.d): {+,-,×,x^3}	**CC**	0.83	0.99	0.83	0.99	0.83	0.99
	MAE	3.87E5	2.35E4	4.00E5	2.10E4	3.96E5	2.06E4
	RMSE	4.94E5	3.87E4	4.75E5	3.81E4	4.69E5	3.69E4
(4.e): {+,-,×,e^x}	**CC**	0.83	0.99	0.84	0.99	0.84	0.99
	MAE	3.98E5	2.35E4	3.97E5	2.06E4	3.80E5	2.17E4
	RMSE	4.67E5	3.86E4	4.66E5	3.64E4	4.84E5	3.73E4
(4.e): {+,-,×,ln(x)}	**CC**	0.83	0.99	0.83	0.99	0.83	0.99
	MAE	3.90E5	2.35E4	3.90E5	2.40E4	3.81E5	2.29E4
	RMSE	4.93E5	3.86E4	4.81E5	4.18E4	4.69E5	4.05E4

Figure 8 compares modelled suspended sediment against their observed values, according to which the improvement by GEP is remarkable compared with SRC. Overall, the GEP modelling results follow observed values rather faithfully both in values and patterns, although there are still discrepancies in predicted values.

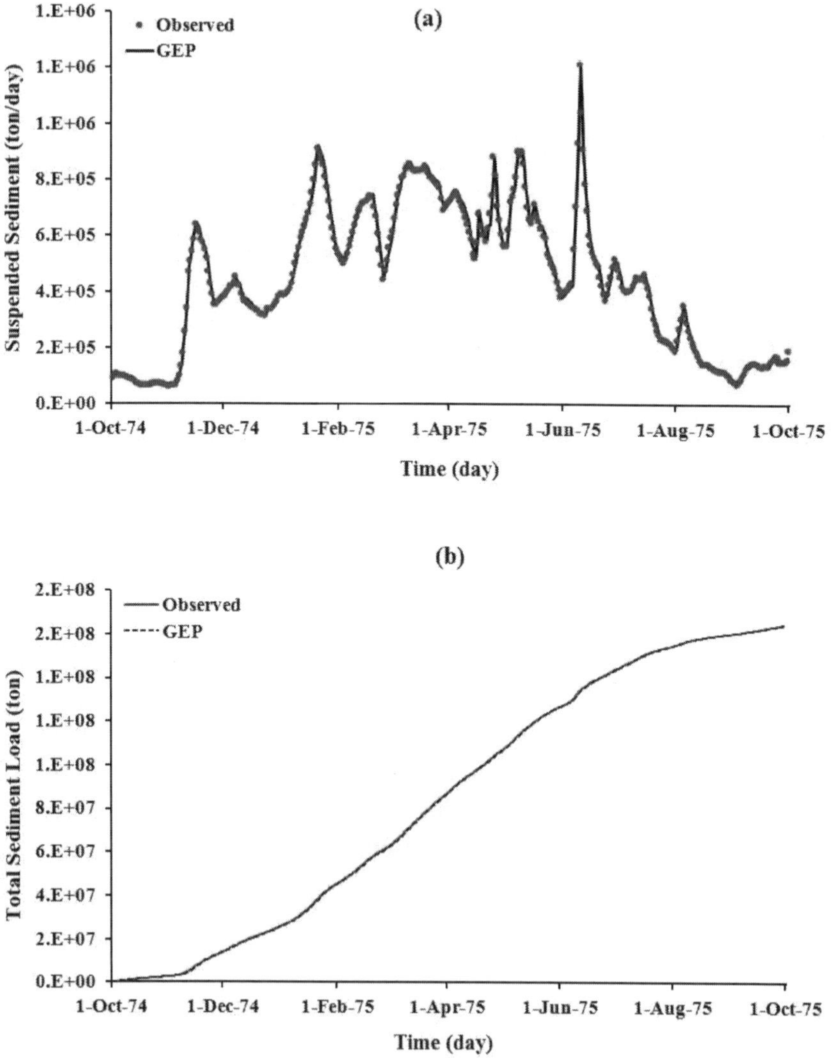

Figure 8. Comparison of Observed Suspended Sediment with that Modelled by GEP; (a) hydrograph, (b) cumulative values

4.3. Implementation of Ann

ANN implements another AI approach to the data represented in Figure 2 by another strategy, as described in Section 3.4.3. A preliminary investigation was carried out to make decisions on the choice of the models given in Table 2 (Models 1-6) and the ANN structure in terms of the neuron structure of the various layers.Table 5 presents model structures investigated. The preliminary modelling task also included a normalisation function for the data. In this study, MATLAB was employed to develop the ANN model and its mapstd function was selected for the normalisation (further defaults values are given in Table 11). The investigated ANN model structures are defined in Table 5 and their results for both the training and testing periods are presented in Table 6.

Table 5. ANN Structure (number of nodes in layers)

Model Identifier	Model Inputs	Training	Testing
Model 1	Q_t	2-5-1	2-5-1
Model 2	Q_t , S_{t-1}	3-5-1	3-5-1
Model 3	Q_t ,Q_{t-1}	3-7-1	3-7-1
Model 4	Q_t , Q_{t-1} , S_{t-1}	4-6-1	4-6-1
Model 5	Q_t,Q_{t-1},Q_{t-2}	4-9-1	4-9-1
Model6	Q_t,Q_{t-1},Q_{t-2},S_{t-1}	5-12-1	5-12-1

The performances of Models 1-6 are shown in Table 6 in terms of the values of three statistical indices of CC, MAE and RMSE. The performance of different models in terms of CC is remarkably high but Model 4 (Q*t*, Q*t1*, S*t-1*) produce less deviations, which is selected for the final run.

4.4. Implementation of the MLR Model

The MLR modelling strategy was implemented using Mathematica to derive regression coefficients for both periods of model fitting (training in the AI terminology) and testing using different statistical indices (CC, MAE and RMSE) given in Table 7, which shows that Model 2 (Q*t*, S*t-1*) performs

Table 6. Statistical Performance of the Selected Model Structure for the Training and Testing periods

	Model Training			Model Testing		
Model Inputs	CC	MAE	RMSE	CC	MAE	RMSE
Q_t	0.999	2.32E4	2.70E4	0.999	2.16E4	2.30E4
Q_t, S_{t-1}	0.999	2.59E4	3.12E4	0.996	2.17E4	2.64E4
Q_t, Q_{t-1}	0.999	2.00E4	2.79E4	0.981	4.19E4	4.84E4
Q_t, Q_{t-1}, S_{t-1}	**0.999**	**2.01E4**	**2.51E4**	**0.998**	**1.18E4**	**1.37E4**
Q_t, Q_{t-1}, Q_{t-2}	0.991	7.57E4	8.42E4	0.942	8.47E4	8.41E4
Q_t, Q_{t-1}, Q_{t-2}, S_{t-1}	0.995	5.66E4	6.42E4	0.976	4.63E4	5.47E4

relatively better than the others. The regression equation suggested by this technique is given by:

$$S_t = 0.24Q_t + 30.99S_{t-1} \tag{6}$$

Table 7. Statistical analysis of the estimated values for the train and test period

Model Inputs	CC	MAE	RMSE	CC	MAE	RMSE
Q_t	0.77	2.41E5	4.05E5	0.833	3.85E5	4.96E5
Q_t, S_{t-1}	**0.994**	**3.90E4**	**8.40E4**	**0.988**	**2.40E4**	**3.90E4**
Q_t, Q_{t-1}	0.78	2.40E5	3.97E5	0.837	3.85E5	4.98E5
Q_t, Q_{t-1}, S_{t-1}	0.993	3.30E4	7.60E4	0.987	2.50E4	4.10E4
Q_t, Q_{t-1}, Q_{t-2}	0.779	2.40E5	3.95E5	0.840	3.84E5	4.96E5
Q_t, Q_{t-1}, Q_{t-2}, S_{t-1}	0.993	3.30E4	7.70E4	0.987	2.50E4	4.10E4

4.5. Implementation of the Deterministic Chaos Model

A visual assessment for the existence of chaotic behaviour in the suspended sediment time series was presented in Figure 9, although it was not conclusive evidence but just invoked the possibility of the existence of a low-dimensional chaos. Traditionally, several techniques are employed to show the existence of low-dimensional chaos and below the results of the determination of the dimensions of the phase-state diagram are given:

1. Using the AMI method, the delay time, is estimated for the data as the intercept with the x-axis of the curves by plotting the values of the AMI evaluated by the TISEAN package (Hegger et al., 1999) against delay times progressively increased from 1 to 100. The value of delay time is calculated as the first (local) minimum in the variation of AMI against varying delay time from 1 to 100 day. The results are shown in Figure (9.a), signifying a well-defined first minimum at delay time of 94 day. The delay time is then used in the determination of the sufficient embedding dimension using the percentage of false nearest neighbours for the time series. Figure (9.b) shows the results of the false nearest neighbours method for embedding dimension m, by allowing it to vary from 1 to 40 and hence its value is 28.

2. The presence of chaotic signals in the data is further confirmed by the correlation dimension method. Figure (10.a) shows the relationship between correlation function C(r) and radius r (i.e. lnC(r)versus ln(r)) for increasing m, whereas Figure (10.b) shows therelationship between the correlation dimension valuesD_2(m) and the embedding dimension values m. It can be seen fromFigure (10.b) that the value of correlation exponent increases with the embedding dimension up to a certain value and then saturates beyond it. The saturation of the correlation exponent is an indication of the existence of deterministic dynamics. The saturated correlation dimension is 3.5, (D_2=3.5). The value of correlation dimension also suggests the possible presence of chaotic behaviour in the dataset. The nearest integer above the correlation dimension value ($D2$=4) is taken as the minimum dimension of the phase space.

3. Local prediction algorithm is used to predict suspended sediment time series. The procedure involves varying the value of the embedding dimension in a range, say 3-8, and estimating the CC and RMSE. The embedding function with the highest coefficient of correlation is selected as the solution. These are given in Table 8 for Mississippi River basin for the dataset with daily time interval, as well as a selection of other time steps. It shows that the best predictions are achieved when the embedding dimension is m=3 produce the best results.

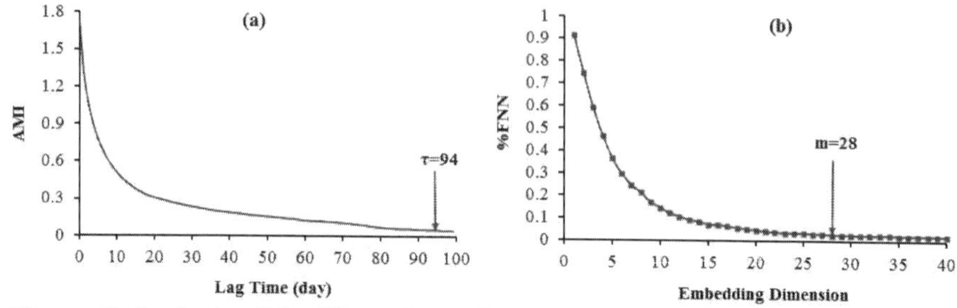

Figure 9. Analysis of the Phase-Space Diagram of Suspended Sediment Data in the Mississippi River basin; (9.a): Average Mutual Information; (9.b) Percentage of false nearest neighbours

Table 8. Local Prediction Using Different Embedding Dimension for the Mississippi River Dataset

m	CC	RMSE
3	**0.988**	**4.00E4**
4	0.988	4.10E4
5	0.986	4.30E4
6	0.985	4.60E4
7	0.986	4.40E4
8	0.987	4.20E4

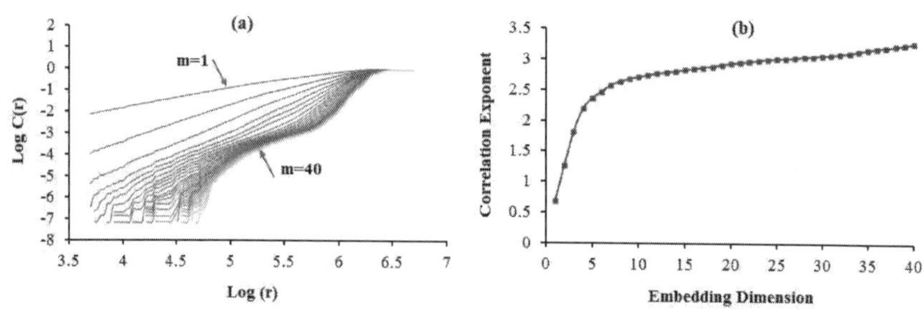

Figure 10. Correlation Dimension Method to Identify the Presence of Chaos Signal in the Dataset; (10.a): Convergence of logC(r) versus log(r); (10.b): saturation of correlation dimension D2(m) with embedding dimension m – this signifies chaotic signals in the Dataset 5. Inter-comparison of the models and discussion of results

Table 9 summarises the performance and main features of each and all of the modelling strategies. The results presented so far confirms the experience that the traditional SRC model performs poorly and may only be used for rough-and-ready assessments. However, the results by the GEP model show that considerable improvements are likely by using it. This section also analyses the relative performance of the various modelling strategies. An overall visual comparison of all the results is presented in Figure 11, according to which GEP, ANN, MLR and local prediction models perform remarkably well and similar to one another.

Table 9. Qualitative Overview of the Performances of Various Modelling Strategies

Model	Performance	Model Structure	Outcome	Comments
SRC	Poor	Model 1	Eq. (3)	For rough-and-ready estimates
GEP	Good	Model 4	Eq. (4.e)	
ANN	Good	Model 4	→	The model is bounded to software
MLR	Good	Model 2	Eq. (6)	
Chaos	Good	Model 0	→	Needs expertise to implement

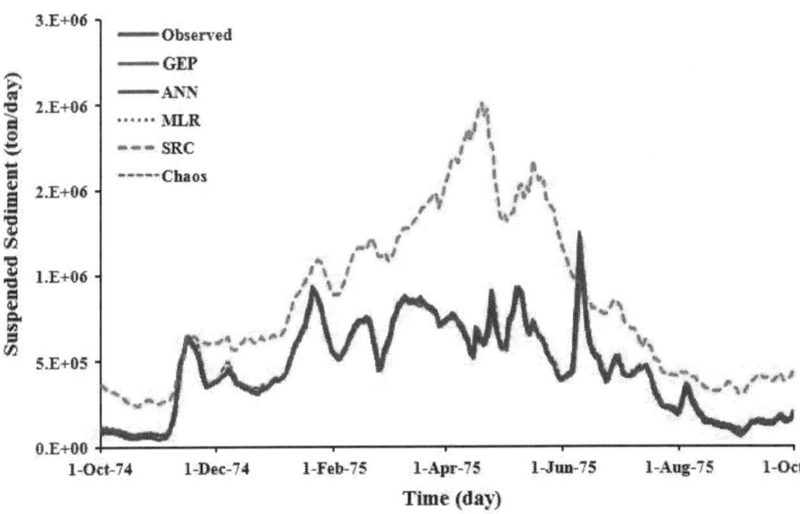

Figure 11. Model Predictions for Suspended Sediment – Performances of GP, ANN, MLR, Chaos (closest to observed), and SRC (poor)

Scatter diagrams are also a measure of performance. These are presented in Figures 12, which provides a quantitative basis that (i) SRC performs poorly and (ii) there is little to choose between the other models, although the performance of ANN stands out.

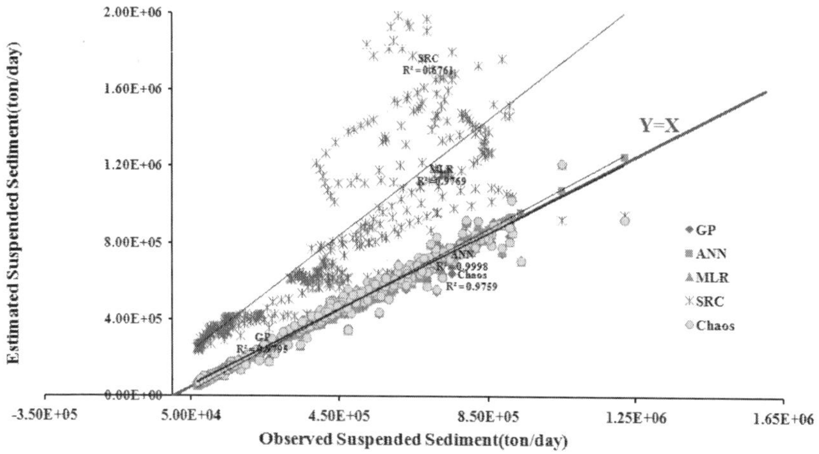

Figure 12. Scatter between Modelled and Observed Suspended Sediment Load

The relative performances of GEP, ANN, MLR and local prediction models are not still visible fromFigure 12 and therefore attention is focused on the differences between the GEP and ANN models with respect to their corresponding observed values. Figures 13 shows the respective results for both the GEP and ANN models and that of ANN is remarkable, as the differences are nearly zero. It may be reported that those of local prediction model and MLR are very close to that of GEP.

Due to the importance of the volume of transported sediment, the total predicted values are also compared with that of the observed values for the testing period and the results are presented in Table 10. The table show that the traditional SRC model is in error by as much as nearly 50% but the other models perform well, among which the error in the performance of ANN is the lowest. It is also noted that, despite the good performance of ANN models, it is not transferrable, like the GEP models. The implementation of both ANN and deterministic chaos models require considerable expertise.

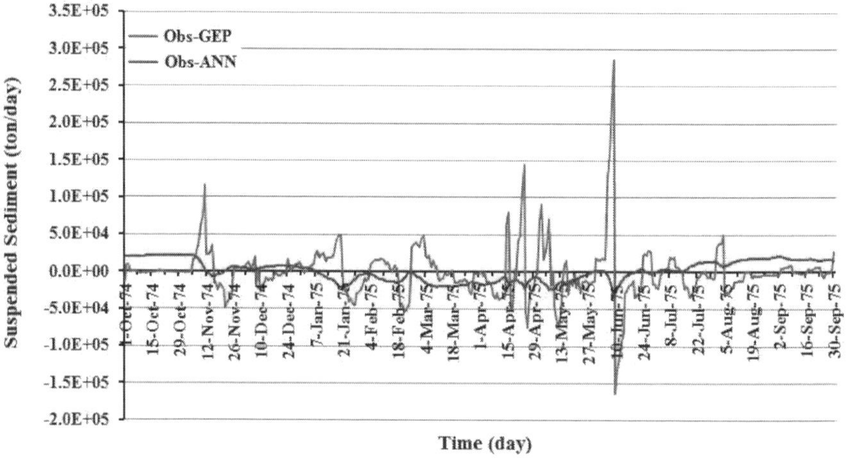

Figure 13. Performances of the ANN and GEP Models – y-ordinates: observed – modelled values

Table 10. Total Volume of Suspended Sediment Predicted by each of the Models at Gauging Station for the Mississippi River basin

Model	Actual Val. (ton/year)	Estimation Val. (ton/year)	Dif. Val. (%)
SRC	1.65E8	3.06E8	+46 %
GEP	1.65E8	1.65E8	- 0.4 %
ANN	1.65E8	1.64E8	- 0.3 %
MLR	1.65E8	1.66E8	+0.6 %
Chaos	1.65E8	1.66E8	+0.7 %

The chapter presents the performance of the GEP model, as a variation of evolutionary programming, to forecast suspended sediment load of the Mississippi River, the USA. GEP is just a modelling strategy, where any other relevant strategy is just as valid if its performance is satisfactory. The overall results show that the information contained in the observed data can be treated by the following modelling strategies:

1. **Evolutionary computing:** this produced a formula to forecast the future values in terms of recorded values of flows and suspended sediment. The results show that the strategy can be successful in identifying a number of different formulae.

2. **Emulation of the working of the brain:** this successfully fitted an inbuilt polynomial to the data. It performs better than the other tested models but is not readily transferrable as it resides in particular software applications.
3. **Regression analysis:** this produced a regression equation, according to which the future values would regress towards average recorded values, in spite of the presence of noise.
4. **Deterministic chaos:** this produced future values of suspended sediment load by identifying an attractor towards which the system performance would converge even when the internal system behaves erratically.

The only common feature in the above modelling strategies is their use of optimisation techniques. Otherwise, they are greatly different from one another but remarkably, they produce models fit for purpose and can explain the data. Undoubtedly, the data can be explained by many more sets of equations or by other possible strategies. This emphasises that models are just tools and the modelling task is to test the performance of the various models to add confidence to the results. Yet the poor performance of the traditional SRC underlines the fact that a good performance cannot be taken for granted.

A review of the data (in Section 3) shows that the overall contribution of the datapoints in the test period is average; its individual characteristics in terms of kurtosis shows that the annual hydrographs are less peaked and more flat but at the same time the suspended sediment load during the year was significantly high. Thus, the minimum values during this year were significantly above the average but persistent and though less dynamic. However, all the four modelling strategies coped well with these data peculiarities. If the data during the test period have a more pronounced feature not very common during the training period, the various local modelling strategies are likely to perform poorly in their own unique way and one of the greatest tasks of research in modelling should be investigations to understand these unique features and not to sweep them under the carpet.

A general view projected by the investigation in this chapter is that the performance of modelling techniques must not be the only basis of practical applications. Equal attention must also be paid to the quality of the data used. If the data suffers from inherent uncertainties, no good model will compensate for the inherent shortfalls.

6. CONCLUSION

This chapter presents an investigation of the performance of the Gene Expression Programming (GEP) models of suspended sediment load of the Mississippi River, the USA. The study employs the Mississippi River data spanning 26 years involving both flows and suspended sediment load, of which the first 25 years of the data is used for training and the remaining for the prediction of one year into the future. This investigation concurs with the past findings that the performance of sediment rating curve, an empirical technique used widely in practice, can lead to gross errors. This alone underlines the value of other modelling techniques capable of producing reliable results with less than 1% of errors.

The chapter promotes a pluralist culture of modelling and although presents the GEP model as the focus, it also presents the application of other techniques to model the same data. The other models comprise: artificial neural networks, multi-linear regression analysis and deterministic chaos. The chapter outlines the modelling strategy underlying each of these techniques and the results show in spite of their differences they produce similar results inflicting less 1% of errors. The lowest errors are associated with the artificial neural networks for this set of data but each of these techniques should be considered as reliable. The volume of sediment load is an important management parameter and the error associated with each model was estimated for each model. The results show that the traditional SRC model suffers from gross errors by as much as 50% but the other tested models perform well, among which the error in the performance of ANN is the lowest. ANN is noted for its good performance but with some drawback that these models are not transferrable, like the GEP models. It is noted that the implementation of ANN requires an ANN-platform for further modelling and deterministic chaos models require considerable expertise.

7. APPENDIX

Symbols

SRC	**Sediment Rating Curve**	
MLR	Multi Linear Regression	
Q_t	Discharge Series	
S_t	Sediment Series	
MLR	X_i	Term of Various Model
	a_i	Values Called Regression
Chaos	T	Delay Time
	$C_m(r)$	Fraction of states
	H	Heaviside Step
	N	Number of Points
	D_2	Correlation Exponent
	Y_j	Vectors of Dimension
	M	Dimensional phase Step
	A	Jacobean Matrix
	$x(t)$	different neighbors
	R	Radius Spherical
	$C(r)$	Correlation Function

Appendix I

Table 11 Defaults Values Employed in Implementing GEP and ANN Models

Table 11. Default Parameter Values Used by the Model

GP		ANN	
Training parameters	**Values**	**Training parameters**	**Values**
Crossover rate	0.1	Goal	Mean Square Error
Mutation rate	0.044	Epochs	10 - 100
Inversion	0.1	Training algorithm	Trainlm
IS Transposition	0.1		
RIS Transposition	0.1		
1-point Recombination	0.3		
2-point Recombination	0.3		
Gene Recombination	0.1		
Gene Transposition	0.1		
Population (Chromosome) size	30		
Head Size	7		
Number of Genes	3		
Linking Function	Addition		
Random Numerical Constants	Yes		
Number of generation	1000		
Arithmetic functions	(4.a)-(4.f)		
Fitness Function	RRSE: RRSE: Root Relative Squared Errors		

REFERENCES

1. A. Aytek, O. Kisi, 2008A genetic programming approach to suspended sediment modeling,J. Hydrol., 351288298
2. H. K. Cigizoglu, O. Kisi, 2006Methods to improve the neural network performance in suspended sediment estimationJ. of Hydrology, 317221238
3. H. K. Cigizoglu, 2004Estimation and forecasting of daily suspended sediment data by multi layer perceptronsAdvances in Water Resources27185195
4. Cohn TA, Caulder DL, Gilroy EJ, Zynjuk LD, Summers RM.1992The validity of a simple statistical model for estimating fluvial constituent loads: An empirical study involving nutrient loads entering Chesapeake BayWater Resources Research28923532363
5. D. J. Farmer, J. J. Sidorowich, 1987aPredicting chaotic time seriesPhys. Rev. Lett. 59845848
6. J. D. Farmer, J. J. Sidorowich, 1987bExploiting chaos to predict the future and reduce noiseIn: Lee, Y.C. (Ed.), Evolution, Learning and Cognition. World Scientific, River Edge, NJ, 277330
7. Ferguson RI.1986River loads underestimated by rating curvesWater Resources Research2217476
8. C. Ferreira, 2001aGene expression programming in problem solving. In: 6th Online World Conference on Soft computing in Industrial Applications (invited tutorial)
9. C. Ferreira, 2001bGene expression programming: a new adaptive algorithm for solving problemsComplex Syst 13287129
10. A. M. Fraser, H. L. Swinney, 1986Independent coordinates for strange attractors from mutual informationPhysical Review A1134 EOF1140 EOF
11. Khatibi. R. Ghorbani, A. Aytek, O. Makarynskyy, J. Shiri, 2010Sea water level forecasting using genetic programming and comparing the performance with artificial neural networksJ Comput Geosci 365620627
12. Glysson GD.1987Sediment transport curves. US Geological Survey Open File Report 87218

13. P. Grassberger, I. Procaccia, 1983Characterization of strange attractorsPhysical review letters, 505

14. R. Hegger, H. Kantz, T. Schreiber, 1999Practical implementation of nonlinear time series methods: The TISEAN packageChaos. 9413435

15. K. Itoh, 1995A method for predicting chaotic time-series with outliersElectron. Commun. Jpn. 78 (5), 44 EOF

16. S. K. Jain, 2001Development of integrated sediment rating curves using ANNsJ. Hydraul. Eng ASCE 127(1), 30 EOF37 EOF

17. M. Kennel, R. Brown, H. D. I. Abarbanel, 1992Determining embedding dimension for phase- space reconstruction using a geometrical construction. Phys Rev A.45340311

18. R. Khatibi, 2011Evolutionary Systemic Modelling for Flood Risk Management Practices," Journal of Hydrology 4011-23652

19. O. Kisi, 2004bMulti-layer perceptrons with Levenberg-Marquardt optimization algorithm for suspended sediment concentration prediction and estimation. Hydrol. Sci. J. 49(6), 1025-1040.

20. O. Kisi, 2005Daily river flow forecasting using artificial neural networks and auto regressive models", Turkish J. Eng. Env. Sci. 29

21. O. Kisi, 2005bSuspended sediment estimation using neuro-fuzzy and neural network approachesHydrol. Sci. J., 50(4), 683 EOF696 EOF

22. Koza JR1992Genetic programming: on the programming of computers by means of natural selection.MIT, Cambridge

23. Miller CR.1951Analysis of flow-duration, sediment-rating curve method of computing sediment yieldUS Bureau of Reclamation Report: Denver, Colorado.

24. A. Porporato, L. Ridolfi, 1997Nonlinear analysis of river flow time sequencesWater Resources Research1353 EOF1367 EOF

25. D. E. Rumelhart, J. L. . Mc Clelland, Eds., (1986), 1986Parallel Distributed Processing". Explorations in the Microstructure of CognitionMIT Press, Cambridge

26. B. Sivakumar, 2002A phase-space reconstruction approach to prediction of suspended sediment concentration in riversJournal of Hydrology149 EOF

27. B. Sivakumar, A. W. Jayawardena, 2002An investigation of the presence of lowdimensional chaotic behavior in the sediment transport phenomenon, Hydrological Sciences Journal, 47(3), 405-416.

28. B. Sivakumar, A. W. Jayawardena, 2003Sediment transport phenomenon in rivers: An alternative perspectiveEnvironmental Modeling and Software, in press.

29. B. Sivakumar, W. Wallender, 2005Predictability of river flow and suspended sediment transport in the Mississippi River basin: a non-linear deterministic approachJ. Earth Surf. Process. Landforms 30665677

30. F. Takens, 1981Detecting strange attractors in turbulence, in Dynamical Systems and Turbulence, Lecture Notes in Mathematics 898, D. A. Rand and L. S. Young (eds.), 366381Springer-Verlag, Berlin.

31. G. Tayfur, V. Guldal, 2006Artificial neural networks for estimating daily total suspended sediment in natural streamsNordic Hydrology376979

32. G. Tayfur, 2002Artificial neural networks for sheet sediment transportHydrol. Sci. J. 47(6), 879 EOF892 EOF

33. J. Theiler, 1986Spurious dimension from correlation algorithms applied to limited time series data.Phys Rev A. 34. 24272432

34. Thomas RB.1988Monitoring baseline suspended sediment in forested basins: The effects of sampling of suspended sediment rating curvesHydrological Sciences Journal335499514

35. K. Ustoorikar, M. C. Deo, 2008Filling up gaps in wave data with genetic programmingMarine Structures21177195

36. Wilks DS.1991Representing serial correlation of meteorological events and forecasts in dynamic decision-analytic models. Monthly Weather Rev 11916401662

37. Yu-Min Wang, Seydou Traore and Tienfuan Kerh2008Monitoring Event-Based Suspended Sediment Concentration by Artificial Neural Network Models" WSEAS TRANSACTIONS on COMPUTERS, 57May 2008

38. D. E. Walling, 1977Limitations of the rating curve technique for estimating suspended sediment loads, with particular reference to British rivers. In: Erosion and solid matter transport in inland waters (Proceedings of the Paris symposium, (July, 1977), IAHS Publ., 1223438

9

CHAPTER

THE USAGE OF GENETIC METHODS FOR PREDICTION OF FABRIC POROSITY

Polona Dobnik Dubrovski[1] and Miran Brezočnik[2]

[1] *Department of Textile Materials and Design, University of Maribor, Faculty of Mechanical Engineering, Slovenia*

[2] *Department of Mechanical Engineering, University of Maribor, Faculty of Mechanical Engineering, Slovenia*

1. INTRODUCTION

Advanced fabric production demands developing strategies with regard to new fabric constructions in which sample-production is reduced to a minimum. It is clear that a new fabric construction should have the desired end-usage properties pre-specified as project demands. Achieving such a demand is a complex task based on our knowledge of the relations between the fabric constructional parameters and the predetermined fabric end-usage properties that fit the desired quality. Individual fabric properties are difficult to predict when confronting the various construction parameters, which can be separated into the following categories: raw materials, fabric structure, design, and manufacturing parameters.

Many attempts have been made to develop predictive models for fabric properties with different modelling tools. There are essentially two types of modelling tools: deterministic (mathematical models, empirical models, computer simulation models) and non-deterministic (models based on genetic methods, neural network models, models based on chaos theory and theory of soft logic), and each of them has its advantages and disadvantages [1].

Deterministic modelling tools present the heart of conventional science and have their basis in first principles, statistical techniques or computer simulations. Mathematical models offer a deep understanding of relations between constructional parameters and predetermined fabric property, but due some simplifying assumptions large prediction errors occur. Empirical models based on statistical techniques show a much better agreement with the real values but the problems with samples preparing, process repeatability, measurements errors and extrapolation occur. They usually refer to the one type of testing method of particular fabric property. The advantage of computer simulation models is their ability to capture the randomness inherent in fabric structure so the predicted values are very near the real ones, but on the other hand they require numerous fabric samples data. The problem with extrapolation still remains. In general, when deterministic modelling is used, the obtained models are the results of strict mathematical rules and/or the models are set in advance. In this case the goal is to discover merely a set of numerical coefficients for a model whose form has been pre-specified. However, nowadays more and more processes and systems are modelled and optimized by the use of non-deterministic approaches. This is due to the high degree of complexity of the systems, and consequently, inability to study them successfully by the use of conventional methods only. In non-deterministic modelling of systems, no precise and strict mathematical rules are used [2, 3, 4, 5, 6, 7]. For example, in genetic programming, no assumptions about the form, size, and complexity of models are made in advance. They are left to the stochastic, self-organized, intelligent, and non-centralized evolutionary processes [1, 8].

Fabrics are porous materials having different porous structures as the consequence of different manufacturing techniques needed to interlace the fundamental structural elements, e.g. fibres, yarns or layers, into fibrous assembly. Fabric porosity strongly determines important physical, mechanical, sorptive, chemical, and thermal properties of the fabrics such as mechanical strength, thermal resistance, permeability (windproofness, breathability), absorption and adsorption properties (wicking, wetting), translucence, soiling propensity, UV light penetration, sound absorption ability, etc. [9, 10]. Knowledge about the fabric's porous structure is, therefore, an important step when characterising fabrics, in order to predict their behaviour under different end-usage conditions regarding a product. Hence, if porosity is estimated or predicted then when developing a new product the desired porosity parameters can be set in advance on the basis of selecting those fabric constructional factors that have an effect on porosity and, in this way sample production trials could be reduced.

This chapter gives some basic information about the porosity, porosity parameters of woven and nonwoven fabrics, and the results of the studies dealing with the prediction of porosity parameters of two types of fabrics, e.g. woven fabrics made from the 100% cotton staple yarns and needle-punched nonwovens made from the mixture of viscose/polyester fibres, using nondeterministic modelling tools, e.g. genetic programming (GP) and genetic algorithms (GA), respectively.

2. POROSITY AND POROSITY PARAMETERS

Flat textile materials, e.g. fabrics, are porous materials which allow the transmission of energy and substances and are therefore interesting materials for different applications. In general, they are used for clothing, interior and wide range of technical applications. Fabric as porous barrier between the human body an environment should support heat and water vapour exchange between the body and environment in order to keep the body temperature within the homeostasis range. Besides thermo-physiological protection, fabrics also play an important role by heat protection due to the flames or convection heat, contact heat, radiant heat as well as due to the sparks and drops of molten metal, hot gases and vapours [11]. Fabrics protect users against micro-organisms, pesticides, chemicals, hazardous particles and radiations (radioactive particles, micro-meteorites, X-rays, micro-waves, UV radiation, etc.). They act very important role also by environmental protection as filters for air and water filtrations, sound absorption and isolation materials against noise pollution, adsorption materials for hazardous gas pollution, etc. [10, 12, 13]. By all mentioned applications dedicated to absorption, desorption, filtration, drainage, vapours transmission, etc., the essential constructional parameter that influences fabric efficiency to protect human or environment is porosity. The fabric in a dry state is a two-phase media which consists of the fibrous material – solid component and void spaces containing air – gas (void) component. The porosity of a material is one of the physical properties of the material and describes the fraction of void space in the material. The porosity (or void volume fraction) is expressed as coefficient ranging between 0 and 1 or as percentage ranging between 0% and 100% (by multiplying the coefficient by 100). Mathematically, the porosity is defined as the ratio of the total void space volume to the total (or bulk) body volume [14, 15]:

$$\varepsilon = \frac{V_v}{V} \tag{1}$$

where, ε is the porosity expressed as coefficient, V_v is the volume of the total void space in cm^3, and V is the total or bulk body volume in cm^3. The total volume of the body consists of the volumes of the solid and void components as follows:

$$V = V_v + V_s \tag{2}$$

where, V is the total volume of the body in cm^3, V_v is the volume of void component in cm^3, and V_s is the volume of solid component in cm^3. If the volume of void component is exposed from the Equation 2, the Equation 1 can be further written as follows:

$$\varepsilon = \frac{V_v}{V} = \frac{V - V_s}{V} = 1 - \frac{V_s}{V} = 1 - \beta \tag{3}$$

$$\beta = \frac{V_s}{V} \tag{4}$$

where, β is the fulfilment (or solid volume fraction) which describes the fraction of solid component volume in the material expressed as coefficient ranging between 0 and 1 or as percentage. If we take into account the common equation for material density (Equation 5), and assume that the mass of the material is actually the mass of solid component (m_s=m_b), the Equation 3 could be further written in the form of Equation 6:

$$\rho = \frac{m}{V} \tag{5}$$

$$\varepsilon = 1 - \frac{V_s}{V} = 1 - \frac{m_s \rho_b}{\rho_s m_b} = 1 - \frac{\rho_b}{\rho_s} \quad (6)$$

where, ε is the porosity expressed as coefficient, V_s is the volume of solid component in cm^3, V is the volume of the body (or bulk volume) in cm^3, m_s is the mass of solid component in g, m_b is the mass of the body (or bulk mass) in g, ρ_b is the bulk density in g/cm^3, and ρ_s is the density of solid component in g/cm^3.

In this way exactly defined porosity of the material is useful parameter, only, when materials with the same porous structure are compared, and gives an indication which material possesses more void space in the bulk volume. It does not give any information about the porous structure of the material, so it is an insufficient parameter for describing fibre assembly characteristics [16]. Namely, the materials with the same porosity could have very different porous structure and consequently, in the case of fabrics, different protection, filtration, sound absorption, etc., properties; so the need to define porous structure and some other porosity parameters is essential. From the theoretical point of view, the porosity parameters could be easily determined on the basis of an ideal geometrical model of the material porous structure. The simpler models consider that all pores, whatever their shape, are the same and regularly arranged in a fibre assembly [16, 17]. Ideal models are based also on some other simplifying assumptions depending on the fibre assembly type. Porosity parameters calculated on the basis of ideal models of porous structures are usually not in a good correlation with the real porosity parameters. Real porous media generally have rather complex structures that are relatively difficult to define. But the advantage of ideal geometric models of porous structures is the possibility to understand the influence of porous structure on some end-usage properties of the material, which is crucial by a new product planning.

The fundamental building elements of the material porous structure are pores (also capillaries, channels, holes, free volume) [15, 18]. Pores are void spaces within the material which are separated between each other, and are classified [19, 20]:

1. according to the position in the material into:
    a. inter-pores, e.g. pores which lie between the structural elements of the material,
    b. intra-pores, e.g. pores which lie within the structural element of the material;
2. according to the pore width (the shortest pore diameter) into:
    a. macropores whose pore-width is greater than 50 nm,
    b. mesopores whose pore-width lies in the range between 2 and 50 nm, and
    c. micropores with the pore-width lower than 2 nm;
3. according to the fluid accessibility into (Figure 1):
    a. closed pores being inaccessible for fluid flow or surroundings,
    b. blind pores which are accessible for fluid but terminate inside the material and prevent fluid flow, and
    c. open (or through) pores which are open to external surface and permit fluid flow;

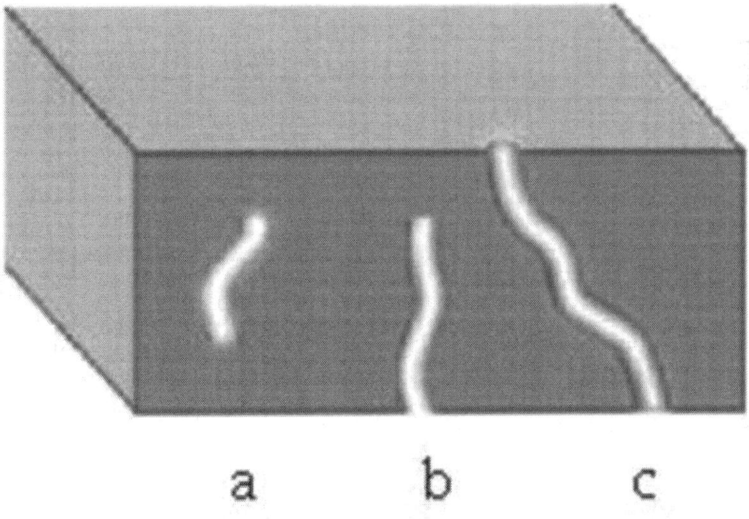

Figure 1. Types of pores according to the fluid accessibility

1. according to the pore shape into (Figure 2):
    a. cylindrical pores,
    b. slit-shape pores,
    c. cone-shape pores, and
    d. ink bottle pores;

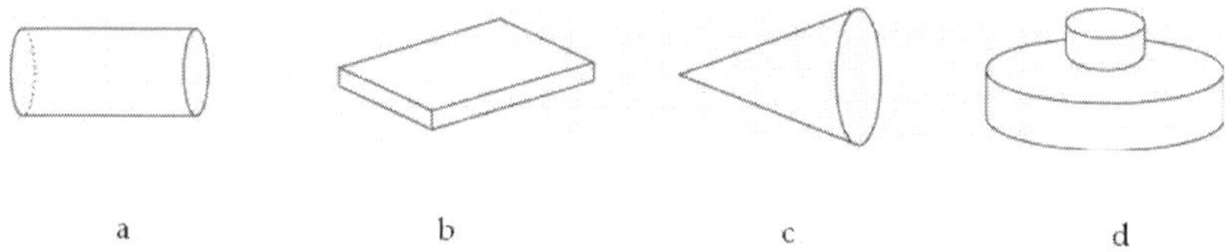

Figure 2. Types of pores according to the pore shape [19]

1. according to the geometry of pore-cross section into (Figure 3):
    a. pores with geometrically regular cross-sectional shape and
    b. pores with geometrically irregular cross-sectional shape,

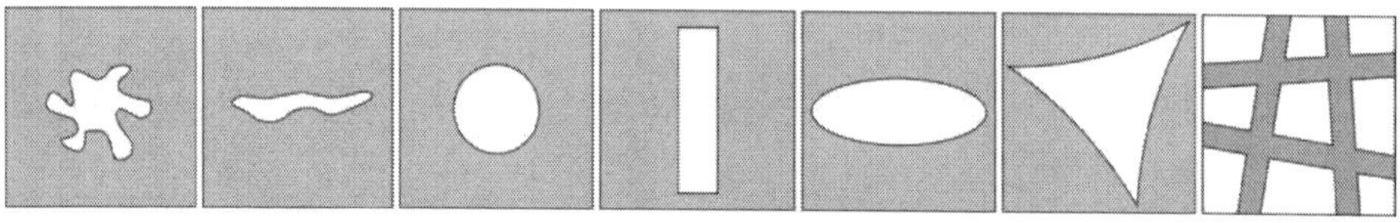

Figure 3. Different shapes of pore cross-sections [20]

1. according to the uniformity of pore cross-section over the pore length into (Figure 4):
    a. pores with a permanent cross-section,
    b. pores with a different cross-sections and for which different diameters are defined (the most constricted, the largest, the mean pore diameters).

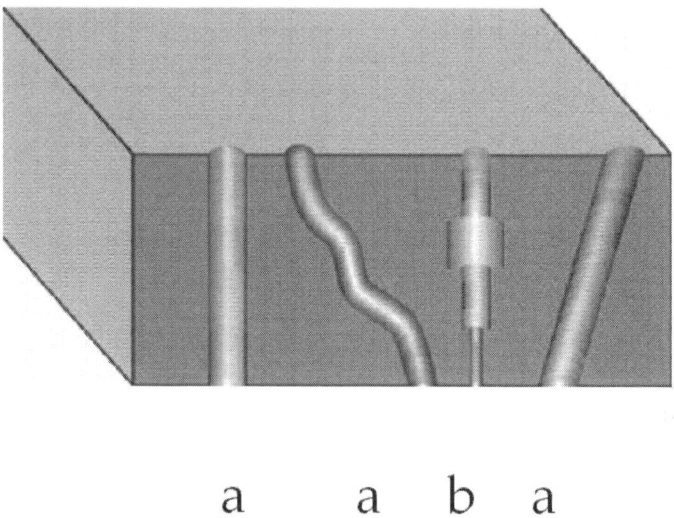

Figure 4. Pores with permanent (a) and non-permanent (b) cross-sections over their length

Four groups of pore descriptors, e.g. size, shape, orientation, and placement, are defined as important parameters [21]. Pores can be mathematically assessed on the basis of known model of pores geometry and constructional parameters of the material with the following parameters: the number of pores, pore size, pore volume, pore surface area, pore length, etc. On the basis of an ideal geometrical model of porous structure, the pore size distribution which is also an important parameter of material porous structure can not assessed while the pores in geometrical model are usually assumed to be the same sizes. Such situation rarely occurs in the real fabrics. The further considerations of ideal geometrical models of material porous structures and porosity parameters will be focused on different types of fabrics.

Fabrics are flat textile materials which are produced by different manufacturing techniques using different fibrous forms of input material (or structural element), and consequently having different porous structures. Following basic types of fabrics are known (Figure 5):

- woven fabrics which are made by interlacing vertical warp and horizontal weft yarns at right angles to each other,
- knitted fabrics which are made by forming the yarn into loops and their interlacing in vertical (warp-knitted fabrics) or horizontal (weft-knitted fabrics) direction,
- nonwoven fabrics which are produced from the staple fibres, filaments or yarns by different web-forming, bonding and finishing techniques.

Figure 5. D schematic presentations of woven-, knitted-, and nonwoven (made from staple fibres) fabrics

While this chapter is focused on the genetic methods in order to predict porosity of woven and nonwoven fabrics, only those types of fabrics and their ideal geometric models of porous structure will be presented.

2.1. Woven Fabric's Ideal Geometric Model of Porous Structure

When a woven fabric is treated as a three dimensional formation, different types of pores are detected [22, 23, 24]: 1. inter-pores, e.g. the pores which are situated between warp and weft yarns (macropores, interyarn pores) and pores which are situated between fibres in the yarns (mesopores, interfiber/intrayarn pores), 2. intra-pores, e.g. the pores which are situated in the fibres (micropores, intrafiber pores). The structure and dimensions of the inter- or intrayarn pores are strongly affected by the yarn structure and the density of yarns in the woven structure [22]. As fibrous materials, woven fabrics have, with regard to knitted fabrics or nonwovens, the most exactly determined an ideal geometrical model of a macro-porous structure in the form of a tube-like system, where each macropore has a cylindrical shape with a permanent cross-section over all its length (Figure 6) [25]. Because the warp density is usually greater than the weft density, the elliptical shape of the pore cross-section is used to represent the situation in Figure 6. Macropores are opened to the external surface and have the same cross-section area. They are separated by warp or weft yarns, and are uniformly distributed over the woven fabric area.

The primary constructional parameters of woven fabrics which alter the porous structure are:

- yarn fineness, e.g. the mass of 1000 meter of yarn from which the yarn diameter can be calculated,
- type of weave, e.g. the manner how the yarns are interlaced. It has an effect on the pore size as well as on the shape of pore cross-section [26],
- the number of yarns in length unit (warp and weft densities), which directly alters the pore size.

When fibre properties (fibre density, dimension, and shape) are different, two woven fabrics with similar woven structures and geometrical configurations can have distinctly different porosity [22].

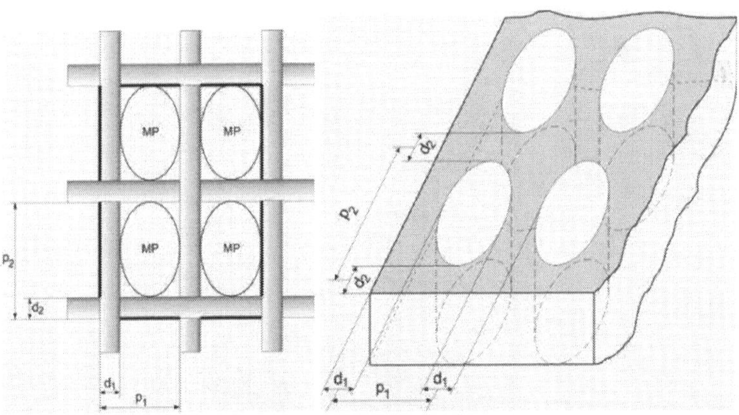

Figure 6. and 3D presentations of an ideal model of the porous structure of a woven fabric [27, 28] (d – yarn thickness, p – yarn spacing, MP - macropore; 1, 2 indicates warp and weft yarns, respectively)

To compare woven fabrics with porosity, the following porosity parameters can be calculated on the basis of the woven fabric primary constructional parameters and the ideal model of porous structure in the form of a tube-like system:

- (total) porosity by using Equation 6 where the bulk density of the material is actually the woven fabric density and the density of solid component is the yarn density. If the fibre volume fraction (yarn packing factor) is exposed from the Equation 7 which represents the yarn diameter calculation, and then inserted in Equation 8 by assuming Equation 9 for woven fabric density at the same time, the porosity of woven fabrics can be then written in the form of Equation 10:

$$d = \sqrt{\frac{4T}{10^5 \pi \cdot \rho_{yarn}}} = \sqrt{\frac{4T}{1000 \cdot \pi \cdot \rho_{fib} \cdot \beta_{fib}}} \tag{7}$$

$$\rho_{yarn} = \rho_{fib} \cdot \beta_{fib} \tag{8}$$

$$\rho_{fab} = \frac{m}{D \cdot 1000} \tag{9}$$

$$\varepsilon = 1 - \frac{\rho_b}{\rho_s} = 1 - \frac{\rho_{fab}}{\rho_{yarn}} = 1 - \frac{100 \cdot m \cdot d^2 \cdot \pi}{D \cdot 4 \cdot T} \tag{10}$$

where, d is the yarn diameter in cm, T is the yarn fineness in tex, ρ_{yarn} is the yarn bulk density in g/cm^3, ρ_{fib} is the fibre density in g/cm^3, β_{fib} is the fibre volume fraction (or yarn packing factor), ρ_{fab} is the woven fabric bulk density in g/cm^3, m is the woven fabric mass per unit area in g/m^2, D is the woven fabric thickness in mm, ρ_b is the body bulk density in g/cm^3, and ρ_s is the density of solid component in g/cm^3. It is worth to mention that in this way defined porosity refers to all types of pores regarding their position in the woven fabric, e.g. inter- and intra-pores;

- area of pore cross-section which refers only on macropores in a woven fabric. The ideal model of woven fabric porous structure is based on the assumption that macropores have cylindrical shape with circular cross-section. In real woven fabrics, the macropore cross-section shape is more likely to be irregular rather regular (Figure 7) [26]. The shape of pore cross-section and consequently the area of pore cross-section depend on the type of yarns used. Woven fabrics made from filament yarns have pure macropores with rectangular cross-sections, whilst woven fabrics made from staple yarns have a small percentage of pure macropores, some of partly latticed macropores as well as fully latticed macropores (as the consequence of the phenomenon of latticed pores) with mostly irregular cross-sections. The area of pore cross-section also depends on the phenomenon of changing the position of warp threads according to the longitudinal fabric axis and the phenomenon of thread spacing irregularity [28]. For the theoretical calculations of the macropore cross-section area three types of regular pore cross-section shapes are taken into account, e.g. circular (Equation 11), rectangular (Equation 12) and elliptical (Equation 13) as follows:

$$A_{p/circular} = \frac{\pi}{16}(p_1 + p_2 - d_1 - d_2)^2 = \frac{\pi}{16}\left(\frac{10}{g_1} + \frac{10}{g_2} - d_1 - d_2\right)^2 \quad (11)$$

$$A_{p/rec\tan gular} = (p_1 - d_1)\cdot(p_2 - d_2) = \left(\frac{10}{g_1} - d_1\right)\cdot\left(\frac{10}{g_2} - d_2\right) \quad (12)$$

$$A_{p/elliptical} = \frac{\pi}{4}\cdot(p_1 - d_1)\cdot(p_2 - d_2) = \frac{\pi}{4}\left(\frac{10}{g_1} - d_1\right)\cdot\left(\frac{10}{g_2} - d_2\right) \quad (13)$$

where, A_p is the area of macropore cross-section in mm^2, p is the yarn spacing in mm, d is the yarn diameter in mm, g is the number of yarns per unit length in threads/cm, and subscripts 1 and 2 indicate warp and weft yarns, respectively;

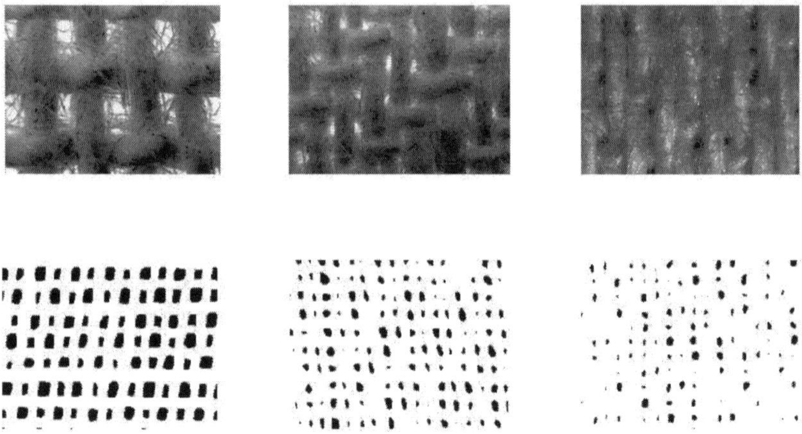

plain, 21/16 threads/cm   twill, 27/22 threads/cm   satin, 30/24 threads/cm

Figure 7. Real and binary images of the pore cross-section shape and the number of pores in real woven fabrics (magnification of binary images: 20 x, magnification of real images: 80 x, yarn fineness: 36 tex, fabric relative density: 83 %)

- number of macropores in the area unit (pore density). It can be seen from Figure 7, that one macropore belongs to one warp yarn and one weft yarn, so the number of macropores can be calculated on the basis of warp and weft densities using Equation 14:

$$N_p = g_1 \cdot g_2 \tag{14}$$

where, N_p is the pore density in pores/cm^2, g_1 is the warp density in threads/cm, and g_2 is the weft density in threads/cm;

- open porosity (open area) which describes the fraction of macropore cross-section area in the area unit of woven fabric. If we assume elliptical macropore cross-section area (Figure 7), the open porosity is calculated as follows:

$$\varepsilon_{open} = \frac{A_p}{A_p + A_y} = \frac{\pi(p_1 - d_1) \cdot (p_2 - d_2)}{4 \cdot p_1 \cdot p_2} \tag{15}$$

where, ε_{open} is the open porosity, A_p is the macropore cross-section area in mm^2, A_y is the projection area of warp and weft yarns, which refers to one macropore in mm^2, p is the yarn spacing in mm, d is the yarn diameter in mm, and subscripts 1 and 2 indicate warp and weft yarns, respectively. Open porosity can be calculated also on the basis of cover factor (Equation 16) or pore density (Equation 17)[26, 29]:

$$\varepsilon_{open} = 1 - K = 1 - \left[\frac{\left(d_1 g_1 + d_2 g_2 - \left\{ \frac{d_1 d_2 g_1 g_2}{10} \right\} \right)}{10} \right] \tag{16}$$

$$\varepsilon_{open} = N_p \cdot A_p \tag{17}$$

where, ε_{open} is the open porosity, K is the woven fabric cover factor, d is the yarn diameter in mm, g is the warp/weft density in threads/cm, N_p is the pore density in pores/cm^2, A_p is the area of macropore cross-section in cm^2, and subscripts 1 and 2 indicate warp and weft yarns, respectively;

- equivalent macropore-diameter. If we assume that macropore has cylindrical shape, then the area of macropore cross-section is equal to the area of circle with radius r (Equation 18). Equivalent macropore diameter is the diameter of macropore with circular cross-section whose area is the same as the area of the macropore with irregular cross-section shape (Equation 19) [30].

$$A_{circle} = \pi \cdot r^2 = \frac{\pi \cdot d^2}{4} \tag{18}$$

$$d_e = \sqrt{\frac{4 \cdot A_p}{\pi}} \tag{19}$$

where, A_{circle} is the circular cross-section macropore area in mm^2, r is the macropore radius in mm, d is the macropore diameter in mm, d_e is the equivalent macropore diameter in mm, and A_p is the macropore cross-section area of macropore with irregular shape in mm^2;

- maximal an minimal macropore diameters which refer to the elliptical shape of macropore cross-section. In the case where warp density is greater than weft density the maximal diameter is equal to p_2-d_2, while minimal diameter is equal to p_1-d_1 (Figure 7);
- macroporosity which describes the portion of macropore volume in volume unit of woven fabric. In general, it is defined using Equation 20. In the case of the elliptical macropore cross-section shape, the macroporosity, defined with Equation 21, is the same as open porosity:

$$\varepsilon_{macro} = \frac{V_p}{V_p + V_y} = \frac{A_p \cdot D}{p_1 \cdot p_2 \cdot D} = \frac{A_p}{p_1 \cdot p_2} \quad (20)$$

$$\varepsilon_{macro} = \frac{V_p}{V_p + V_y} = \frac{\pi(p_1 - d_1) \cdot (p_2 - d_2) \cdot D}{4 \cdot p_1 \cdot p_2 \cdot D} = \frac{\pi(p_1 - d_1) \cdot (p_2 - d_2)}{4 \cdot p_1 \cdot p_2} = \varepsilon_{open}$$

(21)

where, ε_{macro} is the macroporosity, V_p is the macropore volume in cm^3, V_y is the volume of warp and weft yarns which refers to one macropore in cm^3, p is the yarn spacing in mm, d is the yarn diameter in mm, D is the woven fabric thickness in mm, A_p is the macropore area in mm^2, ε_{open} is the open porosity, and subscripts 1 and 2 indicate warp and weft yarns, respectively.

2.2. Nonwoven Fabric's Ideal Geometric Model of Porous Structure

The porous structure of nonwoven fabric is a result of nonwoven construction (the type and properties of fibres or yarns as input materials, fabric mass, fabric thickness, etc.) as well as technological phases, e.g. the type of web production, bonding methods and finishing treatments. According to several different methods to produce non-woven fabrics having consequently very different porous structure, the ideal geometric model of porous structure in the form of tube-like system is partially acceptable only by those nonwovens which are thin and translucence, e.g. light polymer–laid nonwovens and some thin spun-laced or heat-bonded nonwovens (Figure 8). Such model is based on the assumptions that fibres having the same diameter are distributed only in the direction of fabric plane and the distance between fibres and the length of individual fibres is much greater than the fibre diameter. Xu [21] found out that in most nonwoven fabrics, pore shape is approximately polygonal and that pores appear more circular when the fabric density increases. Pore orientation to some extent relates to fibre orientation. If pores are elongated and predominantly oriented in one direction, fibres are likely to be oriented in that direction. The variation in pore size is inherently high. Some regions may contain more pores than others or may have larger pores than those in other regions.

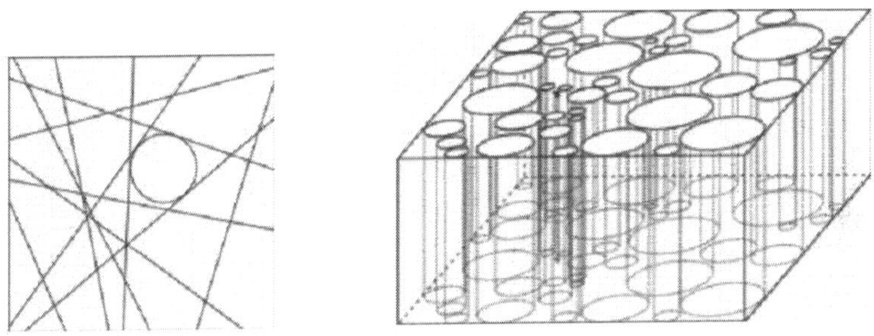

Figure 8. and 3D presentations of an ideal model of the porous structure of a nonwoven fabric (with detail to define opening diameter of pore by 2D presentation)

The primary constructional parameters of nonwoven fabrics which alter the porous structure are:

- fibre fineness, e.g. the mass of 1000 meter of fibre, from which the fibre diameter can be calculated,
- web mass per unit area and
- web thicknesses.

To compare nonwoven fabrics with porosity, the following porosity parameters can be calculated on the basis of the nonwoven fabric primary constructional parameters and the ideal model of porous structure in the form of a tube-like system:

- (total) porosity by using Equation 6 where the bulk density of the material is actually the nonwoven fabric density and the density of solid component is the fibre density. The nonwoven fabric density is calculated on the basis of primary nonwoven constructional parameters, e.g. fabric mass and thickness using Equation 9 where index fab in this case refers to the nonwoven fabric. Substituting Equation 9 into Equation 6, final Equation 22 of nonwoven porosity which refers to inter- (pores between fibres in nonwovens) and intra-pores (pores inside the fibres) is obtained:

$$\varepsilon = 1 - \frac{\rho_b}{\rho_s} = 1 - \frac{\rho_{fab}}{\rho_{fib}} = 1 - \frac{m_{fab}}{D_{fab} \cdot \rho_{fib} \cdot 1000} \tag{22}$$

where, ε is the nonwoven fabric porosity, ρ_b is the body bulk density in g/cm^3, ρ_s is the density of solid component in g/cm^3, ρ_{fab} is the nonwoven fabric density in g/cm^3, ρ_{fib} is the fibre density in g/cm^3, m_{fab} is the nonwoven fabric mass per unit area in g/m^2, and D_{fab} is the nonwoven fabric thickness in mm;

- opening diameter which is the diameter of the maximum circle that can fit in a pore (Figure 8). It is predicted on the basis of nonwoven fabric constructional parameters and refers to the heat-bonded nonwoven fabrics, as follows [17, 21]:

$$d_o = \frac{1}{\sqrt{C} \cdot L} - d_{fib} \tag{23}$$

$$C = \frac{D_{fab}}{d_{fib}} \tag{24}$$

$$L = \frac{8 \cdot m_{fab}}{\pi \cdot D_{fab} \cdot d_{fib} \cdot \rho_{fib}} \tag{25}$$

where, d_o is the opening diameter in μm, C is the thickness factor, L is the specific total length of fibres per nonwoven unit area in mm^{-1}, d_{fib} is the fibre diameter in μm, D_{fab} is the nonwoven thickness in mm, m_{fab} is the nonwoven fabric mass per unit area in g/m^2, and ρ_{fib} is the fibre density in g/cm^3;

- average area of pore cross-section which is for un-needled fabrics (e.g. fabrics made of layers of randomly distributed fibres) predicted using Equation 26 [17]:

$$A_p = \frac{\pi \cdot \varepsilon \cdot d_{fib}^2}{(1-\varepsilon)^2} \tag{26}$$

where, A_p is the average area of pore cross-section in mm^2, ε is the porosity, and d_{fib} is the fibre diameter in μm. On the basis of calculated average area of pore-cross-section, the equivalent pore diameter is then calculated using Equation 19.

Needle-punched nonwoven fabric is a sheet of fibres made by mechanical entanglement, penetrating barbed needles into a fibrous mat [31]. Needle-punched nonwovens represent the largest segment of filtration materials used as dust filters [32]. The geometrical model of three-dimensional needle-punched nonwoven fabric proposed by Mao & Rusell [33], is also known from the literature, and it is constructed on a two-dimensional fibre orientation within the fabric plane, with interconnecting fibres oriented in the z-direction (Figure 10). Such model relies on the following basic assumptions: 1. the fibres in the fabric have the same diameter, and a fraction of the fibres is distributed horizontally in the two-dimensional plane, the rest are aligned in the direction of the fabric thickness, 2. fibre distribution in both the fabric plane and the z-direction is homogeneous and uniform, 3. in each two-dimensional plane, the number of fibres oriented in each direction is not the same, but obeys the function of the fibre orientation distribution $\Omega(\alpha)$, where α is the fibre orientation angle, 4. the distance between fibres and the length of individual fibres is much greater than the fibre diameter. The basic porosity parameters which are based on the mentioned geometrical model of needle-punched nonwoven fabric are still difficult to define due to the fact that in each fabric planes fibres lie in different direction and in this way produce pores with different orientations, diameters, connectivity and accessibility to fluid flow (Figure 9). The only porosity parameters that are calculated from such model are:

- total porosity (Equation 22) and
- mean pore diameter which is deduced from the fibre radius and porosity according to the following relation proposed by White [34]:

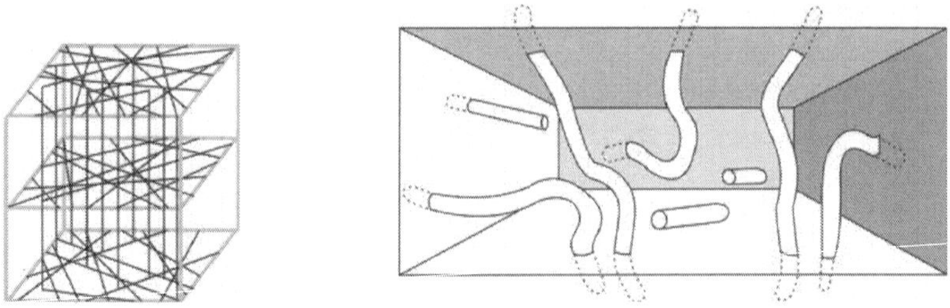

Figure 9. Geometrical models of needle-punched nonwoven fabric and porous structure [14, 34]

$$d_p = \frac{\varepsilon}{1-\varepsilon} \cdot \frac{d_{fib}}{2} \tag{27}$$

$$d_{fib} = 35.68\sqrt{\frac{T}{\rho_{fib}}} \tag{28}$$

where, d_p is the mean pore diameter in μm, ε is the nonwoven fabric porosity, d_{fib} is the fibre diameter in μm, T is the fibre linear density in tex, and ρ_{fib} is the fibre density in g/cm^3.

Three kinds of pores may be present in needle-punched nonwoven fabrics, namely, closed pores, open pores, and blind pores. The important pore structure characteristics of needle-punched nonwoven fabrics as filter media are the most constricted open pore diameter (smallest detected pore diameter), the largest pore diameter (bubble point pore diameter), and mean pore diameter (mean flow pore diameter) [35].

3. THE USAGE OF GENETIC PROGRAMMING TO PREDICT WOVEN FABRIC POROSITY PARAMETERS

Porosity parameters based on an ideal geometrical model of porous structure give woven fabric constructor some useful information about porosity by developing a new product, but they are not in a good agreement with the experimental values. In order to balance the difference between the theoretical and experimental values of porosity parameters, genetic programming was used to develop models for predicting the following macro-porosity parameters of woven fabric: the area of macro-pore cross-section, macro-pore density, open porosity, and equivalent macro-pore diameter. The genetic programming is a variant of evolutionary algorithm methods described in many sources (e.g., [2, 3, 4]). The basic information on the evolutionary algorithms is given at the beginning of the section 4. We implemented Koza's variant of genetic programming [2]. In our research, the independent input variables (the set of terminals) were: yarn fineness T (tex), weave value V, fabric tightness t (%) and denting D (ends/dent in the reed). The set of terminals also included random floating-point numbers between −10 and +10. Variegated reed denting was treated as an average value of treads, dented in the individual reed dent. The dependent output variables were: area of macro-pore cross-section Ap (10^{-3}mm^2), pore density Np (pores/cm^2), and equivalent macro-pore diameter (μm). For all modelling, the initially set of functions included the basic mathematical operations of addition, subtraction, multiplication, and division. In the case of modelling the area of macro-pore cross-section and pore density the initially set of functions also included a power function, whereas the set of functions for modelling of equivalent macro-pore diameter included an exponential function. We then used the genetic programming system to evolve appropriate models consist of above-mentioned sets of terminals and functions. Open porosity was calculated on the basis of predicted values of the area of macro-pore cross-section and macro-pore density and Equation 17. The equivalent macro-pore diameter was calculated on the basis of predicted values of the area of macro-pore cross-section using Equation 19. The fitness measure for modelling by genetic programming was exactly the same as defined byEquation 33 in section 4. The goal of the modelling was to find such a predictive model in a symbolic form, that Equation 33 would give as low an absolute deviation as possible.

The evolutionary parameters for modelling by genetic programming were: population size 2000, maximum number of generations to be run 400, probability of reproduction 0.1, probability of crossover 0.8, probability of mutation 0.1, minimum depth for initial random organisms 2, maximum depth for initial random organisms 6, maximum depth of mutation fragment 6, and maximum permissible depth of organisms after crossover 17. The generative method for the initial random population was *ramped half-and-half*. The method of selection was tournament selection with a group size of 7. For the purpose of this research 100 independent genetic programming runs were executed. Only the results of the best runs (i.e., the models with the smallest error between the measurements and predictions) are presented in the paper.

3.1. Materials and Porosity Measurements

Our experiments involved woven fabrics made from staple yarns with two restrictions: first, only fabrics made from 100% cotton yarns (made by a combing and carding procedure on a ring spinning machine) were used in this research; second, fabrics were measured in the grey state to eliminate the influence of finishing processes. We believe that it is very hard, perhaps even impossible, to include all woven fabrics types to predict individual macro-porosity parameters precisely enough, and so we focused our research on unfinished staple yarn cotton fabrics. We would like to show that genetic programming can be used to establish the many relations between woven fabric constructional parameters and particular fabric properties, and that the results are more useful for fabric engineering than ideal theoretical models. The cotton fabrics varied according to yarn fineness (14 tex, 25 tex, and 36 tex), weave type (weave value), fabric tightness (55% - 65%, 65% - 75%, 75% - 85%), and denting. The constructional parameters of woven fabric samples are collected in Table 1. They were woven on a Picanol weaving machine under the same technological conditions. The weave values of plain (0.904), twill (1.188), and satin (1.379) fabrics, as well as fabric tightness, were determined according to Kienbaum's setting theory [36].

We used an optical method to measure porosity parameters of woven fabrics, since it is the most accurate technique for macro-pores with diameters of more than 10 m. For each fabric specimen, we observed between 50 and 100 macro-pores using a Nikon SMZ-2T computer-aided stereomicroscope with special software. We measured the following macro-porosity parameters: area of macro-pore cross-section, pore density, and equivalent macro-pore diameters.

3.2. Predictive Models of Woven Fabric Porosity Parameters

Equations 29 and 30 present predictive models of the area of macro-pore cross-section A_p and macro-pore density N_p, respectively [37]. Here V is the weave factor, T is the yarn linear density in tex, t is the fabric tightness in %, and D is the denting in ends per reed dent. The open porosity and equivalent diameter are calculated using Equations 17 and 19, respectively, where for Ap and Np the predicted values are taken into account. Because the model of the area of macro-pore cross-section is more complex, the functions f_1, f_2,...f_{10} are not presented here but are written in the appendix. When calculating the values of models, the following rules have to be taken into account: the protected division function returns to 1 if denominator is 0; otherwise, it returns to the normal quotient. The protected power function raises the absolute value of the first argument to the power specified by its second argument.

By a comparison of both GA models (Equations 29 and 30) with the theoretical ones (Equations 11-13 and 14), the complexity of GA models is obvious and derives from the factors involved in the models. Namely, factors involved in GA models don't ignore the irregularity of macro-pores cross-section area as well as the number of pores, due to the phenomenon of latticed pores in the case of staple yarns (which depends on the type of weave – factor V and fabric tightness – factor t) and the phenomenon of thread spacing irregularity (factor D), as theoretical models do. Theoretical model for the macro-pore cross-section area assumes that all macro-pores in woven structure have the same cross-section area regardless the type of used yarns, type of weave, fabric tightness and denting, whilst the theoretical model for the pore density assumes no reduction of the number of pores.

Table 1. The constructional parameters of woven fabric samples

Ref.	Yarn linear density *T*, tex	Weave value *V*	Fabric tightness t, %	Denting D, ends/reed dent
1	14	0.904	62	2
2	14	0.904	70	2
3	14	0.904	84	2
4	14	1.188	62	3

5	14	1.188	70	3
6	14	1.188	80	3
7	14	1.379	59	5
8	14	1.379	69	5
9	14	1.379	79	5
10	25	0.904	62	2
11	25	0.904	73	2
12	25	0.904	83	2
13	25	1.188	63	2
14	25	1.188	73	2
15	25	1.188	84	2
16	25	1.379	60	2+3
17	25	1.379	70	2+3
18	25	1.379	81	2+3
19	36	0.904	62	1
20	36	0.904	71	1
21	36	0.904	83	1
22	36	1.188	63	2

23	36	1.188	72	2
24	36	1.188	83	2
25	36	1.379	58	2+3
26	36	1.379	65	2+3
27	36	1.379	79	2+3

$$A_p = \frac{1}{V^2 t^2}\left(f_1 + \frac{t}{f_2 - f_3}\right) \cdot \left(f_8\left(f_9 + f_{10}\right) + TV\left(f_4 + f_7 + \frac{f_5 f_6}{t(T+t)}\right)\right) \quad (29)$$

$$N_p = \frac{(D+V)(D+t)\left(t+\frac{9+t}{T-V}\right)}{2.93+T} - \frac{D\left(t+\left(T+V-t+\frac{Vt}{D}\right)^{-7}+\frac{-1.4+2D+0.95DV^{-1-T}+\frac{9+D+t}{-6.6+T}}{T+\frac{t}{D+V}}\right)}{(D+T)\left(1.055-0.8816V+\frac{D}{V\sqrt{\frac{T}{VD}}-t}\right)} -$$

$$(30)$$

$$-\frac{D\left(\frac{D\left(1.05-V-\frac{6.3}{(-1+D)DV^{T}}\right)}{DT-t}+\frac{t+\frac{T-\frac{t}{D}}{D+V^2}}{T+\frac{9.5+t}{D-T+V}}\right)}{1.055-V+\frac{3.56\cdot 5.18^{V}(D+T)}{V(1.05+V+Tt)}}$$

Figure 10 presents a comparison of the experimental, predicted, and theoretical values of macro-porosity parameters. Theoretical values of macro-pore density are calculated on the basis of an ideal model of porous structure using Equation 14. By calculation of the theoretical values of the area of macro-pore cross-section, open porosity, and the equivalent pore diameter, the circular, rectangular, and elliptical shape of macro-pore area are taken into account.

Theoretical values of woven fabric porosity parameters deviate from experimental ones on average by 118.3% (min 8.8%, max 452.9%) for the area of the macro-pore with rectangular cross-section, 111.5% (min 14.5%, max 370.6%) for the area of the macro-pore with circular cross-section, 72.8% (min 0.2%, max 335.3%) for the area of the macro-pore with elliptical cross-section, 37.3% (min 0.0%, max 395.0%) for the macro-pore density, 232.6% (min 19.9%, max 1900.1%) for the open porosity of fabrics with rectangular pore cross-section, 221.0% (min 14.3%, max 1558.0%) for the open porosity of fabrics with circular pore cross-section, 166.3% (min 5.9%, max 1479.0%) for the open porosity of fabrics with elliptical pore cross-section, 43.7% (min 4.3%, max 135.1%) for the equivalent pore diameter where rectangular pore cross-section is taken into account, 43.7% (min 7.0%, max 116.9%) for the equivalent pore diameter where circular cross-section is taken into account, and 28.0% (min 0.1%, max 108.6%) for the equivalent pore diameter where elliptical pore cross-section is taken into account.

The results of woven fabric porosity parameters determined with models based on genetic programming show very good agreement with experimental values (Figure 11) and justify the complexity of GA models. The predicted values deviate from experimental ones on average by 1.5% (min 0.0%, max 10.2%) for the area of the macro-pore cross-section, 2.0% (min 0.0%, max 8.0%) for the macro-pore density, 3.2% (min 0.0%, max 10.1%) for the open porosity, and 0.8% (min 0.0%, max 5.2%) for the equivalent macro-pore diameter. The correlation coefficients between the predicted and experimental values are 0.9999, 0.9989, 0.9941, and 0.9997 for the area of macro-pore cross-section, macro-pore density, open porosity, and equivalent diameter, respectively.

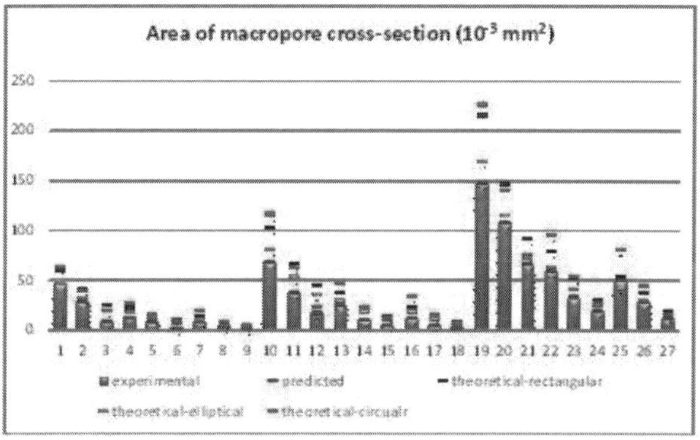

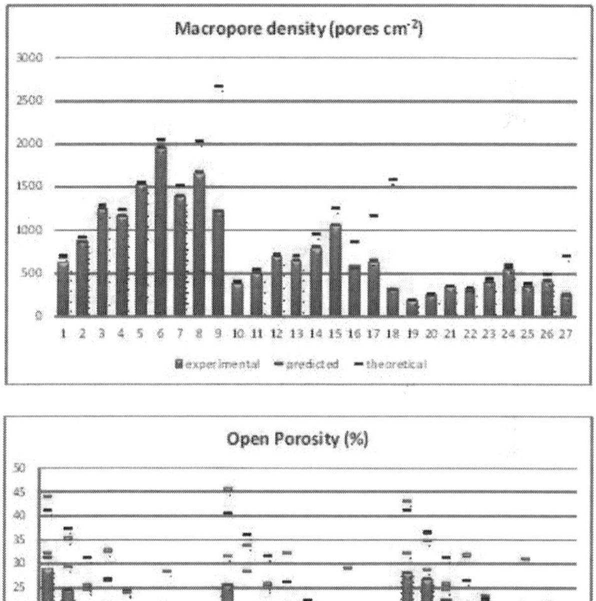

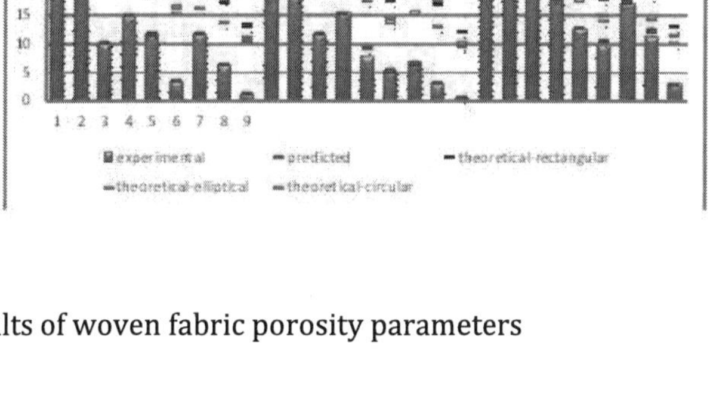

Figure 10. Results of woven fabric porosity parameters

The models are based on image analysis technique and assumption that woven samples are transparent. The boundary limits for the validity of the models are as follows: 1. the minimal values for yarn linear density, weave factor and fabric tightness, are 14 tex, 0.904, and 55%, respectively, 2. the maximal values for yarn linear density, weave factor and fabric tightness are 36 tex, 1.379, and 85%, respectively.

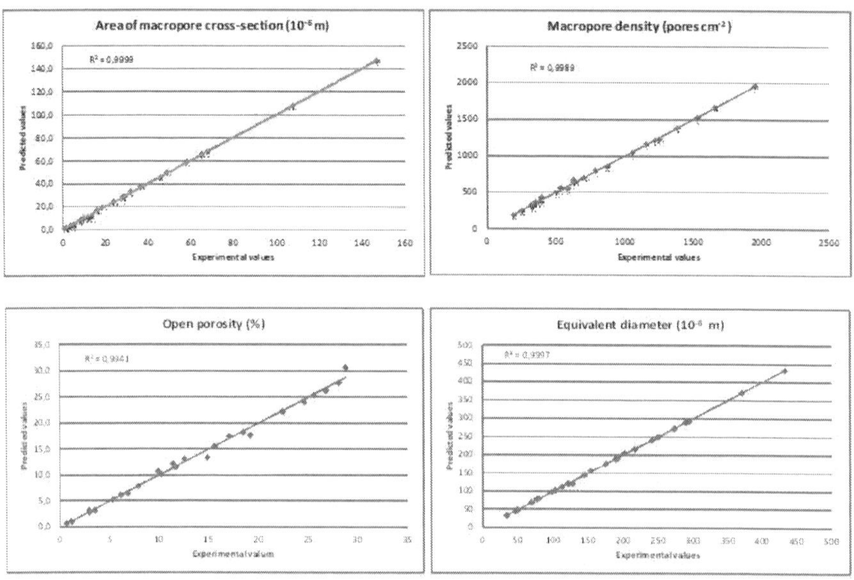

Figure 11. Scatter plots of experimental and predicted porosity parameters using GP models

4. THE USAGE OF GENETIC ALGORITHM TO PREDICT NONWOVEN FABRIC POROSITY PARAMETERS

In this research, the genetic algorithm was used for definition of predictive models of nonwoven fabric porosity parameters. Since needle-punched nonwoven fabrics have completely different porous structure when compared to woven fabrics, it is inappropriate to focus on open porosity through the prediction of the area of macro-pore cross-section and macro-pore density. The most valuable porosity parameters for needle-punched nonwoven porous structure characterisations are total porosity and mean pore diameter, and those parameters were the subjects of our research. Since the basic steps in evolutionary computation are well-known, only a brief description follows. Firstly, the initial population *P(t)* of the random organisms (solutions) is generated. The variable *t* represents the generation time. The next step is the evaluation of population *P(t)* according to the fitness measure. Altering the population *P(t)* by genetic operations follows. The genetic operations alter one or more parental organism(s); thus, creating their offspring. The evaluation and alteration of population takes place until the termination criterion has been fulfilled. This can be the specified maximum number of generations or a sufficient quality of solutions [38]. More comprehensive information on evolutionary computation can be found in [39].

The independent input variables were fibre fineness - T (dtex), nonwoven fabric area mass - m (g/m^2), and nonwoven fabric thickness - D (mm). The dependent output variables were mean pore diameter d_p(μm) and total porosity ε (%). Since the GA approach is unsuitable for the evolution of prediction models (organisms) in their symbolic forms, it is necessary to define them in advance [38]. In this study, a quadratic polynominal equation with three variables was used as a prespecified model for the prediction of porosity parameters as follows:

$$Y = c_1 + c_2 m + c_3 D + c_4 T + c_5 m^2 + c_6 D^2 + c_7 T^2 + c_8 mD + c_9 mT + c_{10} DT + c_{11} mDT \tag{31}$$

where, Y is the dependent output variable, *m* is the nonwoven fabric mass per unit area in g/m^2, *D* is the nonwoven fabric thickness in mm, *T* is the fibre fineness in dtex, and $c_{1...11}$ are constants. The main reasons for this selection were as follows: 1. a polynominal model is relatively simple, 2. for the problem studied we did not expect harmonic dependence of the output variables, 3. some preliminary modelling-runs with different types of prespecified models showed that the quadratic polynominal model provides very good selection in terms of prediction quality. In our research, the initial random population *P(t)* consisted of *N* prespecified models (Equation 31) where *N* is the population size. Of course, in our computer implementation of the GA, the population *P(t)* consisted only of the *N* sets of the real-valued vectors of model constants. The individual vector is equal to:

$$c = (c_1, c_2, , c_{11})$$

The absolute deviation *D(i,t)* of individual model *i* (organism) in generation time *t* was introduced as a fitness measure. It was defined as:

$$D(i,t) = \sum_{j=1}^{n} |E(j) - P(i,j)| \tag{32}$$

where, *E(j)* is the experimental value for measurement *j*, *P(i, j)* is the predicted value returned by the individual model *i* for measurement *j*, and *n* is the maximum number of measurements. The goal of the optimisation task was to find such a predictive model (defined by Equation 31), that Equation 33 would give as low an absolute deviation as possible. Therefore, the aim was to find out appropriate real-valued constants in Equation 32. However, since it was unnecessary that the smallest values of the above equation also meant the smallest percentage deviation of this model, the average absolute percentage deviation of all measurements for individual model *i* was defined as:

$$\Delta(i) = \frac{D(i,t)}{|E(j)|n} \cdot 100\,\% \tag{33}$$

The Equation 33 was not used as a fitness measure for evaluating population, but only for finding the best organism within the population, after completing the run.

The altering of population *P(t)* was effected by reproduction, crossover, and mutation. For the crossover operation, two parental vectors, e.g., c_1 and c_2 were randomly selected. Then the crossover took place between two randomly-selected parental genes having the same index. Two offspring genes were created according to the extended intermediate crossover, as considered by Mühlenbeim and Schlierkamp-Voosen [40]. During the mutation operation, one parental vector *c* was randomly selected. Then, the mutation took place in one randomly selected parental gene. During both the crossover and mutation processes, the numbers of crossover and mutational operations performed on parental vector(s), were randomly selected. The evolutionary parameters for modelling by genetic algorithms were: population size 300, maximum number of generations to be run 5000, probability of reproduction 0.1, probability of crossover 0.8 and probability of mutation 0.1. Tournament selection with a group size of 5 was used. For the purpose of the research 200 independent genetic algorithms runs were carried out. Only the best models are presented in the paper.

4.1. MATERIALS AND POROSITY MEASUREMENTS

Bearing in mind the fact that nonwovens have very different structures and, thus, also porosity parameters due to their sequences when web-forming, bonding, as well as finishing methods, the nonwoven fabric samples were limited to one type of nonwoven fabrics – those needle-punched nonwoven fabrics made from a mixture of polyester and viscose staple fibres. Nonwoven multi-layered webs were first obtained from the same manufacturing process by subjecting the fibre mixtures to carding and then orienting the carded webs in a cross-direction by using a cross lapper to achieve web surface mass ranges of 100-150, 150-200, 250-300, and 300-350 g/m^2, and a web volume mass range of 0.019-0.035 g/cm^3. The webs were made from a mixture of polyester (PES) and viscose (VIS) staple fibres of different content, fineness, and lengths, as follows: samples 1–3 from a mixture of 87% VIS fibres (1.7 dtex linear density, 38 mm length) and 12.5% of PES fibres (4.4 dtex linear density, 50 mm length), samples 4–7 from a mixture of 60% VIS fibres (1.7 dtex linear density, 38 mm length) and 40% PES fibres (3.3 dtex linear density, 60 mm length), samples 8–11 from a mixture of 30% VIS fibres (3.3 dtex linear density, 50 mm length), 40% PES fibres type 1 (6.7 dtex linear density, 60 mm length) and 30% of PES fibres type 2 (4.4 dtex linear density, 50 mm length), samples 12–15 from a mixture of 70% PES fibres type 1 and 30% PES type 2. Multi-layered carded webs were further subjecting to pre-needling using needle-punching machine, under the following processing parameters of one-sided pre-needle punching: stroke frequency 250/min; delivery speed 1.5 m/min; needling density 30/cm, depth of needle penetration 15 mm, and felting needles of 15x18x38x3 M222 G3017. The processing parameters of further two-sided needle-punching were as follows: stroke frequency 900/min; delivery speed 5.5 m/min; needling density 60/cm (30/cm upper and 30/cm lower), depth of upper and lower needle penetrations 12 mm, and felting needles of 15x18x32x3 M222 G3017. The webs were further processed through a pair of heated calendars at under 180 °C with different gaps between the rollers, in order to achieve further changes in fabric density and, consequently, in the porosity within the range of 80–92 %. The constructional parameters of the nonwoven fabric samples are collected in Table 2. All the nonwoven fabric samples were in a grey state to eliminate the influence of finishing treatments. The constructional parameters of the nonwoven fabric samples, e.g. the nonwoven fabric mass per unit area and thickness were measured according to ISO 9073-1 (Textiles – Test Methods for nonwovens – Part 1: Determination of mass per unit area) and ISO 9073-2 (Textiles – Test Methods for nonwovens – Part 2: Determination of thickness).

Table 2. The constructional parameters of nonwoven fabric samples

Ref.	**Average fibre fineness *T*, dtex**	**Fabric mass per unit area *m*, g/m²**	**Fabric thickness *D*, mm**
1	2.0	143	1.202
2	2.0	142	0.941
3	2.0	142	0.576
4	2.3	173	1.509
5	2.3	201	1.558
6	2.3	171	0.941
7	2.3	200	1.071
8	5.0	259	1.360
9	5.0	259	1.261

10	5.0	279	1.182
11	5.0	274	1.112
12	6.0	298	1.400
13	6.0	304	1.266
14	6.0	352	1.347
15	6.0	343	1.235

The porosity parameters of the nonwoven fabric samples were measured using the Pascal 140 computer aided mercury intrusion porosimeter, which measures pores' diameters between 3.8 - 120 μm, and operates under low pressure. The mercury intrusion technique is based on the principle that non-wetting liquid (mercury) coming in contact with a solid porous material can not be spontaneously absorbed by the pores of the solid itself because of the surface tension, but can be forced by applying external pressure. The required pressure depends on the pore-size and this relationship is commonly known as the Washburn equation [9]:

$$P = \frac{-2 \cdot \gamma \cdot \cos\theta}{r} \tag{34}$$

where, P is the applied pressure, Υ is the surface tension of mercury, θ is the contact-angle and r is the capillary radius. The distribution of pore size, as well as the total porosity and the specific pore volume can be obtained from the relationship between the pressure necessary for penetration (the pore dimension) and the volume of the penetrated mercury (pore volume). There are certain main assumptions necessary when applying the Washburn equation: the pores are assumed to be of cylindrical shape and the sample is pressure stable.

Each nonwoven sample of known weight was placed in the dilatometer, then the air around the sample was evacuated and finally the dilatometer was filled with mercury by increasing the pressure up to the reference level. The volume and pressure measurements' data were transferred into the computer programme and the following data were detectable or calculated: the specific pore volume (mm^3/g), the average pore diameter (μm) and the total porosity (%). The volume of penetrated mercury is directly the measure of the sample's pore volume expressed as a specific pore volume in mm^3/g, and is obtained by means of a capacitive reading system. The average pore diameter is evaluated at 50% of the cumulative volume of mercury.

4.2. Predictive Models of Nonwoven Fabric Porosity Parameters

Equations 36 and 37 present predictive models of the total porosity ε and mean pore diameter d_p, respectively. Here T is the fibre fineness in dtex, m is the nonwoven fabric mass per unit area in g/m^2, and D is the nonwoven fabric thickness in mm.

$$\varepsilon = 150.1 - 8.61 \cdot 10^{-2} m + 3.21 \cdot 10^{-2} D - 66.04 \cdot T - 1.09 \cdot 10^{-3} m^2 - 28.74 \cdot D^2 + \\ +0.89 \cdot T^2 + 0.24 \cdot m \cdot D + 0.20 \cdot m \cdot T + 32.16 \cdot D \cdot T - 0.10 \cdot m \cdot D \cdot T \tag{35}$$

$$d_p = 103.12 - 0.39 \cdot m + 6.01 \cdot D - 0.73 \cdot T - 2.12 \cdot 10^{-3} m^2 - 30.77 \cdot D^2 - 3.79 \cdot T^2 + \\ +0.46 \cdot m \cdot D + 0.16 \cdot m \cdot t + 1.13 \cdot D \cdot T - 3.79 \cdot 10^{-3} \cdot m \cdot D \cdot T \tag{36}$$

Figure 12 presents a comparison of the experimental, predicted and theoretical values of porosity parameters, e.g. total porosity and mean pore diameter. The theoretical values of total porosity and mean pore diameters were calculated using Equation 22 and 27-28, respectively.

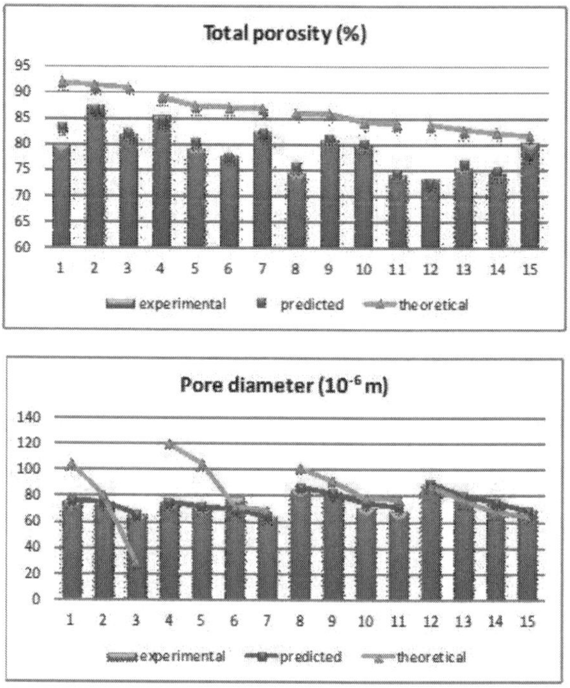

Figure 12. Results of nonwoven fabric porosity parameters

In Figure 12, the theoretical values of total porosity and mean pore diameter as well as predicted values of pore diameter are linked with lines while samples (1-3, 4-7, 8-11, and 12-15) are arranged regarding their decreased porosity. The results show that nonwovens with similar porous structure and lower porosity also have lower pore diameter. The experimental values of total porosity are for some samples not in a good agreement with theoretical ones, while samples which should have the highest porosity actually have the lowest (samples No. 1, 8, and 12). The reason may lie in fact, that these samples contain more closed pores which are not detectable with mercury porosimetry.

The results show that the theoretical values of porosity parameters deviate from experimental ones on average by 8.0% (min 0.0%, max 15.4%) for total porosity and by 19.7% (min 2.9, max 57.3%) for pore diameter, whilst the predicted values, calculated using Equations 36-37, are in better agreement with the experimental ones. The mean predicted error is: 1.1% (from 0.0% to 4.4%) for the total porosity and 1.9% (from 0.0% to 12.4%) for the average pore diameter. The correlation coefficients between the predicted and experimental values are 0.9024 and 0.8492 for the total porosity and the average pore diameter, respectively. Scatter plots of the experimental and predicted values for porosity parameters, are depicted in Figure 13.

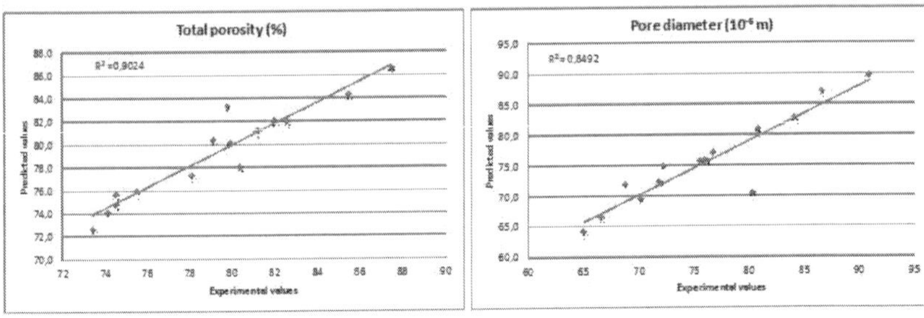

Figure 13. Scatter plots of experimental and predicted porosity parameters using GA models

CONCLUSION

By a new fabric developing, there is a need to know some relationships between the constructional parameters of fabrics and their predetermined end-usage properties in order to produce fabrics with desired quality. Fabric constructors develop a new fabric construction on the basis of their experiences or predictive models using different modelling tools of which deterministic and nondeterministic are distinguished. In general, the models obtained by deterministic modelling tools are the results of strict mathematical rules while in the case of models obtained by nondeterministic modelling tools, there are no precise, strict mathematical rules. Our study focused on the development of predictive models based on the genetic methods, e.g. genetic programming and genetic algorithms, in order to predict some porosity parameters of woven and nonwoven fabrics. Predictive models of the: 1. area of macro-pore cross-section and macro-pore density of woven fabrics based on the constructional parameters of woven fabrics (yarn linear density, weave factor, fabric tightness, denting), image analysis as testing method of porosity measurements, and genetic programming, and 2. total porosity and mean pore diameter of nonwoven fabrics based on the constructional parameters of nonwoven fabrics (fibre linear density, fabric mass per unit area, fabric thickness), mercury intrusion porosimetry as testing method of porosity measurements, and genetic algorithm, were developed. Open porosity and equivalent pore diameter of woven fabric were also predicted using values calculated on the basis of predictive models of the area of macro-pore cross-section and pore density, and known mathematical relationships. All proposed predictive models were created very precisely and could serve as guidelines for woven/nonwoven engineering in order to develop fabrics with the desired porosity parameters.

In general, for prediction of porosity parameters of woven or nonwoven samples both modelling tools can be used, e.g. GA and GP. Usually, GP method is used for more difficult problems. Our purpose was to show usability and effectiveness of both methods. By woven fabric modelling, the range of porosity parameters' measurements was substantial larger with more input variables when compared to the nonwoven fabrics (and this means more difficult problem), so the GP was used as modelling tool. By GP modelling, the models are developed in their symbolic forms, thus more precise models are developed in regard to the GA modelling, where only coefficients of prespecified models are defined. At the same time, for GP modelling more measurements data are desired for better model accuracy, while by GA modelling good results are achieved by lower number of measurements (in our case 27 measurements were available for woven fabrics and only 15 for nonwoven fabrics). The advantage of GP modelling is its excellent prediction accuracy, while its disadvantage is the complexity of the developed models. In general, by GA modelling, the developed models are simple but less accurate.

REFERENCES

1. M. Brezočnik, The Usage of Genetic Programming in Intelligent Manufacturing Systems, Maribor: University of Maribor, Faculty of Mechanical Engineering, 2000.
2. J.R. Koza, Genetic programming II, Massachusetts: The MITPress, 1994
3. J.R. Koza, Genetic programming III, San Francisco: Morgan Kaufmann,CA, 1999
4. M. Brezocnik, J. Balic, "Emergence of intelligence in next-generation manufacturing systems", Robot. Comput. Integrat. Manufact., Vol. 19, pp. 55-63, 2003.
5. P. Udhayakumar and S. Kumanan, "Task Scheduling of AGV in FMS Using Non-Traditional Optimization Techniques", Int. Journal of Simulation Modelling, Vol. 9, pp. 28-39, 2010.

6. N. Chakraborti, R. Sreevathsan, R. Jayakanth and B. Bhattacharya, "Tailor-made material design: An evolutionary approach using multi-objective genetic algorithms", Computational Materials Science, Vol. 45, pp. 1-7, 2009.
7. S. Mohanty, B. Mahanty and P.K.J. Mohapatra, "Optimization of hot rolled coil widths using a genetic algorithm", Materials and Manufacturing Processes, Vol. 18, pp. 447-462, 2003
8. M. Brezočnik and J. Balič, »A Genetic-based Approach to Simulation of Self-Organizing Assembly«, Robot. Comput. Integrat. Manufact., Vol. 17, pp. 113-120, 2001.
9. Porosimeter Pascal Instruction Manual, Milan: Thermo Electron S.p.A, 2004.
10. K. L. Hatch, Textile Sciences, New York: West Publishing Company, 2000.
11. P. Bajaj and A. Sengupta, »Protective Clothing«, in Textile Progress, Manchester, The Textile Institute, 1992, pp. 1-94.
12. Y. Shoshani and Y. Yakubov, »A Model for Calculating the Noise Absorption Capacity of Nonwoven Fiber Webs«, Textile Research Journal, Vol. 69, pp. 519-526, 1999.
13. M. Mohammadi and P. Banks-Lee, »Determing Effective Thermal Conductivity of Multilayered Nonwoven Fabrics«, Textile Research Journal, Vol. 73, pp. 802-808, 2003.
14. N. Pan and P. Gibson, Thermal and moisture transport in fibrous materials, Cambridge: Woodhead Publishing Limited and CRC Press LLC, 2006.
15. K. Dimitrovski, New Method for Assesment of Porosity in Textiles, Doctoral Disertation, Ljubljana: University of Ljubljana, Textile Department, 1996.
16. B. Neckar and S. Ibrahim, »Theoretical Approach for Determing Pore Charachteristics Between Fibres«, Textile Research Journal, Vol. 73, pp. 611-619, 2003.
17. G. Lombard, A. Rollin and C. Wolff, »Theoretical and Experimental Opening Sizes of Heat-Bonded Geotextiles«, Textile Research Journal, Vol. 59, pp. 208-217, 1989.
18. M. J. Park, S. H. Kim, S. J. Kim, S. H. Jeong and J. Jaung, »Effect of Splitting and Finishing on Absorption/Adsorption Properties of Split Polyester Microfiber Fabrics«, Textile Research Journal, Vol. 71, pp. 831-840, 2001.
19. K. Kaneko, »Determination of pore size and pore size distribution«, Journal of Membrane Science, Vol. 96, pp. 59-89, 1994.
20. A. Jena and K. Gupta, »Liquid Extrusion Techniques for Pore Structure Evaluation of Nonwovens«, International Nonwoven Journal, Vol. 12, pp. 45-53, 2003.

21. B. Xu, »Measurement of Pore Charachteristics in Nonwoven Fabrics Using Image Analysis«, Clothing and Textiles Research Journal, Vol. 14, pp. 81-88, 1996.
22. Y. L. Hsieh, »Liquid Transport in Fabric Structures«, Textile Research Journal, Vol. 65, pp. 299-307, 1995.
23. D. Jakšić and N. Jakšić, »Assessment of Porosity of Flat Textile Fabrics«, Textile Research Journal, Vol. 77, pp. 105-110, 2007.
24. V. Nagy and L. M. Vas, »Pore Charachteristic Determination with Mercury Porosimetry in Polyester Staple Yarns«, Fibres & Textiles in Eastern Europe, Vol. 13, pp. 21-26, 2005.
25. D. Jakšić, The Development of the New Method to Determine the Pore Size and Pore Size Distribution in Textile Products, Ljubljana: Faculty of Natural Sciences and Technology, Departmetn of Textile Technology, 1975.
26. P. D. Dubrovski, The Influence of Woven Fabric Geometry on Porosity of Biaxial Fabrics, Doctoral Disertation, Maribor: University of Maribor, Faculty of Mechanical Engineeeing, 1999.
27. P. D. Dubrovski, »Volume Porosity of Woven Fabrics«, Textile Research Journal, Vol. 70, pp. 915-919, 2000.
28. P. D. Dubrovski, »A Geometrical Method to Predict the Macroporosity of Woven Fabrics«, Journal of the Textile Institute, Vol. 92, pp. 288-298, 2001.
29. A. V. Kulichenko and L. Langenhove, »The Resistance to Flow Transmission of Porous Materials«, Journal of the Textile Institute, Vol. 83, pp. 127-132, 1992.
30. J. C. Russ, The image Processing Handbook, CRC Press, 1996.
31. A. T. Purdy, Needle-punching, Manchester: The Textile Institute, 1980, pp. 49.
32. R. D. Anandjiwala and L. Boguslavsky, »Development of Needle-punched Nonwoven Fabrics from Flax Fibers for air Filtration Applications«, Textile Research Journal, Vol. 78, pp. 614-624, 2008.
33. J. Mao and S. J. Rusell, »Modelling Permeability in Homogeneous Three-Dimensional Nonwoven Fabrics«, Textile Research Journal, Vol. 73, pp. 939-944, 2003.
34. X. Chen, F. Vroman, M. Lewandowski and A. Perwuelz, »Study of the Influence of Fiber Diameter and Fiber Blending on Liquid Absorption Inside Nonwoven Structures«, Textile Research Journal, Vol. 79, pp. 1364-1370, 2009.
35. A. Patanaik and R. Anandjiwala, »Some Studies on Water Permeability of Nonwoven Fabrics«, Textile Research Journal, Vol. 79, pp. 147-153, 2009.
36. M. Kienbaum, »Gewebegeometrie and Produktenwicklung«, Melliand Textilberichte, Vol. 71, pp. 737-742, 1990.

37. P. D. Dubrovski and M. Brezočnik, »Using Genetic Programming to predict the Macroporosity of Woven Cotton Fabrics«, Textile Research Journal, Vol. 72, pp. 187-194, 2002.
38. M. Brezočnik, M. Kovačič and L. Gusel, »Comparison Between Genetic Algorithm and Genetic Programming Approach for Modelling the Stress Distribution«, Material and Manufacturing Processes, Vol. 20, pp. 497-508, 2005.
39. T. Bäck, D. B. Fogel and Z. Michalewicz, Handbook of evalutionary computation, New York- Oxford: IOP Publishing and Oxford University Press, 1997.
40. M. Gen and R. Cheng, Genetic algorithms and engineering design, Canada: John Wiley & Sons, Inc., 1997.

10

CHAPTER

PROGRAMMING THE GROUP BEHAVIORS OF BACTERIAL COMMUNITIES WITH SYNTHETIC CELLULAR COMMUNICATION

Wentao Kong[1,2] Venhar Celik[1,2] Chen Liao[1,2] Qiang Hua[3] and Ting Lu[1,2,4]

[1]*Department of Bioengineering, University of Illinois at Urbana-Champaign, 1304 W Springfield Avenue, Urbana, IL 61801, USA 2* [2]*Institute for Genomic Biology, University of Illinois at Urbana-Champaign, 1206 W Gregory Drive, Urbana, IL 61801, USA*

[3] *State Key Laboratory of Bioreactor Engineering, East China University of Science and Technology, 130 Meilong Road, Shanghai 200237, People's Republic of China.*

[4] *Department of Physics, University of Illinois at Urbana-Champaign, 1110 W Green Street, Urbana, IL 61801, USA.*

ABSTRACT

Synthetic biology is a newly emerged research discipline that focuses on the engineering of novel cellular behaviors and functionalities through the creation of artificial gene circuits. One important class of synthetic circuits currently under active development concerns the programming of bacterial cellular communication and collective population-scale behaviors. Because of the ubiquity of cell-cell interactions within bacterial communities, having an ability of engineering these circuits is vital to programming robust cellular behaviors. Here, we highlight recent advances in communication-based synthetic gene circuits by first discussing natural communication systems and then surveying various functional engineered circuits, including those for population density control, temporal synchronization, spatial organization, and ecosystem formation. We conclude by summarizing recent advances, outlining existing challenges, and discussing potential applications and future opportunities.

Keywords: Synthetic biology Gene circuits Bacterial communities Cellular communication Collective behaviors Dynamics

Background

Synthetic biology is a newly emerged research discipline that focuses on the engineering of novel cellular behaviors and functionalities. Since the launch of the field in 2000 [1],[2], a wide range of synthetic gene devices have been created, including switches [3]-[9], oscillators [10]-[13], memory elements [7],[14],[15], and communication modules [13],[16]-[18], as well as other electronics-inspired genetic devices, such as digital logic gates [19]-[22], pulse generators [23], and filters [24],[25]. With designed cellular behaviors and functionalities, engineered circuits have been exploited to understand biological questions and to address various real-world problems [26]. The field has shown tremendous potential for biomedical, environmental, and energy-related applications [27]. For example, towards biomedical applications, engineered genetic circuits contribute to the understanding of disease mechanisms, provide novel diagnostic tools, enable economic production of therapeutics, and enable the design of novel treatment strategies for various diseases including cancer, metabolic disorders, and infectious diseases [28],[29].

In the last few years, the advances of synthetic circuits have been further expedited, empowered by recent breakthroughs in genetic engineering techniques such as novel DNA assembly [30]-[33] and genome editing tools [34]-[37], advances in methodologies including those for rational circuit design and optimization [38]-[40], and quick enrichment of parts and elements [41],[42]. As a result, synthetic biologists are now in a position to engineer desired cellular phenotypes in a larger, faster, and cheaper fashion.

One important class of synthetic circuits that are under active development concerns the programming of bacterial cell-cell communication and the group behaviors of communities [43]-[48]. Successful examples include gene constructs responsible for cellular density control [18], spatiotemporal patterning [13],[16],[49],[50], and ecosystem formation [51],[52]. The engineering of community-based circuits is essential and invaluable towards the implementation of complex but robust cellular functionality because of the following reasons: First, although microbes are single cell organisms, they are present dominantly in the form of communities in nature and in live bodies, such as biofilms [53],[54] and the human microbiome [55],[56]. Second, microbial physiology and functionality are strongly correlated with their forms - for instance, bacterial antibiotic resistance is distinct when cells are in planktonic forms and biofilm forms [57],[58]. Third, recent advances in the biotechnological industry have clearly shown that microbial consortia may provide many compelling advantages in producing products of interest and controlling fermentation processes [59],[60].

We are thus motivated in this article to overview the advances of synthetic gene circuits towards the programming of bacterial cellular communication and community behaviors. We will first discuss basic communication modules that confer cell-cell coordination in communities. We will then overview various functional gene circuits that enable the implementation of desired dynamic group behaviors, including those for population density control, temporal synchronization, spatial organization, and ecosystem formation. We will conclude by summarizing recent advances and discussing existing challenges, potential applications, and future opportunities.

Although not discussed here, it is important to note that there has been considerable progress in developing synthetic cellular communication in eukaryotes such as mammalian cells and yeast, which has been surveyed in the literature [51],[61],[62].

REVIEW

Basic communication modules

Despite their species diversity, bacteria often utilize similar signaling systems for the implementation of their group behaviors [63],[64]. For instance, quorum sensing (QS) is prevalent in bacteria for coordinating their group behaviors such as bioluminescence [65], biofilm formation [66], pathogenesis [67] and antibiotic synthesis [68]-[70].

Bacterial communication via nonvolatile signaling molecules

In Gram-negative bacteria, acyl-homoserine lactones (AHLs) are commonly used as QS molecules for intra-species communication. These molecules are composed of a homoserine lactone ring with an acyl chain of C4 to C18 in length [71],[72]. AHL molecules are synthesized by the LuxI family synthases and detected by the corresponding LuxR-type receptors [73]. One canonical example of this class of communication is the QS system discovered in the bioluminescent marine bacterium *Vibrio fischeri*[74]. As shown in Figure 1A, LuxI, the autoinducer synthase, produces the AHL molecule 3OC6HSL that can diffuse freely across the cell membrane and accumulate with the increase of cell density. Once the AHLs reach a threshold concentration, they form a complex with the LuxR receptor and activate the transcription of the downstream genes (*luxI* and *luxR* in this case). A positive feedback regulatory architecture arises here from the self-activation of LuxI synthesis to facilitate the synchronization of the cellular population. Similar to *V. fischeri*, many other Gram-negative bacteria also possess QS systems, including the LasI/LasR and RhlI/RhlR systems in *Pseudomonas aeruginosa*[75], the CarI/CarR system in*Erwinia carotovora*[76], and the EsaI/EsaR system in *Pantoea stewartii*[77]. From an engineering perspective, these QS systems can be decomposed into two separate modules with one for signal production and the other for signal detection and response - when engineered in different cells, the two functional modules will confer communications between the two cells as shown in Figure 1C.

In Gram-positive bacteria, modified oligopeptides often serve as the signaling molecules for cellular communication with the cooperation of two-component systems. One classic example of this type of system is the Agr system in *Staphylococcus aureus* (Figure 1B) [78]. Here, the auto-inducing peptide (AIP) precursor, encoded by the gene *agrD*, is modified on its thiolactone ring and exported by AgrB protein. Upon the binding of AIP with the transmembrane protein AgrC, the transcriptional factor AgrA inside the cell is phosphorylated and then activated, which leads to the induction of the transcription of the downstream genes (*agrB/D/C/A* here). In addition to the Agr system, there are many communication systems based on auto-inducing peptides, such as the fsr system in *Enterococcus faecalis*[79], the Com system of*Streptococcus pneumonia*[80], and the nisRK system in *Lactococcus*[70]. To program collective behaviors in Gram-positive bacteria, a modular partition of those AI systems can thus been exploited (Figure 1D).

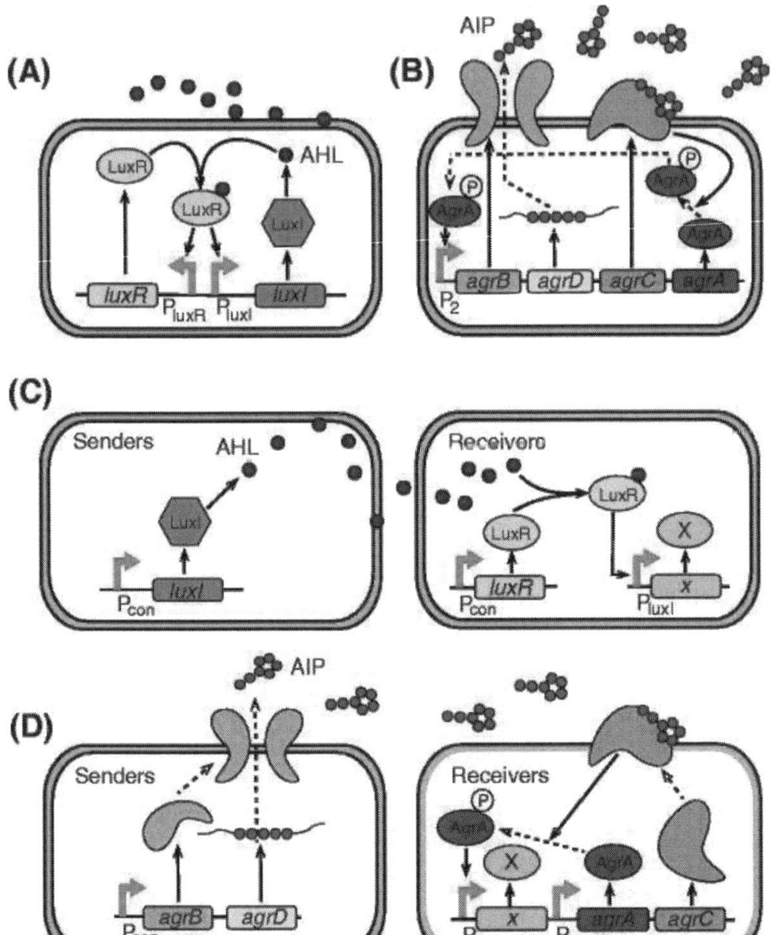

Figure 1. Cellular communication in bacteria. (A) The LuxI/LuxR quorum sensing (QS) system in the Gram-negative bacterium *Vibrio fischeri*. The system consists of the genes *luxI* and *luxR* and the cognate promoter PluxI and PluxR. Its signaling molecule is the acyl-homoserine lactone (AHL) 3OC6HSL. **(B)** The Agr QS system in the Gram-positive bacterium *Staphylococcus aureus*. It consists of the genes,*agrD, agrB, agrC,* and *agrA* and the cognate promoter P2. The auto-inducing peptide (AIP) is the signaling molecule of the system. **(C)**An engineered communication module adapted from the wild-type LuxI/LuxR system in **(A)**. By expressing *luxI*, the sender cell (left) produces the signal AHL that diffuses to the extracellular milieu and further into the receiver cell (right) to alter the expression of the downstream genes *X*. **(D)** A synthetic communication module built from the Agr system in **(B)**. The sender cell (left) produces and secretes the signaling molecule AIP that is sensed by the receiver cell (right), resulting in the expression shift of the gene *X* in the receiver cell.

Other than the QS and AIP systems that are primarily present in intra-species communication, there are inter-species communication systems that coordinate cellular behaviors over multiple bacterial species. One such example is the communication systems mediated by the universal signaling molecule autoinducer-2 (AI-2), a furanosyl borate diester synthesized by LuxS from *S*-adenosylmethionine and present in roughly half of all sequenced bacterial genome [81],[82]. Towards programmable behaviors in multiple bacterial species, AI-2 is hence an ideal candidate for exploitation.

Bacterial communication via volatile and gas molecules

The adoption of nonvolatile molecules, such as AHLs and AIs, as the broadcast signal enables cellular coordination across various species. However, communications via those molecules require the presence of the both sender and receiver species in the same liquid environments or in gel-like setting within a short distance to allow for diffusion of signaling molecules. Volatile molecules, in contrast, can diffuse through air and circumvent the need of physical mediating settings for signaling, allowing for more versatile, rapid, and large-scale communications of communities.

Weber et al. recently established a communication system that utilizes acetaldehyde as signaling molecules [51]. In their study, a bacterial strain (sender) was engineered to constitutively express alcohol dehydrogenase (ADH), an enzyme that converts ethanol in the medium to acetaldehyde. Due to its low boiling point (21°C), acetaldehyde volatized and was broadcast to neighboring cells (receiver) via air to trigger the expression of genes controlled by the cognate acetaldehyde-inducible promoters. Therefore, the sender cells produced a concentric gradient of acetaldehyde that induced the dose-dependent gene expression of the receiver cells with the expression level defined by the distance between the sender and receiver cells.

In another example, Hasty and colleagues constructed *ndh-2,* a gene encoding NADH dehydrogenase II (membrane-bound respiratory enzyme), into an *Escherichia coli* strain to confer the production of hydrogen peroxide (H2O2) [83]. H2O2 is a thermodynamically unstable chemical compound and is able to enter neighboring cells quickly to alter their redox state and inactivate ArcAB, resulting in the shift of the activity of the corresponding downstream genes. Through the exploitation of H2O2, a novel route of airborne signaling molecule was created for fast and large-scale colony coordination.

Other communication mechanisms

In addition to the common signaling mechanisms discussed above, bacteria also exploit a wide range of alternative approaches for communications, such as quinolone signal [84], diffusible signal factor [85], cyclic dipeptide [86], diketopiperazines [86],[87], and others [88],[89]. One such representative mode of signaling is the use of indole, an aromatic heterocyclic organic compound that is produced by over 85 species of Gram-positive and Gram-negative bacteria and used as an extracellular signal for global coordination of various bacterial species [90]. Although little of those mechanisms have been explored for synthetic biology applications, the broad spectrum of signaling systems provides a rich reservoir for engineering multicellular functionality.

Dynamic group behaviors of bacterial communities via engineered communications

Cellular communications enable the coordination of single cells by sending and sensing the states of individuals. Inspired by this natural capability of bacteria, synthetic biologists have developed a set of engineered bacterial populations with their group behaviors programmed from designed artificial cell-cell communications.

Population density control

The first communication-based synthetic circuit was built by You et al. in 2004 with the goal of creating a dynamic, autonomous regulation of the cell density of an *E. coli* population [18]. As illustrated in Figure 2A, the Lux system from *V. fischeri* was introduced to construct cell-cell communication and was coupled to cell survival and killing via the CcdA/B toxin system. Here, the LuxI protein catalyzes the synthesis of a small, diffusible AHL signaling molecule, 3OC6HSL, which accumulates in the extracellular milieu and the intracellular environment as the cell density increases. When cells reach a sufficient density, the AHL binds to LuxR and forms the LuxR/AHL complex that activates the expression of the killer protein LacZα-CcdB, leading to cell death. On the other hand, cell death can cause a reduction of total population density and hence the level of AHL production, which in turn allows the population to recover after killing. The continuous production and degradation of AHL make the cell density approach a steady state. Indeed, a stable cell density was maintained for more than 30 h with the variation within less than 5% in the study. This density control circuit laid a foundation for using cellular communications to program bacterial communities, allowing the extension of the control of population dynamics to the engineering of more sophisticated synthetic ecosystems.

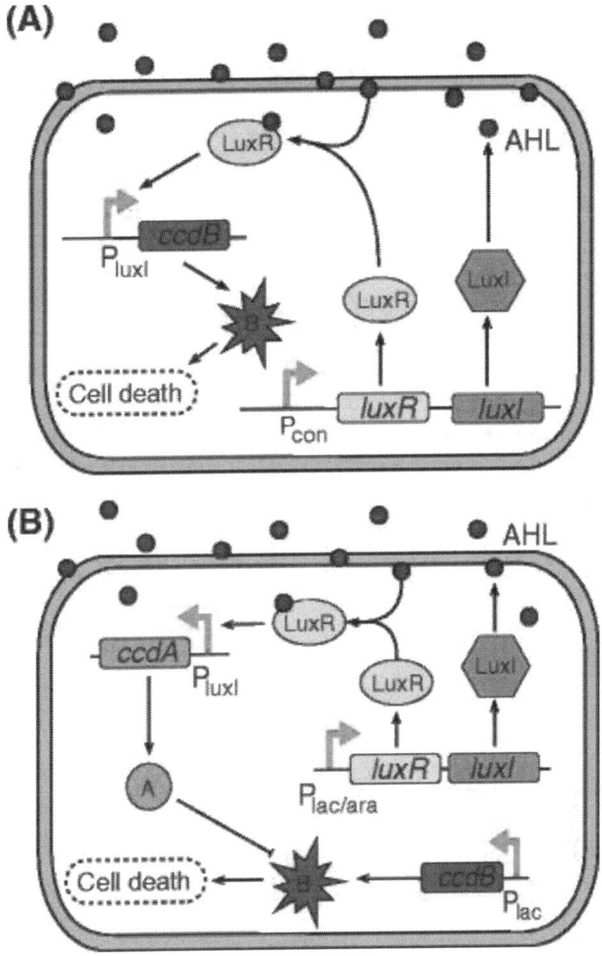

Figure 2: Cellular density control enabled by engineered cellular communications. **(A)** A communication-based gene circuit that confers the auto-regulation of cellular population density. In this system, a positive correlation between cell density and AHL concentration is essential and was created by having the cells constitutively produce LuxI that catalyzes AHL synthesis. At a low density, cells survive and grow normally because the expression of the toxin gene *ccdB* is not activated by a low AHL level. In contrast, when cell density achieves a critical level, *ccdB* expression is triggered by accumulated AHL, causing cellular death. The density-dependent cell death ensures an automatic control of total population density. **(B)** A synthetic gene circuit conferring an Allee effect in an isogenic population. Rather than the toxin CcdB in **(A)**, the antitoxin CcdA was correlated with cellular density via AHL concentration. At a low cell density, the cells cannot survive because of their production of the toxin CcdB. At a high density, the production of the antitoxin CcdA is triggered to neutralize the toxic effects from CcdB, resulting in normal cell growth.

In a recent work, Smith et al. utilized the density control circuit constructed above to create an artificial Allee effect in *E. coli* populations [91]. The Allee effect is a biological phenomenon characterized by a correlation between population density and the mean individual fitness of a population [92]. To create such an effect, a synthetic gene circuit was constructed to contain the LuxI/LuxR system and the CcdA/B toxin-antitoxin system (Figure 2B). In this setting, the expression of LuxR/LuxI and CcdB (killer) is under the control of Plac/ara promoter, while CcdA (rescue) was regulated by the cell density-dependent Plux promoter. When IPTG induction is on, the cellular population growth rate is negative if the initial cell density is less than the critical value (*C* crit) at which CcdA expression is not activated. However, if the initial cell density is above *C* crit, AHL activates the production of LuxR and further drives the production of CcdA which rescues the population by inhibiting the toxicity of CcdB. An Allee effect population was thus established to have a negative fitness below a threshold of cell density but a positive fitness when the density is beyond the threshold. This study provided new implications of engineered cellular communication for controlling invasive species and the spread of infectious diseases.

Temporal synchronization

Complex cellular behaviors, such as biofilm formation and host invasion, often require the temporal coordination and collective action of cellular populations [93],[94]. Towards this need, engineered communications offer a powerful solution.

In a recent study, Hasty and colleagues reported the development of an artificial gene circuit that synchronizes the oscillation of gene expression in individual cells [13]. Figure 3A shows their circuit design based on the QS elements of *V. fischeri* (*luxI, luxR*) and *Bacillus thurigensis* (*aiiA*). The AHL 3OC6HSL, synthesized by LuxI, binds to transcriptional factor LuxR to form a complex (LuxR-AHL) that activates the expression of *luxI*, which leads to a positive feedback loop in regulation. At the same time, the LuxR-AHL complex also activates the expression of *aiiA*, a gene encoding the AHL degradation enzyme, which leads to a negative feedback loop in regulation. The dual positive and negative feedback loops drive the sustained oscillation of gene expression of individual cells, and in the meantime, the signaling molecule AHL confers the synchronization of individual oscillations. Using a custom-tailored microfluidic device, the authors were, for the first time, able to establish and tune synchronized oscillations of an entire cellular population (thousands of cells). Compared with the single cell oscillators developed by the same group [11] and other researchers [1],[10], the engineered cellular communication indeed conferred the synchrony of cellular gene expression dynamics at a robust and yet tunable fashion.

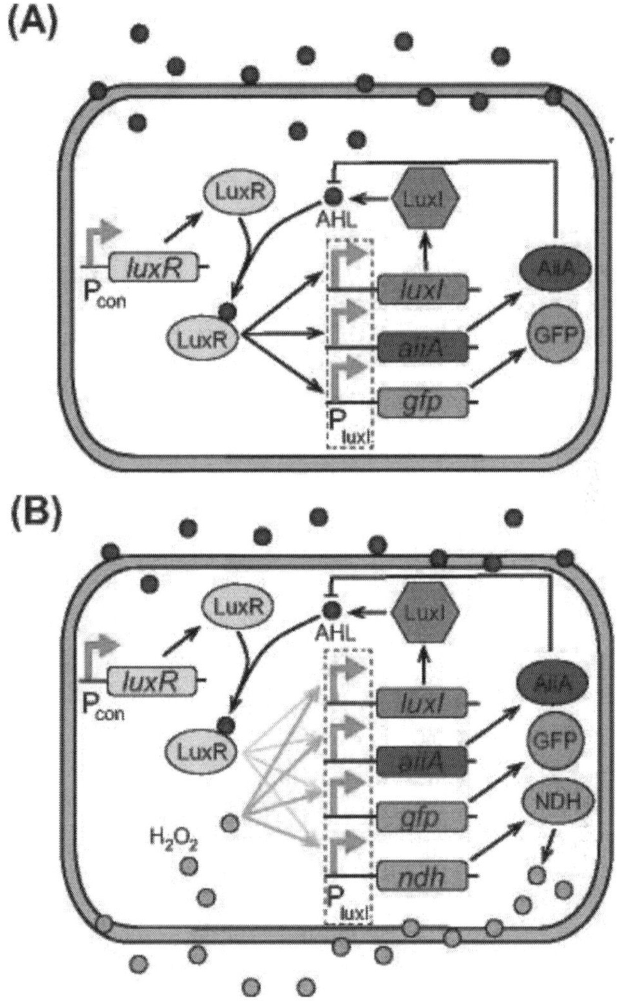

Figure 3: A QS-based gene circuit that synchronizes the oscillation of gene expression in an isogenic bacterial population. The oscillation is enabled by positive feedback, arising from the self-activation of AHL synthesis, and negative feedback, mediated by the AHL-degrading gene *aiiA*. The coupling of the two feedback loops results in robust oscillations of gene expression of an entire bacterial population (thousands of cells). **(B)** An advanced gene circuit modified from **(A)** that enables large-scale synchronization of oscillatory gene expression. In addition to the coupled positive and negative feedback in **(A)**, an additional positive feedback loop is introduced by coupling the production of thermally unstable H2O2 by NADH dehydrogenase (*ndh*) with AHL biosynthesis, leading to global oscillation synchronization of millions of cells.

Building on their success of the synchronized oscillator, the same group further advanced to create a more sophisticated genetic network that is capable of synchronizing oscillatory gene expression of populations across multiple spatial scales [83]. As illustrated in Figure 3B, the researchers placed a copy of the *ndh-2* gene, which encodes NADH dehydrogenase II, under the control of an additional copy of Pluxpromoter (compared with Figure 3A). The NDH-2 produces a low level of H2O2 that vapors and passes through the walls of the oxygen-permeable polydimethylsiloxane (PDMS) chips. Driven by the oscillation of gene expression mediated by the AHL-based synchronized oscillation circuit, H2O2 was periodically produced and exchanged between the cells within individual chambers. When entering cells, H2O2changes the redox state of the cells and inactivates their lux promoter binding protein ArcAB, causing the global activation of the lux promoter of the cells in different chambers. As a result, thousands of oscillating colony 'biopixels' (approximately 2.5 million cells) were synchronized over centimeter-length scales through the use of synergistic intercellular coupling involving both quorum sensing within a colony and gas-phase redox signaling between colonies. As a proof-of-concept application, this system was further employed to sense arsenic in environments via differential modulations of the period of the oscillatory cells that resemble a liquid crystal display (LCD)-like macroscopic clock.

Spatial organization

One of the most fascinating aspects of biological systems is their ability to generate complex but highly reproducible organisms through differential spatial patterning of morphogens across isogenic cells [95]. Towards the ultimate goal of biological engineering for creating desired tissues, organs, or even entire organisms, one critical step is to develop an engineering strategy that enables robust spatiotemporal pattern formation of living cells. Engineered cellular communications hold a great promise towards this goal, in addition to their roles in conferring temporal coordination of cellular behaviors.

In fact, synthetic biologists have already made several interesting attempts through the exploitation of artificial communication-based gene circuits. For instance, Sohka et al. constructed a circuit implementing Wolpert's French flag model [96], enabling the determination of cell fates in a concentration-dependent manner [25]; Payne et al. created a circuit that allows self-organized pattern formation without morphogen gradients in bacteria [97]; Basu et al. engineered a band detector that allows for differential response of gene expression according to the local concentration of AHL, creating a bull's eye-like spatiotemporal pattern [16].

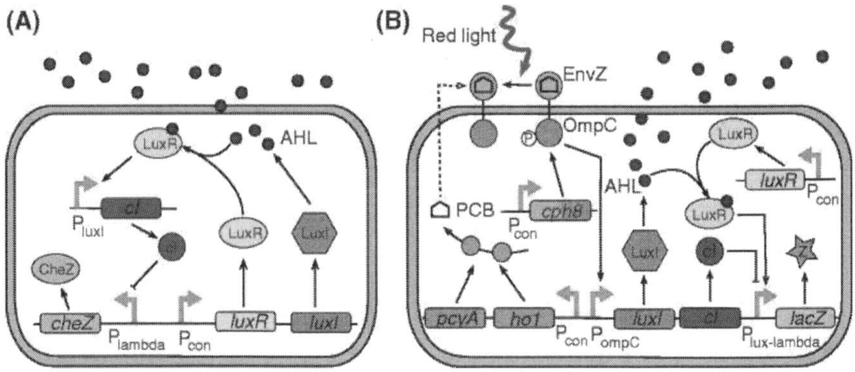

Figure 4: Spatial organization of cellular populations via engineered communication circuits. (A) A genetic circuit that generates periodic stripes in space. The LuxI/LuxR QS system is coupled to cellular motility via the transcriptional repressor gene *cI*, which is induced by AHL via the promoter PluxI and inhibits the expression of *cheZ*, one of the essential genes in bacteria motility. At a low cell density, AHL concentration remains low and no CI is produced, leading to a constant production of CheZ and hence a high cell motility. In a high cell density, sufficient accumulation of the AHL induces CI production which in turn suppresses *cheZ* expression, resulting in a deficiency in cell motility. The density-dependent motility of the population generates periodic stripe patterns in an expanding cell population. **(B)** A multi-module, communication-based synthetic circuit that allows accurate edge detection. Three functional modules are involved, including a light sensor, a cell communication module, and an X AND (NOT Y) gate. Upon exposure to red light, the light-sensing protein Cph8 induces the expression of *cI* and *luxI*: CI represses the expression of *lacZ* in the same cell regardless of AHL concentration while LuxI triggers the production of AHL that can diffuse to neighboring cells in the dark region to induce the production of LacZ. On the other hand, cells far from the light cannot produce LacZ because no AHL is available to trigger the transcription. As a result, only the cells near the edge of the light-exposed area actively express *lacZ*, which results in a dark pigment due to the enzymatic cleavage of a substrate in the plate by LacZ.

One elegant example for this line of applications is the programming of bacterial stripe patterns by Liu and co-workers [49]. As shown in Figure 4A, the gene circuit consists of two functional parts: density-sensing module and motility-control module. The density-sensing module centers on the LuxI/LuxR QS system that enables the synthesis and excretion of the AHL and the activation of the downstream gene *cI* when cell density is sufficiently high. The motility-control module is based on the bacterial motility system that is regulated by the transcription of*cheZ*. Upon the replacement of the wild-type *cheZ* with an inducible version (*cheZ* is under the control of the cI-repressed Plambda promoter), cellular motility becomes regulated by the expression of cI. With the coupling of the two modules, engineered *E. coli* populations were able to form robust but tunable periodic stripes of high and low cell densities sequentially and autonomously. These results established cellular motility as a simple route to create recurrent spatial structures without the need for an extrinsic pacemaker. As a novel mechanism, it offered an alternative solution for the formation of biological spatial patterns that is distinct from the well-acknowledged Turing mechanism [98].

In addition to autonomous pattern formation, the QS-based communication mechanism can also be applied to detect complex spatial signals. Tabor et al. recently developed a multi-module gene circuit system for edge detection, a signal processing algorithm common in artificial intelligence and image recognition [99]. As illustrated in Figure 4B, the biological edge detection algorithm is composed of three modules: a dark sensor (NOT light), cell-cell communication cassette, and an X AND (NOT Y) genetic logic. The darker sensor was engineered based on the light-sensitive protein Cph8, a chimeric sensor kinase. With the covalent association of chromophore phycocyanobilin produced from heme via ho1 and pcyA [100],[101], Cph8 is able to activate the ompC promoter (PompC) by transferring a phosphoryl group to the response regulator OmpR. However, in the presence of red light, the kinase activity of Cph8 is inhibited, which precludes the transcription from PompCand causes a NOT light transcriptional logic gate. The cell-cell communication was implemented through the Lux QS system and was used to convert light information into spatial distribution of AHL. With the incorporation of the converter cI and the hybrid promoter Plux-lambda, the state of PompC is converted via an X AND (NOT Y) logical operation into the state of the promoter Plux-lambda, which is displayed via the production of LacZ that produces black pigment. Upon the loading of the programs, a lawn of isogenic *E. coli* populations was able to sense an image of light, communicate to identify the light-dark edges, and visually present the result of the computation.

Ecosystem formation

Artificial cellular communications can enable not only the coordination of isogenic cell populations but also heterogeneous ecosystems that are composed of multiple species. You and co-works recently developed two gene circuits into a predator-prey ecosystem that consists of two *E. coli* populations [52].

Figure 5A shows the design of the ecosystem that involves two QS modules, LuxI/LuxR from *V. fischeri* and LasI/LasR from *P. aeruginosa*, for two-way communications. The predator cell (top) produces and secretes the AHL 3OC12HSL that induces the expression of the toxin gene*ccdB* in the prey cell

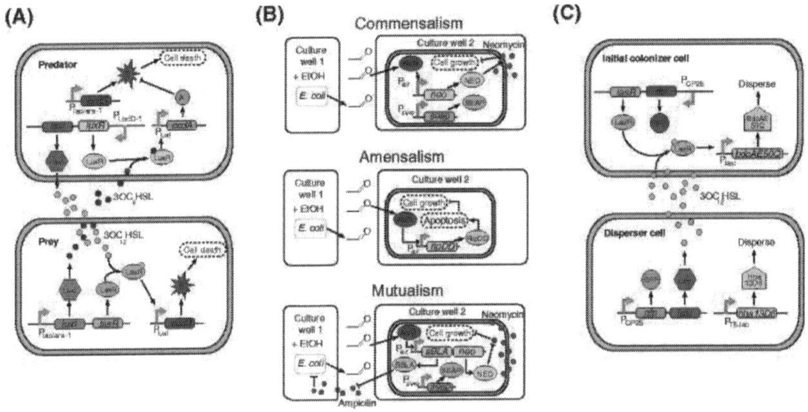

Figure 5: Programmed ecosystems developed from designed cellular communications. (A) A synthetic predator-prey ecosystem in *E. coli*. The predator cell (top) produces the QS signal 3OC12HSL that induces the expression of the toxin gene *ccdB* in the prey cell (bottom) and causes cell death. Meanwhile, the prey produces another QS signal, 3OC6HSL, which triggers the expression of *ccdA*, an antitoxin gene whose expression rescues the predator by neutralizing the toxin CcdB accumulated inside the cell. **(B)** Synthetic ecosystems with*E. coli* and Chinese hamster ovary (CHO) cells. The three ecosystems were based on the same foundation - an airborne transmission of transcription system, through which the sender (*E. coli*) converts ethanol into volatile acetaldehyde and broadcasts it to the receiver (CHO-K1) to alter corresponding gene expression. Top panel: The volatile acetaldehyde produced by *E. coli* induces antibiotic resistance in CHO-K1 cells, leading to a commensal community. Middle panel: The acetaldehyde from the sender induces the apoptosis of the receiver, creating amensalism between the two species. Bottom panel: *E. coli* rescues the CHO-K1 cell by triggering antibiotic resistance through volatile acetaldehyde, and in the meantime, the CHO-K1 cell benefits *E. coli* by degrading ampicillin that is toxic to *E. coli*, resulting in a mutualistic consortium. **(C)** An engineered biofilm-forming system that consists of two communicating *E. coli* species. The disperser cell (bottom) produces AHL (3OC12HSL) to trigger the expression of the gene *bdcAB50Q* in the initial colonizer cell (top), leading to the dispersion of the biofilm formed by the initial colonizer cells. Meanwhile, the biofilm formed by the disperser cells can also be dispersed by inducing the expression of the dispersal protein Hha13D6 with external inducer IPTG. The combination of the two steps allows the replacement and removal of biofilms in a programmed manner.

(bottom), leading to the death of the prey. In the meantime, the prey produces another AHL molecule, 3OC6HSL, which rescues the predator by inducing the production of antitoxin CcdA that neutralizes the toxin from CcdB. With appropriate modulations of the system parameters, the researchers were able to create a bacterial version of predation with different population dynamics generated, including extinction, coexistence, and oscillation. Similar to this work, another bidirectional intercellular communication network was also engineered by Brenner et al. [50], in which the LasI/LasR and RhlI/RhlR QS systems from *P. aeruginosa* were adopted to create a two-species microbial consensus consortium. In that ecosystem, the gene expression of any of the two species mutually depends on the presence of the other.

Beyond predation and consensus, designer cellular communications can be used to create a wide spectrum of inter-species interactions. As revealed by metagenomics and 16S pyrosequencing, microbial interactions in nature such as biofilms and the microbiome are extremely complicated and diverse - for instance, there can be parasitism, predation, commensalism, mutualism, competition, and amensalism within a single pair of species [102]. As one of the earliest efforts towards the programming of complicated cellular consortia, Weber and Fussenegger developed a set of pairwise interactions between *E. coli* and Chinese hamster ovary (CHO) cells [51].

As illustrated in Figure 5B, the designs of the ecosystems center on an airborne transmission of the transcription system that allows one species (*E. coli*) to convert ethanol into volatile acetaldehyde and broadcast this airborne signal (boiling point: 21°C) to another species (CHO-K1 cell line) for the activation of functionally specific, rationally engineered genes. The commensal ecosystem (top) was created by constructing an *E. coli* strain capable of converting ethanol into acetaldehyde for air broadcast and placing a neomycin resistance gene (*neo*) under the control of an acetaldehyde-induced promoter (Pair) in a CHO-K1 cell line. In addition, secreted alkaline phosphatase (SEAP) was used as a reporter of the CHO-K1 cells. When cultivated proximate to synthetic CHO-K1, the engineered *E. coli* cells confer survival of the mammalian cells while keeping their own growth unaffected by the mammalian cells cultured in a separate dish. The amensal ecosystem (middle) was synthesized by cultivating an acetaldehyde-broadcasting *E. coli* strain in close proximity to a CHO-K1 cell line that was engineered to have acetaldehyde-controlled expression of RipDD, a gene that encodes an apoptosis-inducing human receptor interacting protein. As a result, the CHO-K1 cells survive only in the absence of the *E. coli* cells because, otherwise, they induce the death of the CHO-K1 cells by producing acetaldehyde. To create a mutualistic interaction between *E. coli* and CHO-K1 cells (bottom), the commensal ecosystem developed earlier (top) was modified to incorporate a mammalian beta-lactamase gene *sBLA* under the control of the acetaldehyde-inducible promoter (Pair). Here, sBLA can be secreted to the extracellular milieu to hydrolyze the bacterial antibiotic ampicillin in the culture medium to promote the survival of co-cultured *E. coli*, resulting in bidirectional benefits between the two cell species. Following a similar idea, three additional types of ecosystem interactions were created, including parasitism, third party-inducible parasitism, and predator-prey interaction (not shown in Figure 5). This example demonstrated the ability of programming microbial consortia via rational design of cellular interactions by rewiring cellular communication systems, providing novel insights in understanding and programming microbial community patterns that orchestrate the complex coexistence of living systems.

In addition to programming planktonic bacterial populations, synthetic communication circuits have also been exploited in controlling complex communities such as biofilms. Hong et al. recently developed quorum-sensing circuits to program the formation and dispersal of artificial *E. coli* biofilms [103]. As shown in Figure 5C, the circuits have two functional parts with one belonging to the initial colonizer cell (top) and the other belonging to the disperser cell (bottom). The initial colonizer part consists of the constitutively expressed repressor gene *lasR* and its cognate promoter PlasI that drives the expression of the biofilm dispersion gene *bdcAB50Q*; the disperser part is composed of the AHL-producing gene *lasI* that is constitutively expressed and another biofilm dispersion gene, *hha13D6*, controlled by external inducer IPTG. Such a design allows the disperser cell to trigger the expression of the gene *bdcAB50Q* in the initial colonizer cell by producing AHL (3OC12HSL), leading to the dispersion and replacement of the biofilm formed by the initial colonizer cells. Meanwhile, the circuit in the disperser enables the biofilm formed by the dispersers to be removed with the external signal inducer IPTG. These types of functional circuits can be powerful in creating designer biofilms and enabling precise manipulation of community composition in the fields of biorefinery, medicine, and bioproduction.

CONCLUSIONS

With the advances of synthetic biology technologies and a consensus on the need for community-based functionality engineering, synthetic microbial consortia have undergone a rapid development in the past few years. This review has surveyed recent advances of engineered biological systems that utilize cell-cell communication to program bacterial group behaviors, covering both the basic communication modules and functional gene circuits that confer desired community-based dynamic behaviors.

Although there has been significant progress, the engineering of microbial communities is still in its infancy and is subject to a set of challenges. In fact, almost all synthetic circuits to date have involved many rounds of trial and error before achieving the desired functionality. Difficulties in the efficient construction of engineered circuits often stem from a lack of biological knowledge. Specifically, to facilitate gene circuit engineering, it is needed to have a deep understanding of stochasticity in gene expression [104]-[106], the inherent interplay between a synthetic circuit and the host organism [1], and issues related to multicellular physiology and metabolism [107]. Another big challenge arises from the technical side of synthetic biology, which includes the lack of powerful rational design platforms, limited availability of parts and modules, efficient systematic optimization strategies and toolkits, and high-throughput assays for circuit validation. Addressing the above challenges will foster our engineering capability and help to achieve the ultimate goal of efficient and reliable development of synthetic circuits with defined functionality.

Despite the challenges, the future of engineered microbial communities is bright. In fact, synthetic consortia have already started to show tremendous potential in both understanding biological questions and addressing real-world concerns. For example, extended from the programming of cellular dynamics, synthetic bacterial systems have been applied to understand ecological and evolutionary questions that are difficult to address with natural communities [108]. Towards real-world applications, bacterial consortia synthesized with designer communication modules have been used for information processing [109],[110], bio-computation [111], and therapeutics [112]-[114], as well as material and chemical productions [115]-[117]. There are a variety of research fields where synthetic bacterial consortia have started to play an important role: In metabolic engineering, cellular communication can be used to implement self-regulated control between cellular growth and product manufacturing in bioreactors for autonomous bioproduction. In biomedical applications, custom-tailored probiotic bacteria can be introduced into the human body to alter the composition and hence the function of the gut microbiota for disease treatment. In areas relating to the environment, biofilms and microbial consortia in soil and other natural settings can be perturbed and even reprogrammed with engineered microbes for desired purposes. We thus expect that microbial communities programmed via engineered cellular communication will become a versatile strategy in addressing both scientific and practical challenges in the near future.

REFERENCES

1. Elowitz MB, Leibler S: A synthetic oscillatory network of transcriptional regulators. Nature 2000,403(6767):335–338.
2. Gardner TS, Cantor CR, Collins JJ: Construction of a genetic toggle switch in Escherichia coli . Nature 2000,403(6767):339–342.
3. Atkinson MR, Savageau MA, Myers JT, Ninfa AJ: Development of genetic circuitry exhibiting toggle switch or oscillatory behavior in Escherichia coli . Cell 2003,113(5):597–607.
4. Kramer BP, Viretta AU, Daoud-El Baba M, Aubel D, Weber W, Fussenegger M: An engineered epigenetic transgene switch in mammalian cells. Nat Biotechnol 2004,22(7):867–870.
5. Bayer TS, Smolke CD: Programmable ligand-controlled riboregulators of eukaryotic gene expression. Nat Biotechnol2005,123(3):337–343.
6. Deans TL, Cantor CR, Collins JJ: A tunable genetic switch based on RNAi and repressor proteins for regulating gene expression in mammalian cells. Cell 2007,130(2):363–372.
7. Friedland AE, Lu TK, Wang X, Shi D, Church G, Collins JJ: Synthetic gene networks that count. Science 2009,324(5931):1199–1202.
8. Ellis T, Wang X, Collins JJ: Diversity-based, model-guided construction of synthetic gene networks with predicted functions. Nat Biotechnol 2009,27(5):465–471.
9. Wu M, Su R-Q, Li X, Ellis T, Lai Y-C, Wang X: Engineering of regulated stochastic cell fate determination. Proc Natl Acad Sci U S A2013,110(26):10610–10615.
10. Fung E, Wong WW, Suen JK, Bulter T, S-g L, Liao JC: A synthetic gene–metabolic oscillator. Nature 2005,435(7038):118–122.
11. Stricker J, Cookson S, Bennett MR, Mather WH, Tsimring LS, Hasty J: A fast, robust and tunable synthetic gene oscillator. Nature2008,456(7221):516–519.
12. Tigges M, Marquez-Lago TT, Stelling J, Fussenegger M: A tunable synthetic mammalian oscillator. Nature 2009,457(7227):309–312.
13. Danino T, Mondragón-Palomino O, Tsimring L, Hasty J: A synchronized quorum of genetic clocks. Nature 2010,463(7279):326–330.

14. Ham TS, Lee SK, Keasling JD, Arkin AP: Design and construction of a double inversion recombination switch for heritable sequential genetic memory. PLoS One 2008,3(7):e2815.

15. Ajo-Franklin CM, Drubin DA, Eskin JA, Gee EP, Landgraf D, Phillips I, Silver PA: Rational design of memory in eukaryotic cells. Genes Dev 2007,21(18):2271–2276.

16. Basu S, Gerchman Y, Collins CH, Arnold FH, Weiss R: A synthetic multicellular system for programmed pattern formation. Nature2005,434(7037):1130–1134.

17. Kobayashi H, Kærn M, Araki M, Chung K, Gardner TS, Cantor CR, Collins JJ: Programmable cells: interfacing natural and engineered gene networks. Proc Natl Acad Sci U S A 2004,101(22):8414–8419.

18. You L, Cox RS, Weiss R, Arnold FH: Programmed population control by cell–cell communication and regulated killing. Nature2004,428(6985):868–871.

19. Guet CC, Elowitz MB, Hsing W, Leibler S: Combinatorial synthesis of genetic networks. Science 2002,296(5572):1466–1470.

20. Rackham O, Chin JW: Cellular logic with orthogonal ribosomes. J Am Chem Soc 2005,127(50):17584–17585.

21. Anderson JC, Voigt CA, Arkin AP: Environmental signal integration by a modular AND gate. Mol Syst Biol 2007, 3: 133.

22. Win MN, Smolke CD: Higher-order cellular information processing with synthetic RNA devices. Science 2008,322(5900):456–460.

23. Basu S, Mehreja R, Thiberge S, Chen M-T, Weiss R: Spatiotemporal control of gene expression with pulse-generating networks.Proc Natl Acad Sci U S A 2004,101(17):6355–6360.

24. Hooshangi S, Thiberge S, Weiss R: Ultrasensitivity and noise propagation in a synthetic transcriptional cascade. Proc Natl Acad Sci U S A 2005,102(10):3581–3586.

25. Sohka T, Heins RA, Phelan RM, Greisler JM, Townsend CA, Ostermeier M: An externally tunable bacterial band-pass filter. Proc Natl Acad Sci U S A 2009,106(25):10135–10140.

26. Church GM, Elowitz MB, Smolke CD, Voigt CA, Weiss R: Realizing the potential of synthetic biology. Nat Rev Mol Cell Biol2014,15(4):289–94.

27. Khalil AS, Collins JJ: Synthetic biology: applications come of age. Nat Rev Genet 2010,11(5):367–379.

28. Ruder WC, Lu T, Collins JJ: Synthetic biology moving into the clinic. Science 2011,333(6047):1248–1252.

29. Weber W, Fussenegger M: Emerging biomedical applications of synthetic biology. Nat Rev Genet 2011,13(1):21–35.

30. Gibson DG, Young L, Chuang R-Y, Venter JC, Hutchison CA, Smith HO: Enzymatic assembly of DNA molecules up to several hundred kilobases. Nat Methods 2009,6(5):343–345.

31. Engler C, Kandzia R, Marillonnet S: A one pot, one step, precision cloning method with high throughput capability. PLoS One2008,3(11):e3647.

32. Zhang Y, Werling U, Edelmann W: SLiCE: a novel bacterial cell extract-based DNA cloning method. Nucleic Acids Res2012,40(8):e55-e55.

33. Quan J, Tian J: Circular polymerase extension cloning for high-throughput cloning of complex and combinatorial DNA libraries.Nat Protoc 2011,6(2):242–251.

34. Wang HH, Isaacs FJ, Carr PA, Sun ZZ, Xu G, Forest CR, Church GM: Programming cells by multiplex genome engineering and accelerated evolution. Nature 2009,460(7257):894–898.

35. Ellis HM, Yu D, DiTizio T: High efficiency mutagenesis, repair, and engineering of chromosomal DNA using single-stranded oligonucleotides. Proc Natl Acad Sci U S A 2001,98(12):6742–6746.

36. Jiang W, Bikard D, Cox D, Zhang F, Marraffini LA: RNA-guided editing of bacterial genomes using CRISPR-Cas systems. Nat Biotechnol 2013,31(3):233–239.

37. Gaj T, Gersbach CA, Barbas CF III: ZFN, TALEN, and CRISPR/Cas-based methods for genome engineering. Trends Biotechnol2013,31(7):397–405.

38. Slusarczyk AL, Lin A, Weiss R: Foundations for the design and implementation of synthetic genetic circuits. Nat Rev Genet2012,13(6):406–420.

39. Salis HM, Mirsky EA, Voigt CA: Automated design of synthetic ribosome binding sites to control protein expression. Nat Biotechnol2009,27(10):946–950.

40. Hillson NJ, Rosengarten RD, Keasling JD: j5 DNA assembly design automation software. ACS Synth Biol 2011,1(1):14–21.

41. Lou C, Stanton B, Chen Y-J, Munsky B, Voigt CA: Ribozyme-based insulator parts buffer synthetic circuits from genetic context. Nat Biotechnol 2012,30(11):1137–1142.

42. Smolke CD: Building outside of the box: iGEM and the BioBricks Foundation. Nat Biotechnol 2009,27(12):1099–1102.

43. Chuang JS: Engineering multicellular traits in synthetic microbial populations. Curr Opin Chem Biol 2012,16(3):370–378.

44. Brenner K, You L, Arnold FH: Engineering microbial consortia: a new frontier in synthetic biology. Trends Biotechnol2008,26(9):483–489.

45. Pai A, Tanouchi Y, Collins CH, You L: Engineering multicellular systems by cell–cell communication. Curr Opin Biotechnol2009,20(4):461–470.

46. Payne S, You L: Engineered cell–cell communication and its applications. Adv Biochem Eng Biotechnol 2013, 146: 97–121.

47. Tsao C-Y, Quan DN, Bentley WE: Development of the quorum sensing biotechnological toolbox. Curr Opin Chem Eng2012,1(4):396–402.

48. Teuscher C, Grecu C, Lu T, Weiss R: Challenges and promises of nano and bio communication networks. In Networks on Chip (NoCS), 2011 Fifth IEEE/ACM International Symposium on. IEEE, Pittsburgh; 2011:247–254.

49. Liu C, Fu X, Liu L, Ren X, Chau CK, Li S, Xiang L, Zeng H, Chen G, Tang L-H: Sequential establishment of stripe patterns in an expanding cell population. Science 2011,334(6053):238–241.

50. Brenner K, Karig DK, Weiss R, Arnold FH: Engineered bidirectional communication mediates a consensus in a microbial biofilm consortium. Proc Natl Acad Sci U S A 2007,104(44):17300–17304.

51. Weber W, Daoud-El Baba M, Fussenegger M: Synthetic ecosystems based on airborne inter- and intra-kingdom communication.Proc Natl Acad Sci U S A 2007,104(25):10435–10440.

52. Balagaddé FK, Song H, Ozaki J, Collins CH, Barnet M, Arnold FH, Quake SR, You L: A synthetic Escherichia coli predator–prey ecosystem. Mol Syst Biol 2008, 4: 187.

53. O'Toole G, Kaplan HB, Kolter R: Biofilm formation as microbial development. Annu Rev Microbiol 2000,54(1):49–79.

54. Stoodley P, Sauer K, Davies D, Costerton JW: Biofilms as complex differentiated communities. Annu Rev Microbiol 2002,56(1):187–209.

55. Structure, function and diversity of the healthy human microbiome Nature 2012,486(7402):207–214.

56. Cho I, Blaser MJ: The human microbiome: at the interface of health and disease. Nat Rev Genet 2012,13(4):260–270.

57. Costerton J, Stewart PS, Greenberg E: Bacterial biofilms: a common cause of persistent infections. Science 1999,284(5418):1318–1322.

58. Stewart PS, William Costerton J: Antibiotic resistance of bacteria in biofilms. Lancet 2001,358(9276):135–138.

59. Koizumi S, Endo T, Tabata K, Ozaki A: Large-scale production of UDP-galactose and globotriose by coupling metabolically engineered bacteria. Nat Biotechnol 1998,16(9):847–850.

60. Minty JJ, Singer ME, Scholz SA, Bae C-H, Ahn J-H, Foster CE, Liao JC, Lin XN: Design and characterization of synthetic fungal-bacterial consortia for direct production of isobutanol from cellulosic biomass. Proc Natl Acad Sci U S A 2013,110(36):14592–14597.

61. Chen M-T, Weiss R: Artificial cell-cell communication in yeast Saccharomyces cerevisiae using signaling elements fromArabidopsis thaliana . Nat Biotechnol 2005,23(12):1551–1555.

62. Williams TC, Nielsen LK, Vickers CE: Engineered quorum sensing using pheromone-mediated cell-to-cell communication inSaccharomyces cerevisiae . ACS Synth Biol 2013,2(3):136–149.

63. Bassler BL, Losick R: Bacterially speaking. Cell 2006,125(2):237–246.

64. Waters CM, Bassler BL: Quorum sensing: cell-to-cell communication in bacteria. Annu Rev Cell Dev Biol 2005, 21: 319–346.

65. Engebrecht J, Nealson K, Silverman M: Bacterial bioluminescence: isolation and genetic analysis of functions from Vibrio fischeri .Cell 1983,32(3):773–781.

66. Davies DG, Parsek MR, Pearson JP, Iglewski BH, Costerton J, Greenberg E: The involvement of cell-to-cell signals in the development of a bacterial biofilm. Science 1998,280(5361):295–298.

67. De Kievit TR, Iglewski BH: Bacterial quorum sensing in pathogenic relationships. Infect Immun 2000,68(9):4839–4849.

68. Latifi A, Winson MK, Foglino M, Bycroft BW, Stewart GS, Lazdunski A, Williams P: Multiple homologues of LuxR and LuxI control expression of virulence determinants and secondary metabolites through quorum sensing in Pseudomonas aeruginosa PAO1.Mol Microbiol 1995,17(2):333–343.

69. Thomson N, Crow M, McGowan S, Cox A, Salmond G: Biosynthesis of carbapcnem antibiotic and prodigiosin pigment in Serratia is under quorum sensing control. Mol Microbiol 2000,36(3):539–556.

70. Kleerebezem M: Quorum sensing control of lantibiotic production; nisin and subtilin autoregulate their own biosynthesis.Peptides 2004,25(9):1405–1414.

71. Fuqua C, Parsek MR, Greenberg EP: Regulation of gene expression by cell-to-cell communication: acyl-homoserine lactone quorum sensing. Annu Rev Genet 2001,35(1):439–468.

72. Thiel V, Kunze B, Verma P, Wagner-Döbler I, Schulz S: New structural variants of homoserine lactones in bacteria. Chem Bio Chem2009,10(11):1861–1868.

73. Fuqua WC, Winans SC, Greenberg EP: Quorum sensing in bacteria: the LuxR-LuxI family of cell density-responsive transcriptional regulators. J Bacteriol 1994,176(2):269.

74. Nealson K, Hastings JW: Bacterial bioluminescence: its control and ecological significance. Microbiol Rev 1979,43(4):496.

75. Pesci EC, Pearson JP, Seed PC, Iglewski BH: Regulation of las and rhl quorum sensing in Pseudomonas aeruginosa . J Bacteriol1997,179(10):3127–3132.

76. Welch M, Todd DE, Whitehead NA, McGowan SJ, Bycroft BW, Salmond GP: N-acyl homoserine lactone binding to the CarR receptor determines quorum-sensing specificity in Erwinia . EMBO J 2000,19(4):631–641.

77. Minogue TD, Trebra MW, Bernhard F, Bodman SB: The autoregulatory role of EsaR, a quorum-sensing regulator in Pantoea stewartii ssp. stewartii : evidence for a repressor function. Mol Microbiol 2002,44(6):1625–1635.

78. Novick RP, Geisinger E: Quorum sensing in Staphylococci . Annu Rev Genet 2008, 42: 541–564.

79. Hancock LE, Perego M: The Enterococcus faecalis fsr two-component system controls biofilm development through production of gelatinase. J Bacteriol 2004,186(17):5629–5639.

80. Pestova E, Håvarstein L, Morrison D: Regulation of competence for genetic transformation in Streptococcus pneumoniae by an auto-induced peptide pheromone and a two-component regulatory system. Mol Microbiol 1996,21(4):853–862.

81. Winzer K, HARDIE K, Williams P: LuxS and autoinducer-2: their contribution to quorum. Adv Appl Microbiol 2003, 53: 291.

82. Pereira CS, Thompson JA, Xavier KB: AI-2-mediated signalling in bacteria. FEMS Microbiol Rev 2013,37(2):156–181.

83. Prindle A, Samayoa P, Razinkov I, Danino T, Tsimring LS, Hasty J: A sensing array of radically coupled genetic 'biopixels'. Nature2012,481(7379):39–44.

84. Pesci EC, Milbank JB, Pearson JP, McKnight S, Kende AS, Greenberg EP, Iglewski BH: Quinolone signaling in the cell-to-cell communication system of Pseudomonas aeruginos a. Proc Natl Acad Sci U S A 1999,96(20):11229–11234.

85. Ryan RP, Dow JM: Communication with a growing family: diffusible signal factor (DSF) signaling in bacteria. Trends Microbiol2011,19(3):145–152.

86. Holden MT, Ram Chhabra S, De Nys R, Stead P, Bainton NJ, Hill PJ, Manefield M, Kumar N, Labatte M, England D: Quorum-sensing cross talk: isolation and chemical characterization of cyclic dipeptides from Pseudomonas aeruginosa and other gram-negative bacteria. Mol Microbiol 1999,33(6):1254–1266.

87. Tommonaro G, Abbamondi GR, Iodice C, Tait K, De Rosa S: Diketopiperazines produced by the halophilic archaeon, Haloterrigena hispanica , activate AHL bioreporters. Microb Ecol 2012,63(3):490–495.

88. Flavier AB, Clough SJ, Schell MA, Denny TP: Identification of 3-hydroxypalmitic acid methyl ester as a novel autoregulator controlling virulence in Ralstonia solanacearum . Mol Microbiol 1997,26(2):251–259.

89. Chen H, Fujita M, Feng Q, Clardy J, Fink GR: Tyrosol is a quorum-sensing molecule in Candida albicans . Proc Natl Acad Sci U S A2004,101(14):5048–5052.

90. Lee JH, Lee J: Indole as an intercellular signal in microbial communities. FEMS Microbiol Rev 2010,34(4):426–444.

91. Smith R, Tan C, Srimani JK, Pai A, Riccione KA, Song H, You L: Programmed Allee effect in bacteria causes a tradeoff between population spread and survival. Proc Natl Acad Sci U S A 2014,111(5):1969–1974.

92. Stephens PA, Sutherland WJ, Freckleton RP: What is the Allee effect? Oikos 1999, 87: 185–190.

93. Shapiro JA: Thinking about bacterial populations as multicellular organisms. Annu Rev Microbiol 1998,52(1):81–104.

94. Parsek MR, Greenberg E: Sociomicrobiology: the connections between quorum sensing and biofilms. Trends Microbiol2005,13(1):27–33.

95. Gurdon J, Bourillot P-Y: Morphogen gradient interpretation. Nature 2001,413(6858):797–803.

96. Wolpert L: Positional information and the spatial pattern of cellular differentiation. J Theor Biol 1969,25(1):1–47.

97. Payne S, Li B, Cao Y, Schaeffer D, Ryser MD, You L: Temporal control of self-organized pattern formation without morphogen gradients in bacteria. Mol Syst Biol 2014, 9: 697.

98. Turing AM: The chemical basis of morphogenesis. Phil Trans R Soc Lond B 1952,237(641):37–72.

99. Tabor JJ, Salis HM, Simpson ZB, Chevalier AA, Levskaya A, Marcotte EM, Voigt CA, Ellington AD: A synthetic genetic edge detection program. Cell 2009,137(7):1272–1281.

100. Gambetta GA, Lagarias JC: Genetic engineering of phytochrome biosynthesis in bacteria. Proc Natl Acad Sci U S A2001,98(19):10566–10571.

101. Levskaya A, Chevalier AA, Tabor JJ, Simpson ZB, Lavery LA, Levy M, Davidson EA, Scouras A, Ellington AD, Marcotte EM: Synthetic biology: engineering Escherichia coli to see light. Nature 2005,438(7067):441–442.

102. Faust K, Raes J: Microbial interactions: from networks to models. Nat Rev Microbiol 2012,10(8):538–550.

103. Hong SH, Hegde M, Kim J, Wang X, Jayaraman A, Wood TK: Synthetic quorum-sensing circuit to control consortial biofilm formation and dispersal in a microfluidic device. Nat Commun 2012, 3: 613.

104. Lu T, Hasty J, Wolynes PG: Effective temperature in stochastic kinetics and gene networks. Biophys J 2006,91(1):84–94.

105. Lu T, Shen T, Zong C, Hasty J, Wolynes PG: Statistics of cellular signal transduction as a race to the nucleus by multiple random walkers in compartment/phosphorylation space. Proc Natl Acad Sci U S A 2006,103(45):16752–16757.

106. Lu T, Shen T, Bennett MR, Wolynes PG, Hasty J: Phenotypic variability of growing cellular populations. Proc Natl Acad Sci U S A2007,104(48):18982–18987.

107. Mao J, Blanchard AE, Lu T (2014) Slow and steady wins the race: a bacterial exploitative competition strategy in fluctuating environments. ACS Synth Biol doi:10.1021/sb4002008

108. Song H, Payne S, Gray M, You L: Spatiotemporal modulation of biodiversity in a synthetic chemical-mediated ecosystem. Nat Chem Biol 2009,5(12):929–935.

109. Prindle A, Selimkhanov J, Li H, Razinkov I, Tsimring LS, Hasty J: Rapid and tunable post-translational coupling of genetic circuits.Nature 2014,508(7496):387–91.

110. Qi H, Blanchard A, Lu T: Engineered genetic information processing circuits. Wiley Interdiscip Rev Syst Biol Med 2013,5(3):273–287.

111. Tamsir A, Tabor JJ, Voigt CA: Robust multicellular computing using genetically encoded NOR gates and chemical 'wires'. Nature2011,469(7329):212–215.

112. Saeidi N, Wong CK, Lo TM, Nguyen HX, Ling H, Leong SSJ, Poh CL, Chang MW: Engineering microbes to sense and eradicatePseudomonas aeruginosa , a human pathogen. Mol Syst Biol 2011, 7: 521.

113. Hwang IY, Tan MH, Koh E, Ho CL, Poh CL, Chang MW: Reprogramming microbes to be pathogen-seeking killers. ACS Synth Biol2013,3(4):228–237.

114. Duan F, March JC: Engineered bacterial communication prevents Vibrio cholerae virulence in an infant mouse model. Proc Natl Acad Sci U S A 2010,107(25):11260–11264.

115. Chen AY, Deng Z, Billings AN, Seker UO, Lu MY, Citorik RJ, Zakeri B, Lu TK: Synthesis and patterning of tunable multiscale materials with engineered cells. Nat Mater 2014, 13: 515–523.

116. Nocadello S, Swennen EF: The new pLAI (lux regulon based auto-inducible) expression system for recombinant protein production in Escherichia coli . Microb Cell Fact 2012,11(1):1–10.

117. Tsao C-Y, Hooshangi S, Wu H-C, Valdes JJ, Bentley WE: Autonomous induction of recombinant proteins by minimally rewiring native quorum sensing regulon of E. coli . Metab Eng 2010,12(3):291–297.

INDEX

H

N

O

P

R

S